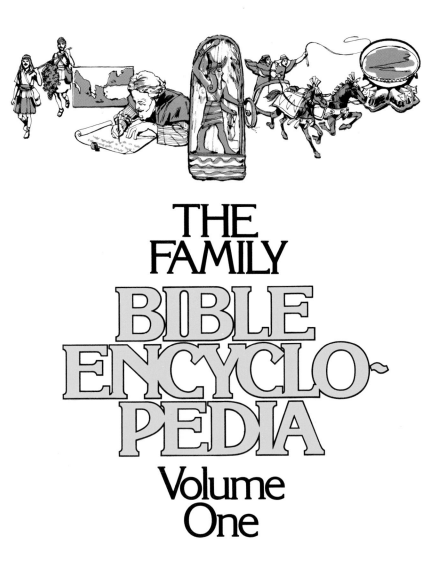

THE FAMILY
BIBLE ENCYCLO-PEDIA

Volume One

A-J

BERKELEY AND ALVERA MICKELSEN

David C. Cook Publishing Co.

ELGIN, ILLINOIS—WESTON, ONTARIO
FULLERTON, CALIFORNIA

PHOTO CREDITS

Bettman Archives, page 36
Ewing Galloway, pages 29, 113
Matson Photo Service, pages 27, 62, 102, 141, 198
Gladys Peterson, page 32
Religious News Service, page 100
Paul Schrock, page 99
Toronto Star Syndicate, pages 24, 25, 30, 69, 88,
133, 137, 157, 187, 188

Published by David C. Cook Publishing Co.
Elgin, Ill.   Weston, Ont.   Fullerton, Calif.
Edited by Dean Merrill, Marshall Shelley, and Sharrel Keyes
Designed by Marita Root
Cover by Kurt Dietsch
Printed in the United States of America

ISBN 0-89191-100-6
LC 78-55384

PREFACE

The Family Bible Encyclopedia has been written for one purpose—to help children and other readers understand more fully the most important book in the world, the Bible. We believe the Bible is God's Word and that it speaks to the reader with divine authority. For this reason, it is crucial for Christians to understand it as it was meant to be understood.

The Bible is not a theology book. It is a book about God's past acts and teachings among his people. It is a book that shows their reactions to God, to life around them, and to their own problems. It is a book that reveals God himself and his plans and purposes for people through all time.

The Bible is a book about real people and real events in real history. Its history and culture sometimes seem far removed from us. *The Family Bible Encyclopedia* will help children understand both the likenesses with and the differences from their own time and thus better understand God's will and work in their own lives.

To help readers understand that the Bible is about real people in real places, geographical locations are given in terms of current geography as well as ancient geography. For example, "Ephesus was the capital city of the Roman province called Asia (now a part of Turkey)." Authentic art and photographs help people and places come alive.

Arranged alphabetically, *The Family Bible Encyclopedia* includes every significant person, place, and term mentioned in the Bible, plus many current religious terms not mentioned in the Bible, such as *Hanukkah, Dead Sea Scrolls,* and *Septuagint.* In addition, there is a short summary of every book in the Bible. Entries make no effort to tell everything known about the people, places, or terms, or to deal with complex critical problems, but rather to answer the basic questions of young readers.

Most of the writing was done by Alvera Mickelsen, with help from a few others with experience in writing for children. They include Lorraine Eitel, Pamela Harris, and Steve Harris. Every entry was carefully checked for biblical accuracy by Berkeley Mickelsen and by one other biblical scholar. The biblical scholars who participated in reading and checking were Dr. George R. Beasley-Murray of the Southern Baptist Theological Seminary, Louisville, Kentucky; David Scholer of Gordon-Conwell Theological Seminary, South Hamilton, Massachusetts; Kermit Ecklebarger of Conservative Baptist Theological Seminary, Denver, Colorado; and Dr. Gerald Hawthorne of Wheaton College, Wheaton, Illinois.

For us, preparing these volumes has been an enriching learning experience. The effort demanded in this work to express complex and profound ideas simply has forced us to think through and further refine our own concepts. Preparing this encyclopedia has stretched and enlarged our understanding of God's Word and its meaning for our own lives.

We hope those who use these volumes will catch something of the excitement and growth that comes from understanding God's Word in greater depth.

Aaron was a better speaker than his brother Moses—especially when they had to face the Pharaoh.

AARON *(AIR-run)* was Israel's first high priest. He was three years older than his brother, Moses, and was a good speaker and leader.

When God told Moses to lead the Hebrew people out of their slavery in Egypt, Moses said he was afraid because he was not a good speaker. God reminded him that his brother Aaron *was* a good speaker and that Aaron would help him. Together Aaron and Moses tried to convince the Pharaoh (king) of Egypt to let the Hebrews go. After God sent ten terrible plagues, Pharaoh finally agreed.

Aaron was Moses' helper all through the forty years the Hebrews spent in the wilderness before they entered the Promised Land. While Moses was on the mountain receiving the Ten Commandments, Aaron committed a terrible sin. He helped the people make a golden calf, an idol to worship.

However, God forgave Aaron, and later Aaron did some heroic things. Once a large group of Israelites revolted against the two brothers. God sent a terrible disease as a judgment, and many people died. Aaron took a container with fire and incense from the Tabernacle altar and ran among the people so

Aaron and his four sons were anointed with oil.

God would forgive them. God stopped the disease.

Aaron and his four sons became the first priests to serve in the Tabernacle. They were given beautiful robes and were anointed with holy oil—a symbol that God had specially appointed them to his holy work.

Aaron died at age 123 before the Hebrew people entered the Promised Land.

Where to find it

God says he is a good speaker *Exodus 4:14-16*
Meets his brother Moses *Exodus 4:27-31*
Helps lead Israelites out of Egypt *Exodus 5–15*
Makes golden calf *Exodus 32*
Helps stop a plague *Numbers 16*
Is anointed high priest *Leviticus 8–9*

AARON'S ROD *(AIR-run's rod)* was probably a straight piece of wood made from an almond tree. It was a sign of authority; God sometimes told Aaron to use it to work miracles. It turned into a serpent when he threw it down before Pharaoh; it changed the rivers and lakes of Egypt into blood; and it brought plagues of frogs, then lice.

Later, when some people rebelled against Aaron's authority as high priest, his rod became part of a test to show that Aaron was God's choice. Twelve rods (one for each tribe of Israel) were placed in the Tabernacle. The next morning, Aaron's rod—but no one else's—had buds, blossoms, and ripe almonds.

Aaron's rod was then placed permanently either in front of or inside the ark of the Covenant (the text isn't clear).

Where to find it

Rod used in miracles *Exodus 7:8-10; 19-22; 8:16-18*
Rod blossoms *Numbers 17:1-11*
Placed inside or in front of the ark *Numbers 17:10; Hebrews 9:4*

ABBA *(AB-uh)* is the Aramaic word like "Daddy"—it's what a child called his father. (Aramaic was the language spoken by Jesus and the Jews of his time.) *Abba* appears in Mark 14:36, Romans 8:15, and Galatians 4:6. Each time it shows the loving relationship Christ had with God, his Father. If we are believers we may have the same closeness with God, our Father.

ABEL *(AY-bul)*, the second son of Adam and Eve, was the first person in the Bible to die. He was murdered by his older brother, Cain. Abel was a shepherd and had brought to God an offering—a lamb from his flock. Cain, a farmer, had brought some vegetables he had grown.

God was pleased with Abel's offering but not with Cain's. The Bible does not say why, but it may have been because Abel's life pleased God and Cain's did not. 1 John 3:12 says Cain's "deeds were evil and his brother's righteous."

Cain was angry. He urged Abel to go out into a field with him, and there he killed him.

Where to find it: *Genesis 4*

ABIATHAR *(uh-BY-uh-thar)* was the only survivor of 86 priests from a town called Nob whom King Saul ordered to be killed. Saul was angry because Abiathar's father, Ahimelech, the high priest, had helped his enemy, David. The priest had given David some of the bread from the Tabernacle altar. He had also given him the sword David had used to kill Goliath several years before.

When Abiathar escaped, he brought David an ephod (see *Ephod),* a special garment worn by priests. David apparently thought the ephod had some power to reveal the future or God's will.

Later David asked Abiathar to help carry the ark back to Jerusalem. When David's son Absalom led a rebellion against his father, Abiathar stayed loyal to David.

Shortly before David's death, a struggle grew between Adonijah, David's oldest living son, and Solomon over who would be the next king. Abiathar was on Adonijah's side. Even after Solomon became king, Abiathar favored Adonijah, and because of this, Solomon made him leave Jerusalem and stop being a priest.

Jesus mentioned Abiathar in Mark 2:26.

Where to find it

Escapes Saul's killing   *1 Samuel 22:20-23*
Brings ephod to David   *1 Samuel 23:6-14*
Carries ark to Jerusalem   *1 Chronicles 15:11-28*
Stays loyal to David   *2 Samuel 15:24-37*
Helps Adonijah   *1 Kings 1:5-7*
Removed as priest   *1 Kings 2:26-27*

Abigail got to David and apologized just in time.

ABIGAIL *(AB-uh-gale)* was the intelligent, charming wife of a very rich sheepherder named Nabal, a mean and stingy man. Abigail's wise acts as a peacemaker saved her community from disaster.

Nabal's sheep grazed in a place where David and his men had been hiding. They had protected Nabal's men. When David heard that Nabal was having a feast, he sent his men to ask for an invitation. Nabal said no and insulted them. David was so angry about this that he threatened to kill Nabal and his men.

When Abigail heard what her husband had done, she quickly gathered a large amount of food and took it to David. David was so impressed by her graciousness that he canceled the raid.

The next morning, when Abigail told Nabal how close he had come to disaster, the Bible says "his heart died within him"—in other words, he probably had a stroke that paralyzed him. Ten days later, he died.

Abigail later became the third wife of David. They had one son, Chileah.

Where to find it: *1 Samuel 25*

ABIHU *(uh-BY-who)* was the second of Aaron's four sons. He became one of the first priests of Israel.

Abihu, his father, brother, and 70 elders went with Moses partway up the mountain to receive the Ten Commandments.

Abihu died after he and his brother Nadab offered "strange fire" before God. We aren't sure what was wrong with their offering, but it must have been contrary to God's command.

Where to find it

Goes with Moses up Mount Sinai   *Exodus 24:1-13*
One of the first priests   *Exodus 28:1*
Offers "strange fire" and dies   *Leviticus 10:1-7*

ABIJAH or **ABIJAM** *(uh-BY-juh)* is the name of nine different people in the Old Testament.

1. The most important is Abijah, king of Judah, grandson of Solomon. He reigned for three years. During his reign, his country was at war with Israel (the Northern Kingdom). Before one battle, Abijah made a speech to both armies. He said that the other side had left the worship of God and could not win. In the battle that followed, Abijah's army won a clear victory.

Later, however, Abijah turned away from God. He "walked in all the sins which his father did before him; and his heart was not wholly true to the Lord his God."

Where to find it: *2 Chronicles 12:16–14:1; 1 Kings 15:1-8*

2. Another Abijah was the son of Jeroboam, king of Israel. A prophet from God told his mother that Abijah would die, and that's what

happened. His death was a judgment on the evil of his father, Jeroboam.

Where to find it: *1 Kings 14:1-18*

3. Abijah was the name of the second son of the prophet Samuel. His father appointed him to be a judge, but he became dishonest.

Where to find it: *1 Samuel 8:1-3*

ABIMELECH *(uh-BIM-i-leck)* is the name of several persons in the Old Testament, including two kings of the Philistines.

1. One was the king of Gerar, a Philistine city. Abraham and Sarah were afraid of him, and when Abimelech wanted to make Sarah one of his wives, Abraham pretended that she was his sister. Later God appeared to Abimelech in a dream and told him to give Sarah back to Abraham, so he did. Abraham later made a covenant (agreement) with Abimelech after their servants argued about who owned a certain well.

Where to find it: *Genesis 20:1-18; 21:22-32*

2. A second King Abimelech took Isaac's wife in a case very much like that of Abraham. This story also includes an argument over a well.

Where to find it: *Genesis 26:1-33*

3. Abimelech the son of Gideon led a revolt that killed all 70 of his brothers except the youngest, Jotham. Abimelech then became king of Shechem. But the people revolted against him twice. The first revolt, when he had been king three years, he put down cruelly. In the second revolt, a woman threw a grindstone from a roof and hit Abimelech in the head. He was dying—yet he didn't want people to say a woman had killed him, so he asked his young armor-bearer to kill him instead with his sword.

Where to find it: *Judges 9*

4. A priest named Abimelech was the son of Abiathar and served during the time of David.

Where to find it: *1 Chronicles 18:16*

ABINADAB *(uh-BIN-uh-dab)* lived on a hill in Kiriath-jearim. The ark of God was suddenly left at his house after many people had died because they disobeyed God by looking into the ark. The ark stayed in his house for 20 years until David took it to Jerusalem.

Where to find it: *1 Samuel 6:19–7:2; 2 Samuel 6:1-15*

ABISHAG *(AB-ih-shag)*, a beautiful young girl, was brought to King David when he was old and dying to keep him warm at night in his cold palace.

After David died, his son Adonijah asked Solomon (his younger brother, now king of Israel) if Abishag could be his wife. Solomon angrily said no and ordered Adonijah to be killed. In ancient times, when a man died, his concubines and women servants were considered to belong to his heir. To let Adonijah have Abishag would have been to admit that Adonijah might have a right to the throne of David.

Where to find it: *1 Kings 1:1-4; 2:13-25*

ABISHAI *(uh-BISH-ay-eye)*, a nephew of David, was one of the chief officers in David's army. He worked closely with David in many daring battles.

He was loyal to David, but he was very cruel to David's enemies. One time he went with David to Saul's camp and found Saul sleeping. Abishai wanted to kill him on the spot, but David said no.

Abishai once conquered an army of 18,000 Edomites. Another time he rescued David from death at the hands of a giant. Abishai and Joab were in charge of the army that stopped the rebellion of Sheba.

Where to find it

Chief officer   *2 Samuel 23:18*
Conquers Edomites   *1 Chronicles 18:12-13*
Rescues David   *2 Samuel 21:15-17*
Stops rebellion   *2 Samuel 20*

ABNER *(AB-ner)* was Saul's cousin and commander of Saul's army. When David defeated the giant Goliath, Abner brought David back to meet Saul.

Later, when Saul was trying to kill David, Abner helped Saul look for David and stayed close to Saul to protect him. After David got into Saul's camp one night and took his sword and jug of water as proof, David shouted from

"Whose spear and water jar are these, Abner?"

across the valley about Abner's failure to protect Saul.

After Saul's death, Abner helped make Ish-bosheth, son of Saul, the king. This brought two years of war between David's men and those following Ish-bosheth.

Abner later decided to help unify Israel under David's rule. He worked to convince the followers of Saul to transfer their loyalty to David. After meeting with David to make an agreement, Abner started home.

But Joab, commander of David's forces, had heard about the meeting and was angry. He thought Abner was a spy. So, without David's knowledge, he followed Abner and killed him.

When David found out, he proclaimed a curse on Joab. David's sincere mourning and fasting for Abner, whom he described as "a prince and a great man," convinced Abner's followers that David had nothing to do with his death. This kept further war from breaking out.

Where to find it: *2 Samuel 2:8–3:39*

ABOMINATION *(uh-BOM-i-NAY-shun)* refers to actions that offend God or men for religious or social reasons. Usually the Bible uses this word about things that offend God, but sometimes it refers to things that offend people. For example, Genesis 43:32 says that for Egyptians to eat bread with Hebrews was an "abomination to the Egyptians."

Among the many actions and attitudes that the Bible says are abominations to God are:

> imperfect offerings—*Deuteronomy 17:1*
> witchcraft and sorcery—*Deuteronomy 18:9-12*
> homosexuality—*Leviticus 18:22*
> adultery and other wrong sexual acts—*Ezekiel 22:11*
> dishonesty and other activities that hurt someone else—*Proverbs 6:16-19*
> idolatry—*Ezekiel 8:15-17*
> unlawful foods—*Leviticus 11:10-12*
> pretending to be religious—*Proverbs 15:8*

ABOMINATION OF DESOLATION: This unusual phrase appears in Daniel 8:13; 9:27; 11:31; and 12:11. Jesus referred back to these words in Matthew 24:15 and Mark 13:14. A better translation might be "detestable thing, or sin that causes horror."

Many scholars think Jesus used Daniel's phrase to foretell the awful destruction of the Temple in Jerusalem in A.D. 70 when Roman soldiers fought Jewish Zealots. Others believe Jesus was referring to the "man of sin (or lawlessness)" mentioned in 2 Thessalonians 2:1-12, who will appear near the end of time.

Most Jews believed that the prophecy in Daniel was fulfilled in 167 B.C. when the wicked Antiochus Epiphanes *(an-TYE-oh-cuss Ee-PIF-an-ees)*, king of Syria, entered the Temple in Jerusalem, set up an altar to the Greek god Zeus (ZOOS) over the sacred altar, and ordered a pig (offensive to the Jews) to be sacrificed there. This act led to a war for freedom called the Maccabean *(MACK-ah-BEE-an)* Revolt.

ABRAHAM *(AY-bruh-ham)* is called the father of the Israelites or Hebrew people. He is the spiritual father of all Christians because of his deep faith in God. His story is told in Genesis, chapters 12—25.

When Abraham and his family moved, they made up quite a caravan.

In the beginning, his name was Abram. His family lived in a city called Ur. Then the whole clan moved nearly 800 miles northwest to Haran. They probably traveled by foot and camel.

At Haran, God called Abram to go to Canaan. He took his wife, Sarai, and his nephew, Lot, with him. They lived in Canaan until a famine forced them to move to Egypt, about 750 miles from Haran.

The ruler there, the Pharaoh, tried to take Sarai into his harem. But God sent diseases on the house of the Pharaoh, and she was released. Then Abram and his family left Egypt and went back to Bethel in Canaan.

Abram and his nephew, Lot, were both growing rich; each had many cattle and herdsmen. But there was not enough grass to graze all the cattle, and Lot's workers argued with Abram's. Knowing they must separate, Abram took Lot up on a hill. He told Lot to choose either the land to the east or to the west, and Abram would take the opposite. Lot saw the fertile valleys of the Jordan River to the east and chose that land—and much trouble. (See *Lot.*)

At that time, Abram had no children. But God appeared to him and said that someday he would have as many descendants as the stars in heaven. When Sarai still did not have children, Sarai suggested that Abram and a servant woman named Hagar have a child. (This was a common custom in that day.) A son, Ishmael, was born when Abram was 86.

Thirteen years later, God changed their names from Abram to Abraham and from Sarai to Sarah. He again promised that they would have a son. Both Sarah and Abraham knew this would be a miracle, since they were much too old to have children. But when Abraham was 100 years old, Isaac was born!

God tested Abraham's faith by telling him to offer this son he loved so much as a sacrifice. Abraham followed God's directions. But at

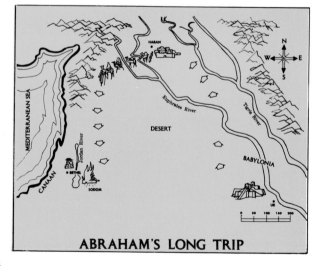

ABRAHAM'S LONG TRIP

6

the last moment, God stopped him from killing his son as a sacrifice. God said he only wanted to see how much Abraham trusted him.

When Abraham was 140 years old, Sarah died. After her death, Abraham married Keturah and had six more children. However, all of the Hebrew people, the nation of Israel, are Abraham's and Sarah's descendants.

Where to find it

The move to the Promised Land   *Genesis 12:1-9*
The trip to Egypt   *Genesis 12:10–13:1*
Abram and Lot separate   *Genesis 13:2-18*
Abram rescues Lot   *Genesis 14*
God's promise   *Genesis 15*
Ishmael is born   *Genesis 16*
Abram's new name   *Genesis 17:1–18:15*
Abraham with the Philistines   *Genesis 20; 21:22-24*
Isaac is born   *Genesis 21:1-7*
Hagar and Ishmael leave   *Genesis 21:8-21*
Isaac as a sacrifice   *Genesis 22*
Sarah dies   *Genesis 23*
A wife for Isaac   *Genesis 24*
Abraham's second family; his death   *Genesis 25:1-10*
Abraham, the spiritual father of all Christians   *Romans 4; Galatians 3:6-29*

ABRAHAM'S BOSOM *(AY-bruh-ham's BOO-zum).* This is a word picture used in Luke 16:22-23 to represent paradise after death. The idea comes from the Roman custom of stretching out on cots at a meal. People would eat this way, propped up on one elbow. With the head of each cot near the table, one person's head was close to the chest of the person next to him.

Since Abraham was the founder of the Jewish nation, to be next to him at a feast would be a great honor.

ABRAM *(AY-brum)* was the original name of Abraham before God changed it. Names were often changed in some way after people met God.

ABSALOM *(AB-suh-lum)* was the third son of King David. He was handsome and had long, beautiful hair. He planned the murder of his older brother Amnon. He then had to get away from his father's anger and stayed away for three years. Finally he returned, and David forgave him.

However, in a few years, Absalom turned the loyalty of many Israelites away from King

Absalom liked to impress people with his chariot.

David to himself. In a terrible battle between Absalom's men and those of King David, Absalom was riding a mule, and his long hair caught in the branches of a tree. The mule ran off and left Absalom hanging there. Some of David's men found him and killed him, even though David had forbidden them to hurt Absalom. This caused David great grief.

Where to find it: *2 Samuel 13–18*

ABSTAIN, ABSTINENCE *(ab-STAIN, AB-stin-ens).* These words mean "to stay away from." They are often used in the New Testament to tell Christians to stay away from sins and from actions that offend other people.

ABYSS *(uh-BISS)* means "bottomless" in Greek. In the New Testament this word is usually used of the home of demons, or the after-death prison of those who disobey God. It is used this way in Luke 8:31; Revelation 9:1, 2, 11; 11:7; 17:8; 20:1-3. In Romans 10:7 it simply means "the place of the dead."

ACACIA (see *Plants*)

ACCO (see *Ptolemais*)

ACCURSED *(uh-CURST)* means to be condemned or cut off from God.

ACELDAMA (see *Akeldama*)

ACHAIA *(uh-KAY-uh)* was a Roman province in what is now the southern half of Greece.

Corinth was the capital, although Athens may have been a more important city. Paul visited this area on two of his three missionary journeys.

ACHAICUS and **FORTUNATUS** *(uh-KAY-uh-cuss* and *for-to-NAY-tuss)* were two Christians from the church at Corinth who visited the apostle Paul at Ephesus, encouraging him. They are mentioned in 1 Corinthians 16: 17-18.

Achan's secret loot didn't stay secret for long.

ACHAN *(AY-kun)* was an Israelite who disobeyed God and brought defeat to his nation's army. At the battle of Jericho, God commanded the warriors to take no loot for themselves. Everything made of metal (gold, silver, bronze, iron) was to be devoted to God; everything else was to be destroyed. But Achan took some clothing, gold, and silver for himself and buried it beneath his tent.

Because of his disobedience, God let the Israelites be badly defeated in the battle for the city of Ai. Then he told Joshua there was sin among his men. God also told him how to identify the guilty person. Achan finally confessed. Achan and his family were put to death for the sin. (In ancient Israel, the family was considered a unit, and what the father did involved everyone in his family.)

Where to find it: *Joshua 7: 1-26*

ACHISH *(AY-kish)* was a king of the Philistines. David ran to his city once when he was running from Saul, but the soldiers there didn't trust him. So David pretended he was insane so he could escape.

Later, David with his 600 warriors returned to the kingdom of Achish. This time Achish trusted him and even invited him and his men to join his army in a war against Israel and King Saul. David agreed, but the Philistine commanders objected, saying that in battle David and his men might turn against them. Reluctantly, Achish sent David and his men away.

Where to find it: *1 Samuel 21: 10–22: 1; 29: 1-11*

ACHSAH *(OX-uh)* was a young woman given as a bride to Othniel as a reward after he conquered the city of Kiriath-sepher. Although her father had given her a field as a wedding present or dowry, it was a dry area, so she asked her father for some springs of water also. Her request was granted.

Where to find it: *Joshua 15: 16-19; Judges 1: 12-15*

ACRE (see *Measures*)

ACROSTIC *(uh-CROSS-tick)* is a kind of Hebrew poem in which verses or lines begin with letters of the Hebrew alphabet in order, like our A, B, C, D, etc.

For example, in Psalms 25 and 34 and in Lamentations 1 and 2, each stanza begins with one of the 22 letters of the Hebrew alphabet, in order. Psalm 119 has 22 whole sections of 8 verses each, and each section starts with a letter of the Hebrew alphabet, in order. This is why Psalm 119 is the longest chapter in the Bible.

Psalms 37, 111, 112, 145, and Proverbs 31: 10-31 are all acrostic poems.

ACTS OF THE APOSTLES *(uh-PAH-suls)* is the fifth book in the New Testament. It was prob-

ably written by Luke, the doctor who went with Paul on parts of his second and third missionary journeys. He probably wrote it about A.D. 61 or 62.

Acts shows how the Church grew from a small group of frightened believers who huddled in one room to a courageous, growing Church spread across the Roman Empire.

Acts centers mostly on the work of two men—Peter and Paul. Peter is the main person until the end of chapter 12. Beginning in chapter 13, Paul becomes the main character.

The most important happening in the early part of the book is the Day of Pentecost, when the Holy Spirit came on the believers in Jerusalem. From that time on, the Church began to grow. At first, the growth was just in Jerusalem itself, but beginning in chapter 8, the Church spread to the rest of Judea and Samaria and then to Antioch and other places.

Beginning in chapter 13, Paul's missionary journeys are traced as the gospel is told in Asia Minor, Greece, and Rome. The letters of Paul in the New Testament are written to some of the churches he started while on those journeys or to pastors and Christian workers in those churches.

The story in Acts also shows some of the problems that came when the Christian faith became separate from the Jewish faith. Most of the very early Christians were Jews, and it was hard to bring them together with non-Jews in one church. But Acts shows that the gospel of Christ and the Holy Spirit break down barriers that divide people so that all can become part of the "Body of Christ"—his Church.

ADAM *(AD-um)* is the name of the first person God created. The name *Adam* also sometimes means all people or mankind. It is used this way in Genesis 5:2.

Genesis 1:27 says that God created the first man and the first woman. He told them to take care of all he had created, a beautiful world in the Garden of Eden, rich with fruits, vegetables, and animals.

The Bible does not say how long Adam and Eve lived in the beautiful garden before they sinned by eating the fruit of the one tree God had said they were to leave alone. When Adam and Eve disobeyed God, sin, with all its

ugliness, entered the world.

After that, Adam and Eve no longer had a good, open feeling toward God. Their harmony with nature and with each other was also destroyed. God told them they must leave the Garden of Eden and that they would die.

From that time on, every person born into the world would, like Adam and Eve, choose the way of sin. Only the coming of Jesus Christ, God's Son, could remove the barriers between people and God. Jesus is called the "second Adam" in Romans 5:14-21 and in 1 Corinthians 15:22, 45.

After Adam and Eve left the Garden of Eden, they had many children, but the best known are Cain and Abel. Adam lived to be 930 years old.

Where to find it

God creates him   *Genesis 1:26–2:7*
Names the animals   *Genesis 2:19-20*
God creates Eve   *Genesis 2:21-25*
Eats the forbidden fruit   *Genesis 3:1-7*
Is punished   *Genesis 3:8-24*
Becomes a father   *Genesis 4:1-2, 25*

ADAMANT *(AD-uh-munt)* was very hard stone—as hard as diamond.

ADAR (see *Calendar*)

ADDER (see *Animals*)

ADJURE *(ad-JOOR)* means to speak very seriously or to command seriously.

ADONI-BEZEK *(uh-DOH-ni BEE-zek)* was king of the city of Bezek. He was a cruel man who admitted that 70 kings whom he had captured had had their thumbs and big toes cut off. When Adoni-Bezek was captured, he was punished the same way. He said God was paying him back for what he had done.

Where to find it: *Judges 1:4-7*

ADONIJAH *(AD-oh-NY-juh)* was the handsome, spoiled fourth son of King David. His three older brothers died while they were young men, leaving Adonijah the oldest at the time of David's death. He wanted to become king, even though he knew his younger brother Solomon had been chosen by God to

ADONIRAM

be the next king. When David was old, Adonijah convinced some of David's right-hand men to help make him king.

Adonijah planned a great feast where he would be crowned. He was careful, of course, not to invite Solomon or those who still supported David.

When Nathan, a prophet loyal to David, heard about the plan, he told Solomon's mother, Bathsheba. She told David that Adonijah was proclaiming himself king. David immediately ordered Solomon to ride upon the king's mule and be anointed king. In this way Solomon was proclaimed king.

When the news came to Adonijah at his feast that Solomon already had been anointed, Adonijah's supporters ran away. Adonijah knew his life was now in danger because he had tried to take the throne. He ran to the altar in the Tabernacle, where fugitives were protected from harm.

Solomon forgave Adonijah, and he returned to Jerusalem. But after David's death, Adonijah asked his brother for permission to marry Abishag, who was David's companion during his last illness. In the eyes of the people, this could have been interpreted as meaning Adonijah was the rightful heir to all that had belonged to David. Solomon was angry at the request and ordered Adonijah to be put to death.

Where to find it: *1 Kings 1:1–2:25*

ADONIRAM *(AD-oh-NY-rum)* was also known as **ADORAM.** He was the official in charge of slaves under King David, King Solomon, and King Rehoboam. Rehoboam (son of Solomon) made the life of the slaves so difficult that they revolted and killed Adoniram, their supervisor.

Where to find it: *1 Kings 4:6; 5:14; 12:18*

ADONI-ZEDEK *(uh-DOH-ni ZEE-dek)* was the Amorite (pagan) king of Jerusalem when the Israelites began taking over Canaan. When he heard that Joshua and his armies had destroyed the big city of Ai, and that the city of Gibeon (a few miles northwest of Jerusalem) had made peace with Joshua, Adoni-Zedek was afraid. He invited the kings of four other cities south of Jerusalem to fight against the

When the battle wasn't finished at sundown, Joshua asked for a miracle.

people of Gibeon. They appealed to Joshua for help, and Joshua and his army came to rescue them. Joshua prayed for help, and the Bible says the sun and the moon stood still until the Israelites won the battle.

During the battle, the five kings hid in a cave. When Joshua heard where they were, he ordered that the cave be sealed with a large stone. After the battle, Adoni-Zedek and the other kings were brought out of the cave and killed. Later they were buried in the same cave, and the cave again was sealed with stones.

Where to find it: *Joshua 10:1-27*

ADOPTION *(uh-DOP-shun)* describes how a person can become a member of a family even though he or she was not born into it. The word is used by the apostle Paul to explain how people who are naturally sinners can by "adoption" become children of God, with many privileges and joys. In Ephesians 1:3-5, Christians are said to be adopted into God's family through Jesus Christ, God's Son.

Paul shows the difference between being a slave and being a son in Galatians 4:1-7. He says Christ came to redeem those who were slaves (of sin) so they could receive the adoption of sons.

In Romans 8:14-17, Paul says the Holy Spirit is the witness that we are now sons of God. He may have been referring to the Roman law

10

requiring witnesses to an adoption.

Christians are children of God, not simply because he created them, but because they have been adopted into God's family.

ADORAM (see *Adoniram*)

ADRAMMELECH *(uh-DRAHM-eh-lek)* was a pagan god brought to Samaria by settlers after the Assyrians conquered the land in 722 B.C. People sometimes burned their children as offerings to Adrammelech. These new settlers said they "feared Jehovah" (whom they thought was the "god of this land"), but they kept on worshiping their own gods also.

Where to find it: *2 Kings 17:24-41*

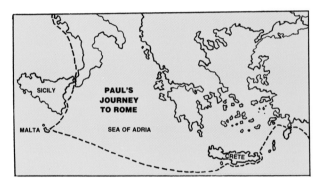

ADRIA *(AY-dree-uh)* was the part of the Mediterranean Sea between the island of Crete and the island of Sicily. Paul was shipwrecked in this sea on his voyage to Rome and finally landed on the island of Malta, south of Sicily.

Where to find it: *Acts 27:27–28:1*

ADULLAM *(uh-DULL-um)* was a very old and beautiful city about 13 miles southwest of Bethlehem. Near it were many limestone caves, where David and his men and family sometimes hid when Saul was trying to kill David. While hiding there, David once said he wished for some water from the well at Bethlehem. Three of his men risked their lives to get it, but David refused to drink it because of the risk they had taken. He poured it out as an offering to God.

Where to find it: *2 Samuel 23:13-17*

ADULTERY *(uh-DUL-ter-ee)* refers to sexual intercourse between a man and a woman when either of them is married to someone else. Another term, *fornication*, means sexual intercourse between any man and woman who are not married to each other. Both adultery and fornication are wrong according to the Bible.

The term *adultery* is also used as a figure of speech meaning "idolatry." In the Old Testament, the Jewish people are referred to as the "wife" of God, and when they turned from God to idols, they were said to be "committing adultery."

Where to find it: *Exodus 20:14; Matthew 15:19; Jeremiah 3:9*

ADVENT *(AD-vent)* means the coming of Christ. The term *Advent Season* means the four Sundays before Christmas—the time of getting ready to celebrate the coming of Christ. It is a time when Christians think about Christ's birth and what it means.

ADVERSARY *(AD-ver-sair-ee)* means an enemy or someone who is against you. The enemy can be a person, a nation, or Satan. Satan is called our adversary in 1 Peter 5:8.

ADVOCATE *(AD-vo-kate)* is someone who gives help, strength, comfort, or advice. Jesus Christ and the Holy Spirit are called advocates of the believer.

Where to find it

Jesus, our advocate   *1 John 2:1, 2*
Holy Spirit, our advocate   *John 14:16, 26; 15:26; 16:7*

AFFLICTION *(af-FLICK-shun)* (see *Suffering*)

AGABUS *(AG-uh-bus)* was a New Testament prophet from Jerusalem who went to the Christians at Antioch and foretold a famine. After hearing his prophecy, the Antioch Christians decided to send Paul and Barnabas to Judea with help for the believers there. Agabus appeared again many years later, where he foretold that Paul would be arrested if he went to Jerusalem.

Where to find it

Foretells a famine   *Acts 11:27-30*
Foretells Paul's arrest   *Acts 21:10-11*

AGAG *(AYE-gag)*, king of the Amalekites, was captured by King Saul after a battle in which the Israelites destroyed everyone else. However, God had ordered Saul to kill *every* person and every animal. When the prophet Samuel reminded Saul that he had disobeyed God, Saul made excuses, saying that the best cattle and sheep had been saved to offer to God. Samuel told Saul that because he disobeyed, God was rejecting him as king. Agag was then brought to Samuel and killed.

Where to find it: *1 Samuel 15*

AGATE *(AG-ut)* is a crystallized stone or quartz with colored bands or cloudy spots.

AGE in the Bible often refers to a long or unknown period of time. It probably means "eternity" in Hebrews 6:5. In Matthew 24:3, Jesus' disciples speak of "the close of the age," meaning the end of the world as we now know it. In Matthew 12:32, Jesus speaks of "this age or the age to come," meaning this world and the world of life after death.

Old age in biblical times was thought of as a sign of God's favor. To live long was an honor. Older people looked at their gray hair as "a crown of glory." Older people were important in the social and political life of the Hebrew people. They were seen as a valuable source of knowledge, and they were always expected to speak first.

Where to find it: *Job 12:12; 32:4, 6*

AGONY *(AG-un-ee)* is a word used only once in the New Testament. It describes Jesus' suffering in the Garden of Gethsemane just before his crucifixion. Christ suffered so much that "his sweat was like great drops of blood falling down upon the ground." His agony was because he knew he would die in terrible pain upon the cross and—even worse—he would be deserted by God, because he was dying for the sins of the world.

Where to find it: *Luke 22:44*

AGRICULTURE, or farming, is the oldest occupation in the world. It began in the Garden of Eden when Adam and Eve were told to care for the garden. Cain, their oldest child, was a farmer; Abel, their second son, was a herdsman. Most people in the ancient world

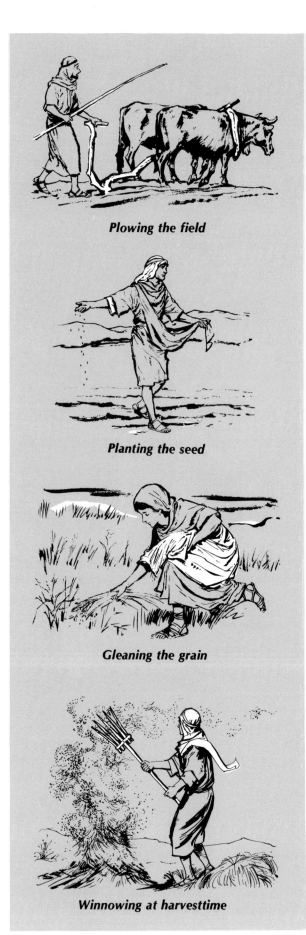

Plowing the field

Planting the seed

Gleaning the grain

Winnowing at harvesttime

farmed or raised cattle and sheep.

Farming the land that is now Israel was never easy. The land was very stony, and the first job of every farmer was to pick up the rocks, usually using them to build fences or dividers. The land was also hilly; farmers often had to build terraces to raise crops.

The climate made farming difficult. Every year there was a five-month summer season without rain and sometimes with hot, searing winds. While the farmer knew there would be a hot, dry season from May to October, the rainy season (the rest of the year) was unpredictable. If it did not rain often from November through April, he knew the summer would bring famine.

Farmers in Bible times tried to prepare for dry seasons by building storage places for the water that fell during the rainy season. Archaeologists have dug up these cisterns all over Palestine. Farmers also carried water from streams or springs.

In addition to problems of rocky land and not enough water, farmers struggled with plant diseases and insects. Locusts, a kind of grasshopper, were a constant threat. A plague of locusts could eat everything green in a few days, leaving only dry stubble. The Book of Joel was written about a locust plague.

Common crops were grapes, olives, wheat, and barley. However, the Bible says people also grew figs, pomegranates, onions, leeks, beans, and garlic.

The farmer of Bible times had few tools. He plowed with oxen pulling a wooden stick with a small metal point. He cut grain by holding the stalks in his hand and cutting them off close to the ground with a large curved knife called a sickle.

To separate the kernels of grain from the stalks, the farmer might beat the grain with a stick or drive his cattle around on piled-up stalks until their hoofs trampled out the grain. Or he might drag some heavy instrument or sledge over the grain.

When the grain had been threshed (kernels separated from stalks), it had to be winnowed. The farmer threw the grain into the air when the wind was blowing. The wind would blow away the lighter chaff, and the heavier seeds would fall to the ground.

During harvesttimes, every healthy person worked in the fields—owners and slaves, women and children. At night, many men would stay in their fields to guard their threshed grain or their ripening crops from robbers or animals.

The religious life of the Hebrew people centered in part around the harvest periods. They gave a tithe (one tenth) of their seed to God. The first sheep born into a flock would be sacrificed to God. At the time of the Passover Feast, usually in April, the fields were just beginning to bear barley, and the people brought to God an offering of the first stalks of grain, "the sheaf of first fruits."

Fifty days later, at the Feast of Pentecost, the wheat would be ripe, and the Jewish people brought two loaves of fresh bread as an offering to the Lord. Later on, the Feast of Booths marked the end of the harvesttime and lasted eight days. (See *Feasts*)

AGRIPPA (*uh-GRIP-uh*) was the name of two rulers in the time of Paul.

1. Herod Agrippa I began ruling a small territory in A.D. 37 and ruled all of Palestine from A.D. 40 to 44. The Bible simply calls him "Herod." Acts 12:1-2 tells that he had James, the brother of John, put to death "to please the Jews." He also had Peter arrested. He died suddenly at age 54 after he permitted his followers to say he was a god.

2. Herod Agrippa II, the son of Herod Agrippa I, is called "Agrippa" in the Bible. He was the ruler before whom Paul gave a speech defending himself. After the speech, Agrippa said he thought Paul did not deserve to be in prison.

Where to find it

Herod Agrippa I   *Acts 12:1-23*
Herod Agrippa II   *Acts 25:23–26:32*

AHAB (*AY-hab*) was the seventh and most evil king Israel ever had. He was also a strong political and military leader who defeated Syria twice. He reigned from about 874 to 853 B.C.

He married Jezebel, who was not an Israelite. She brought her pagan gods to Israel and led the people to worship them. She persecuted the prophets of God and killed many of them.

Ahab was king during the famous conflict between the prophet Elijah and the prophets

"Put this prophet in prison!"
King Ahab ordered when he didn't like
the message God had given Micaiah to say.

of Baal on Mount Carmel, when God sent fire to consume Elijah's offering.

Although Ahab was very rich and lived in a beautiful ivory palace, he always wanted more. Next to his place was a vineyard—but it belonged to a man named Naboth. Ahab offered to buy it, but Naboth did not want to sell, because the land had belonged to his ancestors. Ahab pouted and refused to eat. To get the vineyard for Ahab, Jezebel lied and accused Naboth of crimes for which he was put to death. For this sin, God allowed Ahab to lose his life in the next battle with Syria.

Where to find it

Contest with Elijah   *1 Kings 18:1–19:1*
Gets Naboth's vineyard   *1 Kings 21*
Rejects Micaiah's message   *1 Kings 22:1–28*

AHASUERUS *(uh-HAZ-oo-EAR-us)* was a powerful king of the Medes and the Persians. He is probably the same person known in secular history as Xerxes I, who reigned from about 486 to 465 B.C.

He became angry with his queen, Vashti, when she refused to appear at a huge banquet of many drunken men. So he got rid of her and later chose Esther, the cousin of Mordecai, to be the new queen.

At the request of Haman, his chief officer, Ahasuerus ordered that all Jews were to be killed on a certain day. Esther went to the king about it, and eventually Ahasuerus ordered Haman to be hung in the very place Haman had built for Mordecai. The Jews were al-lowed to protect themselves from harm.

Later, Ahasuerus made Mordecai his chief officer.

Where to find it: *the Book of Esther*

AHAZ *(AY-haz)*, the twelfth king of Judah, was one of its most wicked rulers. He became king at age 20 and ruled from 735 to 715 B.C.

He made idols to false gods called Baals, encouraged his people to sacrifice their children to these gods, and built altars to foreign gods all across the country of Judah. God punished him by letting Judah be defeated by Syria and by Israel. Syria took many captives and so did Israel. However, Israel later sent its captives back to their own land when a prophet of God ordered it.

In desperation, King Ahaz asked the king of Assyria for help. But instead of helping Judah, Assyria attacked. Ahaz took furnishings from his palace and from the Temple of God to use as a gift for the king of Assyria. Then Ahaz destroyed all the other things in the Temple and erected more altars to false gods.

Because of his wickedness, he was not buried with the other kings.

Where to find it: *2 Chronicles 28:1-27; 2 Kings 17–18; Isaiah 7*

AHAZIAH *(AY-haz-EYE-uh)* is the name of two men in the Bible.

1. The first was the eighth king of Israel, the son of wicked Ahab and Jezebel. He was king

14

only one year, in 853 B.C., and died as the result of a fall in his palace. While he was king, the Moabites rebelled against having to pay 100,000 lambs and the wool of 100,000 rams each year to the kings of Israel.

While sick, Ahaziah sent messengers to ask the false god Baal-zebub whether he would recover. God told the prophet Elijah to meet the messengers and tell them they did not have to go to a foreign god to find the answer: Ahaziah was definitely going to die. Hearing this, Ahaziah was so angry he sent several groups of men to capture Elijah. However, two groups of 50 men each were consumed by fire from heaven. When the third group came to Elijah, their leader begged for mercy. Elijah went with them and personally told his message of doom to Ahaziah.

Where to find it: *2 Kings 1:1-17; 3:4-5*

2. The second Ahaziah was the nephew of the first Ahaziah. He became the sixth king of Judah. He, too, reigned only one year, in 841 B.C. He worshiped idols like his grandfather, Ahab, and his mother, Athaliah, had done. While visiting King Joram of Israel, who had been wounded in a battle, he was caught by Jehu, the newly anointed king of Israel. Ahaziah was struck by an arrow as he tried to get away in his chariot, and he died.

Where to find it: *2 Kings 8:25-29*

AHIJAH *(uh-HI-juh)* was the name of seven men in the Bible, two of whom were important.

1. One was the great-grandson of Eli. This Ahijah served as priest in the days of Saul, about 1025 B.C. In a battle between the Israelites and the Philistines, Saul commanded Ahijah to bring the ark to the scene. The Israelites eventually won.

Where to find it: *1 Samuel 14:1-23*

2. Another Ahijah was a prophet from Shiloh who met Jeroboam on a road going out of Jerusalem. Ahijah said God would make Jeroboam ruler of the ten northern tribes of Israel. He dramatized his prophecy by tearing his clothes into twelve pieces and giving ten of them to Jeroboam. This all came true about

930 B.C. Ahijah later foretold the fall of Jeroboam's family and the death of his son.

Where to find it: *1 Kings 11:29-40; 14:1-17*

AHIKAM *(uh-HI-kum)* was one of the men King Josiah asked about the meaning of the Book of the Law that had been found in the Temple. After Josiah died, the leaders of Judah wanted to kill the prophet Jeremiah for warning them of the trouble to come. Ahikam convinced them to let Jeremiah live.

Where to find it: *2 Kings 22:8-20; Jeremiah 26:20-24*

AHIMAAZ *(uh-HIM-ay-az)* carried messages between his father, Zadok, the high priest, and King David during the rebellion of Absalom. Once Ahimaaz and his friend had to hide in a well. To protect them, a woman spread a cloth over the top of the well and scattered grain on it so nothing would look suspicious. Ahimaaz and his friend were saved.

Ahimaaz also carried the news to David of his army's victory over Absalom's. When David asked about Absalom, Ahimaaz hesitated to tell David that his son was dead, and while he hesitated, another man came with the report.

Where to find it

Hides in well   *2 Samuel 17:17-20*
Brings news of Absalom   *2 Samuel 18:24-33*

AHIMELECH *(uh-HIM-eh-lek)* was high priest during the reign of Saul, around 1050 to 1011 B.C. Not knowing that Saul was trying to kill David, Ahimelech helped David one day by giving him holy loaves of bread from the table of showbread in the Tabernacle. He also gave him the sword David had used to kill Goliath, the giant.

A man who was in the Tabernacle reported all this to Saul. He became so angry he ordered Ahimelech and all the priests with him to be killed.

Where to find it: *1 Samuel 21:1-9; 22:6-23*

AHITHOPHEL *(uh-HITH-uh-fel)* was one of David's advisers when he first became king. For reasons not stated in the Bible, Ahithophel joined Absalom (David's son) in rebelling against David. Both David and Absalom considered Ahithophel to be a very wise man. Ahithophel urged Absalom to gather 12,000 men and attack while David and his army were tired and discouraged.

However, Absalom also asked another man, Hushai (who was a counterspy—pretending to serve Absalom, but really on David's side). He suggested that Absalom postpone the battle until he could gather a larger army. Absalom took Hushai's advice instead of Ahithophel's, and the extra time gave David and his men a chance to escape.

When Ahithophel saw that his advice was not followed, he went home and hanged himself.

Where to find it: *2 Samuel 15: 12, 31; 16: 15-23; 17: 1-23*

AHOLAH and AHOLIBAH *(uh-HOLE-uh)* and *(uh-HOLE-uh-buh)*.

In Ezekiel 23 Aholah is a woman who stands for Samaria, the capital of the Northern Kingdom, Israel. Aholibah is a woman who represents Jerusalem, the capital of Judah. In Ezekiel's word picture, these women represent the people of the cities, who have been unfaithful to God. For their idolatry, both cities would be captured by their enemies.

AI *(AY-eye)* was an old city in central Palestine. After Joshua and his army conquered Jericho, Ai was the next city to be attacked. Joshua sent spies to check it out, and they came back saying that the city was small and unprotected; 2,000-3,000 men could easily defeat it.

Joshua sent 3,000 men, but they were beaten by the men of Ai. In despair, Joshua prayed, and God said they were defeated because some Israelites had sinned in the Battle of Jericho by keeping some of the treasures of the city. After the sin was found (see *Achan),* the Israelites returned to the battle, using a clever ambush to draw the warriors out of Ai. The city was destroyed and burned.

It was apparently rebuilt in later years (after the Book of Joshua was written), because some men of Ai were among those who returned from captivity in Babylon.

Where to find it
Battle for the city   *Joshua 7:1–8: 29*
Men from Ai return   *Ezra 2: 28; Nehemiah 7: 32*

AKELDAMA *(uh-KEL-duh-muh)* is the name of the field Judas bought with the money he got for betraying Jesus. The word means "Field of Blood." It may have been bought by the priests in the name of Judas. It was used to bury strangers who died in Jerusalem.

Where to find it: *Matthew 27: 3-10; Acts 1: 18-19*

Alabaster containers held expensive ointment from the spikenard plant. The top was sealed, and had to be broken off in order to use.

ALABASTER *(AL-ah-BAS-ter)* was a soft, creamy-colored stone often used for making perfume flasks and boxes for fragrant salves or creams. Alabaster had streaks of varying shades and colors.

ALEXANDER THE GREAT *(AL-eg-ZAN-der)* is not mentioned in the Bible, but his life is important in understanding the New Testament. The greatest military general of many centuries, he conquered almost all of the then-known world for Greece. In 334 B.C., he crossed from Greece into Asia Minor (now Turkey) and conquered the armies of the Persians and the Medes; then he went as far south as Egypt, which he took without a battle. There he founded Alexandria, today the second largest city of Egypt. He traveled across Palestine to Babylonia and all the way to India.

His army refused to go any farther, and he was forced to stop. He died at age 32 of a fever. He was said to have wept because there were no more worlds for him to conquer.

As the result of his campaigns, Greek became the common language in most of the known world. This was important in the spread of the gospel after Christ's death and resurrection. Most scholars think the "king of Greece" mentioned in Daniel 8: 5-8 and 11: 3-4 was Alexander the Great.

The famous general, Alexander the Great.

ALEXANDRIA *(AL-eg-ZAN-dree-uh)* is the second most important city in Egypt (Cairo is first). It was also important in New Testament times, although it is mentioned only four times. Stephen, in Acts 6:9, debated with men from the synagogue of the Alexandrians; twice "ships of Alexandria" are mentioned in Paul's journeys. Apollos, who became a leader of the church at Ephesus, came from Alexandria.

Alexandria was founded by Alexander the Great in 332 B.C. From its beginning it was a city famous for its learning—art, literature, poetry, medicine, mathematics, and astronomy. Many Jews lived in Alexandria, and in this city, Jewish scholars first translated the Old Testament from Hebrew into Greek, working from about 250 to 150 B.C. Their translation was known as the Septuagint, and it became the Bible of the early church.

ALIEN *(AY-lee-en)* (see *Sojourner*)

ALLEGORY *(AL-luh-gore-ree)* is a kind of story in which objects or people represent something else to teach a particular lesson. The Bible has many allegories. One is found in Psalm 80:8-16, where the Jewish nation is pictured as a vine that came out of Egypt and was planted in other ground, but has been destroyed.

John 15:1-10 is another allegory, in which Christ is pictured as a vine; believers are branches on the vine, and God the Father is pictured as the farmer who takes care of the vine and its branches. The allegory teaches two lessons—it is important for believers to keep close to Christ; and God wants Christians to be "fruitful," showing their faith by their lives.

ALLELUIA (see *Hallelujah*)

ALLIANCE *(uh-LY-unce)* is an agreement between persons or nations, usually to help each other. Most alliances in the Bible involved military help. King Ahaz made an alliance with the king of Assyria to get help in a war against the king of Syria. Other alliances were for business purposes. When Solomon was building the Temple, he made an alliance with Hiram, king of Tyre, to trade cedar and cypress wood for wheat and oil.

The Hebrews were warned not to make alliances with other countries but to trust in God alone. The rulers of Israel often disobeyed that command.

Where to find it

King Ahaz's alliance   *2 Kings 16:5-9*
Warning against alliances   *Exodus 23:32; 34:12-16*

ALLOT, ALLOTMENT *(uh-LOT, uh-LOT-ment)* refers to assigning rights to land or other property. Each of the twelve tribes of Israel was allotted certain parts of the land of Canaan to use. The basis for these allotments is not always clear.

ALMIGHTY *(all-MIGHT-ee)* is a name of God that appears 48 times in the Old Testament and nine times in the New Testament. The Hebrew word means "with great strength," and the Greek word means "all-powerful."

ALMOND (see *Plants*)

ALMS *(ahmz)* are acts of kindness to those who need food, shelter, or other help. Usually it refers to giving money or food to the poor. Jesus taught his followers to give alms and to do it quietly, without letting others know.

Where to find it: *Luke 12:33; Matthew 6:2-4*

ALMUG (see *Plants*)

ALOES (see *Plants*)

ALPHA and **OMEGA** (AL-fuh and oh-MAY-guh) are the first and last letters of the Greek alphabet. When the two are used together, it usually means completeness. In Revelation 1:8, God calls himself "Alpha and Omega, the beginning and the ending." These words are also used of Christ in Revelation 22:13.

Animals were offered to God on altars.

ALTAR (AWL-ter) is a structure made of stone, wood, marble, brick, or other materials; it is used in worship. Altars were common in pagan religions as well as in Judaism. Some altars were very simple; others were fancy. The first altar mentioned in the Bible was built by Noah.

The Jewish Tabernacle had two altars. One was the altar of burnt offering, where sacrifices to God were burned. The other was an altar of incense, sometimes called a golden altar. Incense was burned on this altar twice each day to symbolize believers' prayers (see *Offerings*).

AMALEKITES (uh-MAL-uh-kites) were a fierce, warlike tribe of nomads who descended from one of the sons of Esau. They seemed to wander from what is now the Sinai desert to Palestine. From the time the Israelites came out of Egypt (about 1450 B.C.) to the time of King Hezekiah (about 700 B.C.), the Amalekites always seemed to be enemies of Israel.

The Amalekites first attacked the Israelites as they were coming out of Egypt. In that famous battle, the Israelites kept winning as long as Aaron and Hur held up the arms of Moses. God told Moses at that time, "I will utterly blot out the remembrance of Amalek from under heaven."

In Judges 6:3, the Amalekites appear as a people who swept down upon settlements and took food, animals, and other possessions.

While David and his men were gone from their village of Ziklag, the Amalekites burned it, capturing their wives and children. David later organized a raiding party and rescued the wives and children from the Amalekites.

Saul was told to destroy the Amalekites, but he did not do it completely. They continued to harass the Israelites until the time of Hezekiah, when they were finally destroyed.

Where to find it

Attack Israelites   *Exodus 17:8-16*
Destroy crops   *Judges 6:3-5*
Raid on Ziklag   *1 Samuel 30:1-26*

AMASA (uh-MAY-suh) was the nephew of David. When David's son Absalom rebelled against his father and tried to become king, Amasa became commander of Absalom's army. After Absalom was killed and the rebellion was put down, David made Amasa commander of his army in place of Joab (who had killed Absalom).

Another rebellion arose quickly, led by Sheba, and David sent Amasa out to assemble the army within three days. When Amasa did not come back in three days (reasons not given), David sent another leader, Abishai (brother of Joab), out to fight Sheba.

When Amasa, with his men, joined forces with Abishai, Joab was also there. Joab pretended to greet Amasa as a friend, but instead he ran a sword through him. He was left to die in a field as the army went on.

Where to find it: *2 Samuel 20:1-13*

AMAZIAH (am-ah-ZIE-ah) was the proud ninth king of Judah (796-767 B.C.). He became king when he was 25 years old and reigned 29 years—until he was killed in a plot.

Although Amaziah started out doing the right things, he liked war, and it became his downfall.

At one time he gathered 300,000 men of Judah and then hired an additional 100,000 soldiers from Israel. After he was warned by a prophet against hiring the men, he dismissed them. They were so angry that they looted several cities of Judah along the way.

Amaziah went with his soldiers from Judah against the Edomites and defeated them. He brought back pagan gods and worshiped them. A prophet came to warn him against his evil ways, but Amaziah would not listen.

He was so proud of his military victories that he challenged the king of Israel to come out and have a war with him (like one baseball team challenging another). The king of Israel replied with a fable, suggesting that he should be satisfied with his victory and stay home. But Amaziah kept on insisting on war. When the two armies finally fought, Amaziah was badly defeated. He was captured, and many treasures from Jerusalem were taken by the king of Israel.

Fifteen years later, Amaziah was overthrown in a plot and killed.

Where to find it: *2 Chronicles 25: 5-28*

AMBASSADOR *(am-BAS-uh-door)* in the Bible is usually a messenger sent to another country for a special occasion. He is not like our modern ambassadors, who live in another country as representatives of their government.

AMBER *(AM-bur)* is a shining metal, perhaps a combination of silver and gold.

AMEN *(ay-MEN)* means roughly "It is true." It often appears at the end of important truths such as in Romans 11: 36. The word *Amen* is applied to Christ in Revelation 3: 14, perhaps emphasizing Christ as the truth. *Amen* was part of the Jewish synagogue worship and has been carried over into the Christian church.

AMETHYST *(AM-uh-thist)* is a rare gem ranging in color from purple to blue-violet. It was one of the gems sewn into the breastpiece worn by the high priest in the Old Testament. The amethyst is also mentioned as one of the jewels in the foundation of the Holy City.

Where to find it

Part of breastpiece *Exodus 28: 15-20*
Foundation of Holy City *Revelation 21: 19-20*

AMMON, AMMONITES *(AM-un, AM-uh-nites)*. Ammon was a son of Lot; he became the ancestor of the Ammonites. God told Moses not to make war on them when the Israelites left Egypt for Canaan.

Many years later, however, the Ammonites became persistent enemies of the Israelites. The Ammonites were brutal and fierce. They worshiped idols and sometimes sacrificed humans to the god Molech. Saul once fought and defeated them.

During short periods, they were friendly to David. Solomon had some Ammonite women among his harem. But the Ammonites remained enemies of the Hebrews for nearly a thousand years. When Nehemiah came back from exile to rebuild the walls of Jerusalem about 444 B.C., one of those who opposed him was Tobiah the Ammonite. The Ammonites apparently survived until about 100 B.C.

Where to find it

Moses not to make war on them *Deuteronomy 2: 19*
Saul defeats them *1 Samuel 11: 1-11*
Solomon has Ammonite wives *1 Kings 11: 1-8*

AMNON *(AM-nun)* was the oldest son of David. He once pretended to be ill and asked his half sister, Tamar, to bring him food. When she brought it to his room, he raped her. For this he was murdered by Tamar's brother, Absalom.

Where to find it: *2 Samuel 13*

AMON *(AY-mun)* was the fifteenth king of Judah. He became king in 642 B.C., when he was 22 years old. He was assassinated by his servants after he had reigned only two years. He worshiped idols as his father, Manasseh, had done.

Where to find it: *2 Chronicles 33: 21-25; 2 Kings 21: 19-26*

AMORITES *(AM-uh-rites)* were a very large and powerful group of people who once lived in Mesopotamia, later in Babylon, and still later in Palestine. They were living in Canaan when Joshua was fighting for the land, and he subdued them. They were apparently a very wicked people.

Where to find it: *Genesis 15: 16; Joshua 10: 1–11: 14*

AMOS *(AY-mus)* was a sheepherder and grower of fig trees who became an Old Testament prophet. He lived in Tekoa, a few miles south of Jerusalem in Judah. His preaching and prophesying, however, were mostly

The priest said, "Go on back to Judah, Amos!"

in Samaria, the capital city of Israel, the Northern Kingdom.

In his prophecy, he insisted that people should be treated fairly. He said Israel (Samaria) had become very prosperous under King Jeroboam II. These newly rich people should have used their wealth to help the poor. Instead, they used their power to make poor people even poorer.

Amos said that religious feasts, holy days, and offerings to God only made God angry if the people were not being fair and honest with each other.

Amos pointed out that the Lord is the Creator of the world and he also keeps it running. God decides whether there will be famine or good crops.

We don't know whether the people listened and responded to Amos's prophecy. In the end, he was told by the priest of Israel, Amaziah, to go home to his own land (Judah) and do his prophesying there!

His book of prophecy, like many other parts of the Old Testament, is written in Hebrew poetic style. Although Amos was a sheepherder, his use of words to paint vivid pictures shows that he was a man of great spiritual, moral, and mental strength.

Where to find it

Israel was prosperous *Amos 6:4-7*
Poverty was growing *Amos 5:10-13*
God judges the world *Amos 4:4-13*

AMULET *(AM-you-let)* was usually a stone, gem, or other object that people thought would protect them from snakebites, diseases, or other dangers. Amulets were usually worn around the neck. Although they are mentioned only in Isaiah, archaeological digging has shown that they were common throughout much of the Old Testament period. The New Testament condemns all sorts of "magic" and sorcery.

ANANIAS *(an-uh-NI-us)* is the name of three important people in the New Testament. All appear in the Book of Acts.

1. Ananias and Sapphira were husband and wife; they sold a piece of their land and pretended they were giving the church all the money they received from it. They were actually keeping part of it. When Ananias came to present the gift to the apostles, Peter faced him with his lie, and Ananias fell down dead.

Later Sapphira appeared, repeated the same lie—and she too died. The story shows that their sin was in lying to the Holy Spirit rather than in keeping part of the money.

Where to find it: *Acts 5:1-11*

2. Another Ananias was a devout Jewish Christian who lived at Damascus. After Saul's conversion on the road to Damascus, he became blind and was led into the city. Three days later, God spoke to Ananias, telling him

where to find Saul and saying that he should lay his hands on Saul so that his eyesight would be restored. Ananias was afraid, because he had heard that Saul persecuted Christians. However, he obeyed God, and Saul was healed.

Where to find it: *Acts 9:10-19*

3. Ananias was also the name of the high priest before whom Paul was brought for trial in Jerusalem. Ananias was so angry at Paul that he ordered those near him to slap Paul's mouth. Paul answered back in anger, but then apologized. This same Ananias later went to Caesarea, the capital of Judea, to accuse Paul before the Roman governor.

Where to find it: *Acts 23:1-5; 24:1*

ANCIENT OF DAYS is a term used by the prophet Daniel to describe God as the Almighty, the everlasting ruler of heaven and earth.

Where to find it: *Daniel 7:9, 13, 22*

Andrew was one of the fishermen Jesus called.

ANDREW was one of Jesus' twelve apostles. He and his brother, Peter, were both fishermen.

Andrew was first a disciple of John the Baptist. But one day John pointed to Jesus and said, "Behold, the Lamb of God!" Andrew then became a follower of Jesus and also brought his brother to Jesus.

When Jesus wanted to feed 5,000 people with five loaves and two fish, it was Andrew who found the boy with his lunch. Andrew was one of the four disciples who questioned Jesus about what would happen in the future.

After Acts 1:13, Andrew is not mentioned again in the New Testament. However, tradition says he became a martyr for Christ in Achaia (present-day Greece), where he was crucified on an X-shaped cross. That shape is now known as Saint Andrew's cross.

Where to find it

John points to Jesus   *John 1:35-44*
Finds boy with lunch   *John 6:8-13*
Asks Jesus about future   *Mark 13:3-4*

ANGELS are supernatural beings—thousands and thousands of them—created by God before he created man. Angels appear many times in the Old and New Testaments. Jesus said they do not marry; they also never die. But they are not to be worshiped.

What do angels do? They worship God. They also serve as his messengers. For example, angels told Abraham that Sarah would have a son.

Angels guide God's people. An angel told Philip to go to a certain road where he met an Ethiopian official. An angel opened prison doors for the disciples.

Sometimes an angel brings encouragement to people who need it, as one did for Paul on a boat about to be shipwrecked.

Angels protect God's people in many circumstances.

Angels had a special ministry in the life of Christ. They announced his birth to Mary, Joseph, and the shepherds. Angels helped Christ after his temptation; they strengthened him before the crucifixion; they rolled the stone away from his tomb; and they were with him at his ascension.

Apparently some angels, before the creation of man, decided not to serve God and "fell." What has happened and will happen to them? Evil angels are to be sent to eternal fire, while good angels will go on serving God throughout eternity.

Where to find it

Not to be worshiped   *Colossians 2:18*
Thousands of angels   *Revelation 5:11*
Do not marry or die   *Luke 20:34-36*
They worship God   *Hebrews 1:6*
Are messengers of God   *Genesis 18:1–19:1*
Guide Philip   *Acts 8:26*
Open prison doors   *Acts 5:19*
Encourage Paul   *Acts 27:23-24*
Protect believers   *Psalm 91:11; Hebrews 1:14*
Announce birth of Christ   *Matthew 1:20-24; 2:13-15; Luke 1:26-38; 2:8-15*
Minister to Christ   *Matthew 4:11; Luke 22:43*
Roll stone from tomb and speak to women   *Matthew 28:2-7*
At the ascension   *Acts 1:11*
Some angels sinned   *2 Peter 2:4; Jude 6*
Fallen angels will be punished   *Matthew 25:41*

ANGER is a feeling both in people and in God. People may become angry for many reasons, making them often want to quarrel or fight. But when the Bible says God is angry, it is always because of people's sin, injustice, wrongdoing, or unbelief.

Where to find it: *Psalm 79:5-6; 86:15; 103:8-12*

ANIMALS OF THE BIBLE

Since many of the people in the Bible were farmers or sheepherders, animals are often mentioned. Many of the animals are very similar to animals of the same name today. Others are quite different.

Although cows, pigs, horses, sheep, and dogs were tamed, they were rarely used as pets. Cats are never mentioned in the Bible, and dogs, although mentioned about 40 times, are nearly always seen as snarling, dirty, undesirable creatures.

A man's riches were counted mostly by how many sheep, oxen, camels, cows, and horses he owned. A person's animals were so much a part of his life that when the Israelites were told to destroy cities in Canaan, they were often told to destroy all the animals as well.

Because animals were so important to early people, it is not surprising that they were sometimes thought to be sacred. Idols and images were often made to look like animals. When Moses stayed a long time on the mountain getting the Ten Commandments, the Is- raelites made a golden calf to worship— probably similar to the images they had seen worshiped in Egypt.

The list below does not include all animals mentioned in the Bible, but it includes the most important ones and also those that are unfamiliar to most of us, or are different from animals we know by the same name.

Apes are mentioned in 1 Kings 10:22 as part of the valuable cargo the ships of King Solomon brought to Israel. They were probably more like our rhesus monkeys than our present-day apes.

Adders or **Asps** were poisonous snakes, probably similar to cobras. They are mentioned in Isaiah and in Romans 3:13.

Ants are mentioned in Proverbs 6:6-8 and 30:25 as an example of hard work and planning for the future. Ants store up their food in the summer so they won't be hungry in the winter.

Antelopes *(AN-tuh-lopes)* are something like deer, except they do not shed their horns every year. **Gazelle** is one kind of antelope. The antelope is mentioned in Deuteronomy 14:5, where the King James Version calls it a "wild ox." An antelope is also mentioned in Isaiah 51:20, but the King James Version calls it a "wild bull."

Asses are part of the horse family and are mentioned 150 times in the Bible. They are the same as our modern donkey. They were used for heavy farm work and were also ridden with a saddle. Rulers and great men usually rode asses when they were on a peaceful journey. Horses were used in war. When Jesus rode into Jerusalem on an ass, it was a symbol that he was coming in peace, not as a rebel to overthrow the government.

Badger skins are mentioned in Exodus 25:5 and 26:14 (in the King James Version) as being used to cover the upper part of the Tabernacle. However, other translations say "goatskins" or "sealskins" or "leather" for this word. Our present kinds of badgers are not now found in Bible lands.

Bats, probably similar to modern-day bats, are mentioned in Leviticus 11:19 and Deuteronomy 14:18 as "unclean"—not to be eaten.

Bears are mentioned 14 times in the Old

Testament, always as fierce, threatening animals. They were probably Syrian brown bears, which are still found in modern Lebanon. David is said to have fought and killed a bear while guarding his sheep. The story is told in 1 Samuel 17: 34-37.

Behemoth (buh-HE-muth) is described in Job 40: 15-24 as a powerful creature. Most scholars think the animal was a hippopotamus, although some think it might have been an elephant.

Boar is mentioned in Psalm 80: 13 and was probably a wild pig.

Bulls, bullocks are male cattle, usually mentioned in the Bible as sacrificial animals. To be used for sacrifice, a young bull had to be at least eight days old; in some cases it had to be a year old; in other cases, three years old or seven years old. Bulls were used as sacrifices on many important occasions and feast days such as the consecration of priests, dedication of the altar, the Passover, and the Feast of Booths. Some of the rules are given in Leviticus 9: 2-4 and 22: 27.

Calf, calves are mentioned in the Bible as meat for special festive occasions. When the prodigal son came home, the father killed the fatted calf. Usually only the wealthy could afford such special foods. Calves, like bulls, were also used as sacrifices.

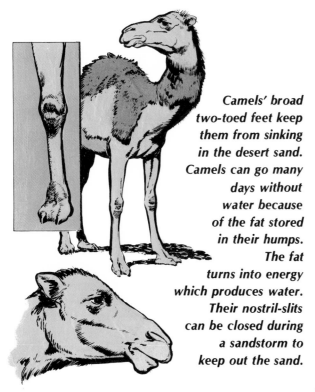

Camels' broad two-toed feet keep them from sinking in the desert sand. Camels can go many days without water because of the fat stored in their humps. The fat turns into energy which produces water. Their nostril-slits can be closed during a sandstorm to keep out the sand.

Camels are mentioned more than 60 times in the Bible. They were important in the Middle East, because they are very hardy and can live 40 to 50 years. They are cud-chewing vegetarians and have a three-part stomach that can store three days' water supply. They carry heavy burdens and travel long distances. The Hebrews were not permitted to eat camel meat, but Arabs often ate it. Camel hair was used in making cloth. Job had 3,000 camels before his troubles began, and later in life he had 6,000. To own camels was a sign of wealth.

Cattle were a sign of wealth among the Israelites and other people in Bible times. The term usually means larger animals such as oxen, asses, horses, and cows rather than sheep and goats. However, sometimes *cattle* refers to all domesticated animals. Because cattle were so important to the life of the Israelites, the Law of Moses said they should be permitted to rest on the Sabbath just like people.

Cattle were used in sacrifices, for food (milk and meat)—and sometimes images of them were made and worshiped.

Cattle were considered part of the loot or bounty of war. A conquering army often took the cattle of the people they had defeated.

Chamois (SHAM-ee), mentioned in Deuteronomy 14: 4-6 as an animal the Israelites could eat, was a mountain sheep, small and sure-footed.

Colts are either young camels, horses, or donkeys (asses). According to John 12: 15, Jesus rode into Jerusalem the Sunday before Easter on the colt of an ass.

Dogs are mentioned 41 times in the Bible, and in most instances they are considered undesirable. They were scavengers and disease carriers. Although they were used to guard sheep, they were not considered pets or companions. Only in the story of a Syrophenician woman in Matthew 15: 26-27 is there any suggestion of a dog as a pet.

Elephants are not mentioned in the Bible. However, *ivory* is mentioned, so elephants must have been somewhere in the area. Records other than the Bible show that elephants were common in Syria.

Foxes are mentioned nine times in the Bible. They were probably similar to the red fox in America.

A wild goat, or ibex, in the wilderness of Judea.

In Israel today, young Bedouins use donkeys to carry things. In the background is this family's flock of goats.

Gazelles *(guh-ZELLS)* were small, swift antelopes that usually lived in hot, barren areas.

Goats are mentioned at least 130 times in the Bible and were important sources for milk and meat. They were also used in sacrifices. Their hair was made into clothing and their skins into containers for water and wine.

Harts (male) and **hinds** (female) were large, fast deer, a bit smaller than American elks.

Heifers *(HEF-ferz)* are young cows. A perfect (unblemished) red heifer was used for an important purification ceremony described in Numbers 19.

Hinds (see *Harts*)

Horses have been tamed for thousands of years. In Bible times, horses were used mostly for war. They pulled chariots and were sometimes ridden—especially by kings and important people. In the story of Esther, Mordecai was honored by riding the king's horse around the capital city.

The Israelites were told in Deuteronomy 17:16 that they were *not* "to multiply horses." However, Absalom disobeyed this command, and so did Solomon and some later kings.

Jackals *(JACK-ulz)* are a kind of wild dog, smaller than a wolf. Jackals move around in packs, usually at night. They eat other small animals, poultry, fruit, vegetables, and garbage. They have a distinctive wailing howl.

Kids are young goats. Kids were used for food on special occasions, and sometimes as sacrifices. In Exodus 23:19 the Jews were told, "You shall not boil a kid in its mother's milk." This command is why many Jews still do not eat meat and milk at the same meal.

Lambs were the animals most frequently used as a Jewish sacrifice. They were used at the Passover feast, in the morning and evening burnt offerings in the Tabernacle, and for many other sacrifices. For the Israelites, the lamb was a symbol of innocence and gentleness.

Leopards of Bible times were similar to modern leopards or cheetahs. They were fierce animals, feared by the people.

Leviathan *(lev-EYE-uh-thun)* appears several times in the Old Testament as some kind of monster. Some scholars think the term refers to a crocodile; others think it is a make-believe creature.

Lions were well known to the Hebrews, but they are now extinct in the Middle East. They were feared as killers, as in the story of Daniel. Lions were respected for their strength and majestic beauty. Jesus is called the "Lion of the tribe of Judah" (Revelation 5:5).

Mice were apparently common in Israel, and the term seems to include small and medium-size rats.

Mules are a cross between male donkeys and female horses. Kings and officers often

A shepherd and his flock of sheep near Bethlehem.

rode mules. David's son Absalom was riding a mule when his hair got caught in branches, leaving him hanging there as the mule went on. He was found and killed as a result.

Oxen are bulls with their sex glands removed. Because they were strong, they were usually used to pull wagons, plows, and other farm implements. Almost every Hebrew farmer had an ox. Oxen were also frequently used as sacrificial animals.

Rams are mature male sheep, often used for sacrifices, but also used for meat. Their skins were used as coverings in the Tabernacle, and their horns were commonly used for trumpets.

Roe, roebuck *(ROW-buck)* is a small deer. It is mentioned in Deuteronomy 14: 5 as an animal the Israelites were permitted to eat.

Sheep are mentioned more often in the Bible than any other animal. The earliest mention is in Genesis 4: 2; where Abel, the son of Adam and Eve, "was a keeper of sheep."

Sheep were kept more for their milk and wool than for their meat. The needs of the sheep kept many of the Hebrews and Arabs living as nomads. The sheep needed pasture and water, so the shepherd and his household moved with the sheep from place to place. Sheep needed constant care. The picture of God as the Good Shepherd in Psalm 23 was based on the well-known habits of shepherds in caring for their sheep.

Swine is the Bible name for pigs and hogs. They were declared "unclean" animals; Hebrews could not eat them. The Hebrews did not raise pigs, but Gentiles in Palestine and surrounding areas did.

Unicorns were probably wild oxen or antelopes.

Weasels *(WEE-sulz)* in the Bible are like today's weasel—a small animal somewhat larger than a mouse. It eats other animals. Israelites were forbidden to eat weasels in Leviticus 11: 29.

Whales mentioned in the Bible are not necessarily the same species as we know today. They could be any of several large, warm-blooded, air-breathing sea mammals. The "great fish" of the story of Jonah might have been some other large marine animal or dolphin.

Wolves are well known in Palestine, although most of the biblical references to wolves are in word pictures comparing them to people. For example, Jesus said false prophets and false teachers were like "ravenous wolves" (Matthew 7: 15).

Vipers were poisonous snakes.

ANKLET BRACELETS were worn by wealthy women in Israel as a decoration. Most were made of bronze.

ANNA *(ANN-uh)* was an 84-year-old prophetess in the Temple when Jesus was brought to be dedicated. She recognized him as the Messiah.

Where to find it: *Luke 2:36-38*

ANNAS *(ANN-us)* was the high priest in Jerusalem from A.D. 6 to A.D. 15, during the time when John the Baptist began to preach in the wilderness. Annas was the father-in-law of Caiaphas, who was high priest when Jesus was crucified. Annas no doubt still had great influence even after the governor of Judea forced him from his position. When Jesus was arrested, he was taken to Annas before he was sent for actual trial before Caiaphas.

Where to find it: *Luke 3:1-3; John 18:13-24*

ANNUNCIATION *(uh-NONE-see-AY-shun)* is the word used to describe the angel Gabriel's visit to Mary, telling her that she would have a son who would be called Jesus.

Where to find it: *Luke 1:26-38*

Young David was anointed by Samuel to be king.

ANOINT *(uh-NOINT)* means to apply oil to a person or a thing. The Bible mentions anointing with oil in three ways:

1. As part of everyday life. People used scented oils as perfume or as a treatment for dry skin. A gracious host always anointed his guests. Anointing was also part of preparing a body for burial.

2. People and things were also anointed with oil as a sign of being dedicated to God. The Tabernacle and its furniture were anointed. Prophets, priests, and kings were anointed as a sign that God had chosen them for special work. The word *Messiah* means "the anointed one."

3. In the Book of James, Christians are told to pray for the sick and to anoint them with oil in the name of the Lord. The New Testament also speaks of Christians being anointed by the Holy Spirit as a sign of God's presence with them. Jesus was said to be anointed by the Spirit of God.

Where to find it

Christians anointed with Holy Spirit   *1 John 2:20*
Jesus anointed by Spirit of God   *Luke 4:18*
Believers anoint the sick   *James 5:14*

ANTICHRIST *(AN-tih-christ)* means an enemy of Christ or one who takes over Christ's name and tries to grab power that really belongs to Christ. Jesus warned his listeners in Matthew 24:24 against "false Christs and false prophets" who would try to deceive Christians.

In 1 John 2:18, 22, and 4:3, the readers are told to expect that antichrists have and will come to deny Jesus.

ANTIOCH *(AN-tee-ock)* was the name of 16 cities founded by Alexander the Great in memory of his father, Antiochus. Two are mentioned in the Bible.

1. **Antioch of Pisidia** *(pih-SID-ee-uh)*. This one was called Antioch near (or of) Pisidia, which was another city nearby. It was on an important trading route in Asia Minor (now Turkey). Paul and Barnabas preached in the synagogue in Antioch on their first journey, and many people were interested in the gospel. Acts 13:44 says, "The next sabbath almost the whole city gathered together to hear the word of God." But some Jews became jealous of Paul's success and stirred up hatred, so Paul and Barnabas had to leave. Paul may also have stopped there on his second and third missionary journeys.

2. **Antioch** in Syria was the city where believers were first called Christians, according to Acts 11:19-26. It was 15 miles from the Mediterranean Sea, with the Orontes River

The city of Antioch (in Syria) as it looks today.

leading to the sea. It was a business center with many caravan routes going through it. In the time of Paul, it may have had a population of 500,000.

Antioch had the first Christian church that was made up mostly of Gentiles rather than Jews. When the church at Antioch began to grow, the church at Jerusalem sent Barnabas to help the new Christians. He, in turn, sent for Paul to help him.

This church sent Paul on his missionary journeys, and between journeys he returned to the Antioch church to tell what had happened.

This city still exists today and is now called Antakiyeh, with a population of about 42,000.

ANTIOCHUS IV (EPIPHANES) *(an-TIE-uh-kus ee-PIF-un-eez)* was a wicked Greek ruler who tried to make the Jews give up their religion. He ordered a pig sacrificed on the altar in Jerusalem. Pigs were considered "unclean" by Jews, so this was a cruel insult to them. Antiochus IV also destroyed all the Old Testament books he could find.

All this made the Jews rebel; Judas Maccabeus led them in what is known as the Maccabean War. Today's Jewish Feast of Hannukah is in memory of their victory over the armies of Antiochus in 165 B.C.

ANTONIA, TOWER OF *(an-TONE-ee-uh)* was a castle attached to the Temple in Jerusalem where a group of Roman soldiers was stationed. From the top of their tower, they could look down inside the Temple to keep

order. When Paul was seized in the Temple by Jews who falsely accused him of bringing in a Gentile, the Roman soldiers rescued him and carried him to the Tower of Antonia. From the stairs of the tower he addressed the people. His speech is found in Acts 21: 27-40.

APOCRYPHA *(uh-POCK-rif-uh)* includes 12 books that the Roman Catholic Church considers part of the Bible but Protestant churches do not. Three additional books, also part of the Apocrypha, were in the old Latin Vulgate Bible but are not a part of the present Roman Catholic Bible. Protestant churches do not include any of the 15 because they were not part of the Jewish Old Testament.

Scholars believe the New Testament writers were well acquainted with some of these books. Early Christian writers who lived between A.D. 100 and 300 often quoted from or referred to them. Saint Jerome, who translated the old Latin Vulgate Bible between A.D. 390 and 410, put these 15 books in a different section from the other 66 books in the Bible.

After the Reformation, Protestant churches did not read or study these books. However, the apocryphal books help us know about the time between the Old and New Testaments—about 400 to 6 B.C.

The books of the Apocrypha are called:
1 Esdras (not in Catholic Bibles) written about 150 B.C.
2 Esdras (not in Catholic Bibles) written between A.D. 66 and 270
Tobit–written between 200 and 175 B.C.
Judith–written between 150 and 50 B.C.
Additions to the Book of Esther–written about 100 B.C.
The Wisdom of Solomon–written between 50 B.C. and A.D. 40
Ecclesiasticus–written about 180 to 132 B.C.
Baruch–written about A.D. 100
A Letter of Jeremiah–written between 323 and 100 B.C.
The Prayer of Azariah (written about 170 B.C.) *and the Song of the Three Young Men* (written 150 B.C.)
Susanna–written between 100 and 75 B.C.
Bel and the Dragon–written between 100 and 75 B.C.
The Prayer of Manasseh (not in Catholic

Bibles)—written between 150 and 100 B.C.

1 Maccabees–written between 90 and 70 B.C.

2 Maccabees–written about 50 B.C.

APOLLOS *(uh-PAHL-us)* was a Christian Jew who came from Alexandria, Egypt. He was well educated, had an excellent knowledge of the Old Testament, and knew the story of Christ. However, he did not know about the Holy Spirit or about Christian baptism.

When he came to the Christians at Ephesus, he met Priscilla and Aquila, who were Paul's fellow workers there. They taught him more about the way of God.

Later Apollos went to Achaia (now Greece), where he became a leader in the church at Corinth and other churches there. When he arrived, he was a great help to the Christians by debating with the Jews in public, showing by the Scriptures that the Christ was Jesus.

Many scholars believe that Apollos was the author of the Letter to the Hebrews.

Where to find it: *Acts 18: 24-28*

APOSTASY *(uh-POSS-tuh-see)* means to turn away from faith in God and the teachings of the Bible. The word is not used in most modern translations of the Bible, but many Bible passages warn Christians about the danger of leaving their faith. Among them are 1 Timothy 4: 1-3 and 2 Peter 3: 17.

APOSTLES *(uh-PAH-suls)* usually refers to the twelve men chosen by Jesus as his special disciples. These twelve were with him during his three years of teaching, traveling, and healing. They were with him before his crucifixion, and they saw him after his resurrection.

The list of the apostles included Peter, Andrew, James the son of Zebedee, John, Philip, Bartholomew, Thomas, Matthew, James the son of Alphaeus, Simon the Zealot, Thaddeus, and Judas Iscariot, who betrayed Jesus. After Judas committed suicide, Matthias was chosen to take his place.

The word *apostle* means "one chosen and sent" and is also applied to Paul and, in a more general sense, to some of the other leaders of the early church.

Although the original twelve apostles were the closest followers of Jesus, they did not really understand his mission until after the resurrection. In spite of what Jesus told them, they expected Jesus to become an earthly ruler, and they were frightened and disappointed when he was crucified. They did not expect him to rise again, but after he did and after the Holy Spirit came, the apostles became leaders and teachers of the early church. According to tradition, most of them were killed as martyrs for Christ.

APPEAL TO CAESAR *(SEE-zur)*. In New Testament times, the Roman government permitted the Jews mostly to rule themselves. If a Jew were accused of a crime, however, and thought he might get a fairer trial from the Romans, he could ask to be tried by the courts of Rome rather than by the Jewish courts—if he held Roman citizenship. This is what Paul did in Acts 25:11 when he said, "I appeal unto Caesar."

The Jewish courts, however, could not put anyone to death; this always had to be approved by Roman authorities.

APPIAN WAY *(AP-ee-un way)* was the oldest of the Roman roads. It was begun in 312 B.C. and ran from Rome south to Naples. Parts of it are still in use today. Paul no doubt traveled to Rome on this road.

APPLE (see *Plants*)

APPLE OF THE EYE is a phrase used several times in the Old Testament to mean something or someone highly treasured or very precious.

APRON in the Bible means a cloth belt. It was usually a square yard of cloth folded into a triangle, then folded into a sash five to eight inches wide, and tied around the waist. People carried small objects or money in its folds.

AQUILA (see *Priscilla*)

ARABIA (*uh-RAY-bee-uh*) was the area roughly the same as what is now Saudi Arabia, a large, dry peninsula between Egypt and the Persian Gulf. It is first mentioned in the Bible when the kings of Arabia brought gold and spices to Solomon. Arabians are mentioned several times in the Old Testament as paying tribute, selling cattle, or being judged by God.

Where to find it: *1 Kings 10:15; Galatians 1:17; 4:25*

ARAMAIC (*air-uh-MAY-ik*), the language Jesus spoke, was the common language of Palestine during the time of Christ. It is something like Hebrew. Some parts of Daniel and Ezra were written in Aramaic, and there are a few Aramaic expressions in the New Testament.

ARARAT (*AIR-uh-rat*) is the name of a country in biblical times that is now a part of Turkey. It is also the name of a mountain in Turkey. Some modern explorers believe Noah's ark is still buried in the ice on this mountain. Genesis 8:4 says, "The ark came to rest on the mountains of Ararat," meaning one of the mountains in the country of Ararat.

ARAUNAH (*uh-RAW-nuh*) was an Israelite who owned a threshing floor near Jerusalem. When David sinned against God by ordering that the Israelites be counted, God sent a plague as punishment. To show he was sorry for his sin, David wanted to buy Araunah's threshing floor to build an altar to God. Araunah offered to give it to David: "Here are the oxen for the burnt offering, and the threshing sledges and the yokes of the oxen for the wood. All this, O king, Araunah gives to the king."

But David insisted on paying the full price for it. "I will not offer burnt offerings to the Lord my God which cost me nothing."

After David offered sacrifices to God there, the plague was stopped.

The Romans built the Appian Way so well that parts of it are still used today.

Later, David bought the area around the threshing floor for the site of the Temple that was erected in the time of his son Solomon.

Where to find it: *2 Samuel 24:15-25.* The same story appears in 1 Chronicles 21:18-25. There Araunah is called Ornan.

ARCHAEOLOGY *(ARK-ay-OLL-uh-jee)* and geology both involve a lot of digging into the earth. Geologists dig to find out how the rocks, minerals, and land were formed. Archaeologists dig to find out how people lived thousands of years ago. They look for old pots, clay tablets, coins, and tools. They keep track of the exact location where they find them. By doing this, archaeologists can learn about the history and life of people who lived long ago.

Archaeology helps us understand the Bible. Archaeologists have also found writings by Egyptians, Assyrians, and others. These add to our information about the people living near the Hebrews and help fill in many details not given in the Bible.

The findings of archaeology also help us understand many biblical customs that seem strange to us. For example, when Rachel became the wife of Jacob and was leaving with him to go back to Canaan, she stole her father's household gods (small images) and hid them in her camel's saddle. The Bible does not explain why Rachel did this. But other evidence found by archaeologists shows that people in that time considered the household gods to be the real owners of the property, and whoever had the gods was therefore the owner of the family property.

Many cities mentioned in the Bible no longer exist. However, the remains of many of them have been located under small hills called *tells.* Most of the cities were quite small, with houses close together. Many cities had walls to protect the people from wandering robbers or from enemies who wanted to conquer them. Individual cities often had their own kings and their own armies and would try to take over nearby cities.

As a result of these frequent battles, cities were often conquered, destroyed, and later rebuilt on the same location. People would level off the rubble and stones left from previous buildings and build a new city on top. Archaeologists can sometimes identify as

Archaeologists put back together some of the pieces of this synagogue at Capernaum, where Jesus taught.

many as ten cities that were erected on one hill. By comparing the pots or tools or old coins found on one layer with those in layers above or below, or with layers found in other tells, archaeologists can estimate how many thousands of years ago that particular layer represents and how people lived at that time.

Many of these findings support information in the Bible.

Archaeology is one of the most popular studies in Israel today. Excavations (called "digs") are carefully controlled by the government and assigned only to highly skilled persons and groups. If you visit Israel, you will see many digs and partial uncoverings of old cities.

ARCHANGEL *(ark-AYN-jull)* is a term applied to the angel Michael in Jude 9. It seems to mean the highest rank among the angels. 1 Thessalonians 4:16 says that the dead who believe in Christ will rise at the call of the archangel.

ARCHELAUS *(ARK-uh-LAY-us)* was also known as Herod Archelaus. He became ruler of Judea about 4 B.C. after the death of his father, Herod the Great. He was such a poor ruler that he was removed from office by the Roman government after ten years.

ARCHER (see *Occupations*)

ARCHIPPUS *(ar-KIP-us)* was a Christian who lived either at Colossae or Laodicea, cities in

Asia Minor, now called Turkey. He is mentioned twice in the letters of Paul and was told to "fulfill the ministry which you have received in the Lord."

Where to find it: *Philemon 2; Colossians 4:17*

AREOPAGUS *(AIR-ee-OP-uh-gus)* was the name of a small hill in Athens, Greece, and also the name of a council that had the right to examine the morals and truth of teachers who spoke in public. It was probably the council (rather than the hill) to which Paul was brought. Paul told them of the true God, who made heaven and earth, who wants all people to repent, and who will judge the world by Jesus Christ, who was raised from the dead.

Most of the Greeks who listened made fun of him, but a few of them believed.

Where to find it: *Acts 17:19-34*

ARISTARCHUS *(AIR-i-STAR-kus)* is mentioned five times in the New Testament, but we still don't know much about him. He came from the city of Thessalonica in what is now northern Greece. He traveled with Paul on his second missionary journey and perhaps stayed with him until the end of his life. He was with Paul on board the ship that was wrecked; he was in prison with Paul at Rome; and Paul speaks of him as his "fellow worker."

Where to find it: *Acts 27:2; Colossians 4:10; Philemon 24*

ARK OF NOAH (see *Noah's Ark*)

ARK OF THE COVENANT *(KUV-un-unt)* was a wooden chest about 4 feet long, 2½ feet wide, and 2½ feet high. God told Moses how it should be built. It was to be covered with gold inside and outside. It was to be carried on poles pushed through four golden rings on the corners. On top were two golden cherubim (winged creatures that looked both animal and human). Inside the ark were the Ten Commandments written on tablets of stone. There was also a pot of manna and Aaron's rod that budded.

The ark was placed in the Tabernacle. God promised to meet and talk with Moses where it was placed.

The people of Israel carried the ark for their

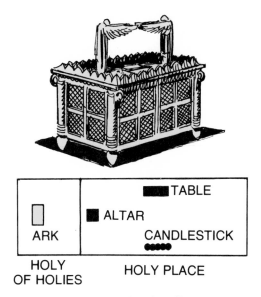

The ark stayed in the Holy of Holies.

forty years in the wilderness. When the priests carried it across the Jordan River into the Promised Land, the waters rolled back and all the people passed over on dry land. At the Battle of Jericho, the priests carried the ark around the outside of the city before the walls fell down.

Once the ark was captured by the Philistines, but they had diseases for seven months until they sent the ark back.

David finally brought the ark to Jerusalem. After Solomon built the Temple, there was a great ceremony as the ark was placed in the Temple.

When Jerusalem and the Temple were destroyed by the Babylonians in 586 B.C., the ark was lost forever. There was no ark in the second Temple nor in the Temple built by Herod the Great shortly before the time of Christ.

Where to find it

Moses' instructions   *Exodus 25:10-22*
Carried around Jericho   *Joshua 6*
Brought to the Temple   *1 Kings 8:1-21*

ARM OF THE LORD is an expression used often in the Bible to show the strength of God or his protection.

Where to find it: *Isaiah 63:12; Deuteronomy 33:27*

ARMAGEDDON *(ARM-uh-GED-dun)* is the name of both a place and of an event. The event is the final battle between the forces of evil and the forces of good at the end of the world. The writer of the Book of Revelation calls the place of this final battle Armageddon, named after the ancient city of Megiddo, where many important battles in the Old Testament took place.

Where to find it: *Revelation 16:16*

ARMLETS *(ARM-lets)* were ornaments worn on the upper arm by both men and women.

ARMOR OF GOD is used in Ephesians 6:11 and 13 as a word picture of how Christians are to defend themselves against evil. The weapons of a Roman soldier in the first century are compared to the spiritual defenses a Christian should use. For example:

Sword—Word of God
Shield—faith
Breastplate (coat of mail)—righteousness
Belt (girdle) from which a sword was hung—truth
Shoes—gospel of peace

ARMOR-BEARER (see *Occupations*)

ARMS, ARMOR (see *Weapons*)

ARMY (see *Weapons*)

ARROW (see *Weapons*)

ART refers to pleasing things that people create. The most common arts are music, painting, sculpture, architecture, dance, drama, and writing—both poetry and prose.

The first mention of art in the Bible is in Genesis 4:21—"Jubal . . . was the father of all those who play the lyre and pipe."

The Hebrews were musical people. They often sang, and the Psalms were probably written to be sung.

The Hebrews were great poets. The Psalms, Proverbs, Job, and most of Hosea, Joel, Amos, Obadiah, Micah, Nahum, Habakkuk, Zephaniah, and some other parts of the Old Testament are written in beautiful, picturesque Hebrew poetry. The King James Version does not show these books as poetry, but most of the modern translations arrange the lines in poetic style (see *Poetry*).

The Hebrews were told not to make "grav-

This temple was carved into the rock at Petra.

en images," probably because they would be tempted to worship images as the people around them did. Their sculpture was mostly specific pieces made for the Tabernacle, such as the cherubim on the ark of the Covenant.

The Tabernacle, although it was a portable tent, had many beautiful pieces of fine embroidery. During the years of traveling in the wilderness and while the Hebrews were conquering Canaan, there was little time for art. But during the reigns of David and Solomon, art began to flourish. Solomon's Temple had ornate wood carvings as well as skilled metal work.

There is little or no record in the Bible of paintings or drawings. However, we know there was pottery, and pottery was often painted or designed.

Where to find it

No graven images *Exodus 20:4*
Wood carvings *1 Kings 6:18, 29*
Metal work *1 Kings 7:23-50*
Embroidery *Exodus 27:16*

ARTAXERXES *(ar-tuh-ZERK-sees)* may have been the *title* of the kings of Persia during 500 to 335 B.C., or it may have been the *name* of two or three different kings during that period. Ezra 4: 7-24 tells of a letter some men wrote to "Artaxerxes the king" complaining that he should stop the rebuilding of the walls of Jerusalem because it would stir up trouble. Artaxerxes did stop the rebuilding as a result.

Artaxerxes (the same king, or another by the same name) appears again in Ezra 6: 14, approving the rebuilding. And Artaxerxes (the same, or still another) in Ezra 7: 1-27 gave full support to restore the sacrifices and worship of God in Jerusalem.

ARTEMIS (AR-tuh-mis) was a goddess whose temple at Ephesus was one of the wonders of the ancient world. It had 100 huge columns, some of them sculptured. Artemis was said to be the daughter of the god Jupiter. She was supposed to be the goddess of hunting and was usually pictured with dogs. Artemis was her Greek name; Diana was her Roman name.

The people in Ephesus were very devoted to the worship of Artemis. But when Paul preached there, many became believers in Christ. The men who made and sold Artemis images feared their business would be hurt, so they began a riot to force Paul and his friends out of Ephesus. The riot was stopped by the town clerk, but Paul soon left the city anyway. The church in Ephesus, however, continued to grow.

Where to find it: *Acts 19: 21-41*

ASA (AY-suh) was the third king of Judah (the Southern Kingdom), and he reigned for 41 years. He began by removing the altars to foreign gods that his father had built.

After ten years of peace, his country was attacked by an army of Ethiopians. Asa called on God for help and defeated the enemy. Asa led his nation in giving thanks to God.

Several years later, Baasha, the king of Israel, threatened war against Judah. This time, instead of relying on God, Asa asked the king of Syria for help. A prophet of God, Hanani, scolded Asa for relying on politics rather than God. Asa became so angry that he ordered the prophet put into stocks. Three years later, Asa developed a disease in his feet. Again, instead of seeking God's help, he tried the cures of

the doctors of his day. He died soon after.

Where to find it: *2 Chronicles 14–16*

ASAPH (AY-suf) was a musician and poet in the time of David. He was appointed by David as the leader of worship in singing. He and his family ("the sons of Asaph") are mentioned many times in the Old Testament, always in connection with singing or playing the cymbals. Asaph is also called a seer (a prophet).

Asaph or his descendants are listed as the authors of 12 psalms. They are Psalms 50 and 73—83.

ASCENSION OF CHRIST (uh-SEN-shun) is Christ's return to heaven after his resurrection. After Jesus rose from the dead, he did not live with his disciples as he had before. Instead, he appeared to them many times, sometimes coming through closed doors.

The ascension happened on a hill outside Jerusalem called Mount Olivet. The eleven disciples were with Jesus. When he was taken up into a cloud before their eyes, it was a sign that they would not see him anymore. From then on, Christ would be "at the right hand of God." Since the ascension, the Holy Spirit has been the presence of God on earth.

After Christ was taken away, an angel appeared to the disciples and told them that Christ would some day return "in the same way as you saw him go."

The hope of Christ's return, known as the Second Coming, has been important to Christians through all the centuries and even now.

Where to find it: *Acts 1: 6-11*

ASHDOD *(ASH-dahd)* was one of the chief cities of the Philistines. Located near the Mediterranean Sea, it was about 12 miles north of what is now the Gaza Strip.

When the Israelites came into Canaan from Egypt, the area around Ashdod was assigned to the tribe of Judah. However, Judah never really conquered Ashdod "because they had chariots of iron." The people of Ashdod worshiped Dagon, the chief god of the Philistines, and had a temple to him.

During a battle with the Philistines, the Israelites carried the ark of the Covenant into battle. The ark was their symbol of the presence of God. They thought it would keep them from being defeated. However, the Philistines won the battle and captured the ark. They took it to Ashdod and set it up in the house of Dagon.

The next day when they went to their temple, they found that the image of their god had fallen face downward before the ark! They put it back in place. The next day the image had fallen again, and its head and hands were broken off. Then a series of terrible diseases came on the people of Ashdod. Finally they sent the ark back to Israel.

In the time of the prophet Nehemiah, the men of Ashdod tried to keep the Jews from rebuilding the walls of Jerusalem. Later some of the Jews married women of Ashdod, but Nehemiah said they were wrong to do that.

In the New Testament, Ashdod is called Azotus and is the town where Philip was found after he talked with the man from Ethiopia on the road to Gaza.

Where to find it

The ark goes to Ashdod   *1 Samuel 4: 1-11; 5: 1– 6: 18*
People try to stop building of walls   *Nehemiah 4: 7-8*
Marrying of Ashdod women   *Nehemiah 13: 23-30*
Philip found in Ashdod   *Acts 8: 40*

ASHERAH *(uh-SHEE-ruh)* is a name of a goddess worshiped by the Canaanites. The word is also used for the wooden images made for the goddess. The Israelites were told to cut down or burn the images. The King James Version calls them "groves," but this is not a good translation.

Where to find it: *Exodus 34: 13; Deuteronomy 12: 3*

ASHERIM (see *Asherah*)

ASHES in the Bible are sometimes mentioned as a symbol. They may stand for something or someone despised, as in Job 30: 19. In other places they mean a person is miserable, as in 2 Samuel 13: 19; or repenting, as in Matthew 11: 21; or mourning, as in Jeremiah 6: 26. The term *sackcloth and ashes* means the same.

ASHIMA *(uh-SHY-muh)* was a pagan god worshiped by some settlers whom the Assyrians sent to Samaria after they conquered the Northern Kingdom in 722 B.C.

Where to find it: *2 Kings 17: 30; Amos 8: 14*

ASHKELON *(ASH-kuh-lon)* was one of the five main cities of the Philistines. It was captured by the tribe of Judah shortly after the death of Joshua, but the Philistines got it back and kept

The Philistines were shocked when their idol, Dagon, fell down in front of God's ark.

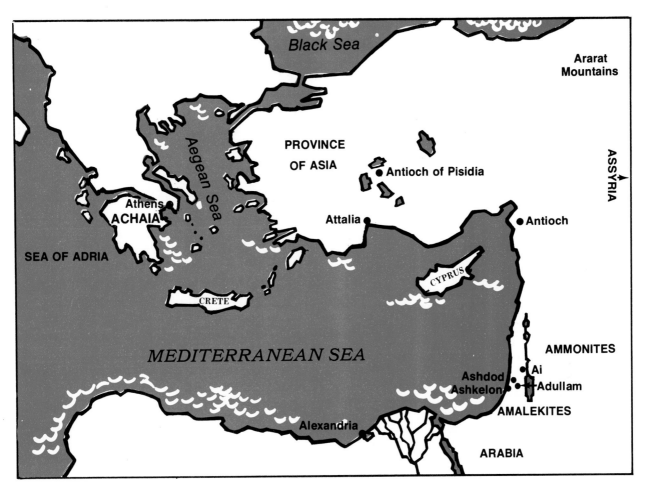

it through much of the Old Testament period. Zephaniah prophesied that Israel would one day be in control of Ashkelon.

A modern city called Ashkelon in Israel has been built near the ruins of the old city, along the Mediterranean coast.

Where to find it: *Zephaniah 2: 4, 7*

ASHTARTE, ASHTORETH, ASHTAROTH, ASTARTE *(ASH-tar-tuh, ASH-tuh-roth)* are all names for a goddess representing love, war, and the ability to have children. Ashtarte was the female goddess and Baal was the male god of the Canaanites. Some Israelites also began worshiping these gods soon after they came into Canaan.

After Saul had been killed by the Philistines, the Philistines took his armor and put it in the temple of Ashtarte.

King Solomon in later life, after he married foreign wives and left the worship of God, became a worshiper of Ashtarte. He built

places to worship the false goddess, and these places were still in use more than 300 years later when King Josiah ordered them torn down about 630 B.C.

Where to find it

Israelites worship Ashtarte   *Judges 2:11-13*
Solomon worships Ashtarte   *1 Kings 11: 4-5*
Josiah tears down places of worship   *2 Kings 23: 13-14*

ASIA *(AY-zhuh)* in the New Testament usually refers to a Roman province that included the western section of Asia Minor (now Turkey). Paul visited this area on two of his missionary journeys and helped begin churches in several of its cities, including Ephesus. The Book of Revelation is written to churches in Asia.

ASP (see *Animals*)

ASS (see *Animals*)

ASSYRIA *(uh-SEAR-ee-uh)* was an old and

35

powerful empire north and east of Israel. It was an enemy of the Israelites for many years, and finally in 722 B.C. it overran the Northern Kingdom (Israel) and took many of its people into captivity. More than 27,000 upper-class Israelites (the wealthy and the leaders) were forced to move to Assyria, and many Assyrians were sent to live in Israel instead. This was a common wartime custom to keep a conquered country from rebelling.

The Assyrians who moved into Israel eventually married Israelites and became the Samaritans mentioned in the New Testament—a people who were looked down upon by the pure Jews who lived around them.

The most important cities of the Assyrian Empire were Nineveh, Assur, and Calah. The Assyrians worshiped idols and had temples to their gods in many cities. The king of Assyria was also his country's religious leader and commander of its huge army.

Assyria is mentioned often in the Bible as a threat or enemy in war. Many of the kings of Israel and Judah paid tribute (money, gifts) to the kings of Assyria to keep them from attacking their country. King Hezekiah gave Sennacherib, the king of Assyria, all the silver in the house of the Lord as well as all the silver he had in his own house. He even stripped the gold from the doors and doorposts of the Temple to give to the Assyrians.

Still, Sennacherib was not satisfied and announced that he was going to capture Jerusalem. However, God did not let him do it. One night, the angel of the Lord killed 185,000 sleeping Assyrians in their camp. Sennacherib was killed by one of his own sons soon after he returned home.

After that, the Assyrian Empire grew weaker and was conquered by Babylonia. It was never again a great power.

Where to find it

Hezekiah's gifts *2 Kings 18:13-16*
Angel of God kills soldiers *2 Kings 19:35-37*

ASTROLOGERS *(as-TRAWL-uh-jers)* are those who try to tell the future from looking at the positions of stars and moon. They are said to be like magicians and wizards, who practice superstitions instead of seeking help directly from God.

They are mentioned in Daniel 2:27; 4:7; 5:7, 11; and Isaiah 47:13.

ASTRONOMY (see *Stars*)

ATHALIAH *(ATH-uh-LY-uh)* was the only woman to reign over Judah. She was the daughter of the wicked Ahab, king of Israel, and Jezebel, his Baal-worshiping wife. After her son, King Ahaziah, was killed by an arrow, she came into power. She was an evil ruler. Normally, one of Ahaziah's sons should have been the next ruler, but Athaliah ordered all of them killed.

However, one infant son, Joash, escaped with the help of his aunt, who was the wife of the priest. His aunt and uncle hid him for seven years in the Temple. Then his uncle, the priest, arranged for the young Joash to be secretly crowned king of Judah.

At the time of the coronation, Athaliah heard crowds gathering, and she went into the Temple, arriving just after Joash was crowned. "Treason! Treason!" she screamed, but the crowd wanted young Joash. At the order of the priest, she was killed as soon as she left the Temple. She had reigned six years.

Where to find it: *2 Chronicles 22–23*

ATHENS *(ATH-enz)* has been an important city for about 3,000 years. It is now the capital of Greece. Its ancient architecture and ruins of old buildings (the Parthenon and several ancient temples) show what a beautiful city it

The Parthenon at Athens, capital of Greece.

was hundreds of years before the time of Christ. It was the center of Greek art, science, and philosophy and was the most important university city of the ancient world. Its time of greatest glory was 459 to 431 B.C. Later it was defeated in war by the Spartans, then by the Romans, later by the Goths and the Turks.

Paul visited the city on his second missionary journey and spoke to a group of people. In the sermon, he called attention to an altar marked "To an Unknown God" that he had seen in the city.

Although some became Christians during his visit, there is no record of Paul beginning a church in Athens.

Where to find it: *Acts 17:15-34*

ATONEMENT *(uh-TONE-ment)* means making up for a wrong act. In the Bible, it usually means to become friends with God after sin has separated us from him.

Because all of us sin, we are all separated from God. Atonement is the way to bridge that separation. In the Old Testament, the Israelites were told to bring sacrifices to atone for their sins. On the Day of Atonement (once a year), the high priest offered a bull and a goat as a sacrifice for himself, his family, and the Tabernacle.

He also took a live goat and confessed over it all the sins of the people. The goat was then led into the wilderness and left there as a symbol that the sins of the people had been carried away (also see *Sacrifices*). We now see this as a picture of Christ's carrying away the believer's sins forever.

The New Testament teaches that the death of Jesus Christ is our atonement. Because Christ was perfect and never sinned, he could be a substitute for sinners. He could "pay the price" or "make up" for our sins. Christ did this willingly—Titus 2:14 says he "gave himself for us to redeem us from all iniquity."

The word *atonement* appears many times in the Old Testament in connection with sacrifices. In the New Testament it is used in the King James Version in Romans 5:11. The newer translations often use the word *reconciliation* instead of *atonement*.

Where to find it
Goat led into wilderness *Leviticus 16:15-22*
Christ's atonement *Romans 5:11; Titus 2:14*

ATONEMENT, DAY OF (see *Day of Atonement*)

ATTALIA *(AH-tuh-LY-uh)* was a seaport in the south of Asia Minor (now Turkey). The town still exists but is now called Antalya. On Paul's second missionary journey, he sailed from this port.

Where to find it: *Acts 14:25*

AUGUSTUS CAESAR *(uh-GUS-tus SEE-zur)* was the ruler of the Roman Empire at the time Jesus was born. He was the grandnephew of Julius Caesar.

Where to find it: *Luke 2:1*

AUTHOR, when used in the Bible, refers to God as the Creator or the cause or source of something. In the King James Version, Hebrews 5:9 speaks of Christ as the "author of eternal salvation unto all them that obey him." This means that Christ is the cause of eternal salvation. In Hebrews 12:2, Jesus is said to be the "author and finisher of our faith." Here it means that Christ is the founder of our faith as well as the one who completes it.

AUTHORIZED VERSION *(AWE-thor-eyezd)*, also known as the King James Version, was published in England in 1611. King James I of England wanted a translation that would show the best work of the finest scholars at Oxford and Cambridge universities. He appointed 54 men to work on it. They were formed into

54 men worked more than two years on the King James Version of the Bible.

committees, each responsible for translating a part of the Bible. They then turned in their work to the other committees for approval. They worked for more than two years without pay.

The men were chosen because they knew Greek and Hebrew (the languages of the first writings), but they also used parts of other translations that had been made earlier. The result was a translation so beautiful and accurate that it is still used today, even though the language is now old-fashioned and the meanings of some words have changed. It has been the most popular translation in America since the beginning of the country.

AWL or **AUL** was a sharp pointed instrument, usually made of bone, used to pierce the earlobe of a person who voluntarily chose to remain a slave. The Law of Moses did not permit a Hebrew to keep another Hebrew as a slave more than six years. The slave must then be freed—unless he loved his master and wanted to remain his slave for the rest of his life.

Where to find it: *Exodus 21:1-6; Deuteronomy 15:12-18*

AX was a common tool in Bible times. It was somewhat similar to axes in our day, except that the head was probably made of bronze or stone.

Axes are often mentioned in the Bible for cutting trees, for shaping things of wood, or as weapons of war. When an army overran a city, the soldiers used their axes to destroy buildings and walls.

A story in the Bible shows that people in Bible times had a hard time fastening axheads securely to the handles. In the story, the head fell off the handle and into the Jordan River. Elisha, the prophet, performed a miracle when he threw a stick into the river where the axhead had sunk—and it floated to the top.

Where to find it: *2 Kings 6:1-7*

AZAZEL *(uh-ZAY-zul)* was a name used in connection with one of the two goats on the Jewish Day of Atonement. While one goat was sacrificed, the other one was sent away into the wilderness "to Azazel." But first the high priest laid his hands on the head of the goat and confessed over it the sins of the people. No one is sure just what *Azazel* meant, but some scholars say the Hebrew word really means "entire removal," showing that the goat being sent away was a symbol of the full forgiveness of God. Some translations use "scapegoat" for the word *Azazel*.

Where to find it: *Leviticus 16:26*

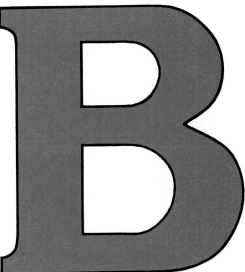

BAAL *(bale)* was the name of many gods worshiped by the people of Canaan. They thought the Baal gods ruled their land, crops, and animals. Gradually *Baal* became a proper name for the chief Canaanite god. The Canaanites believed that each year Baal had a battle with the sea and rivers, bringing them under his power. Baal then made it rain on the fields for a good crop.

The Canaanites made images or idols (see *Idols*) of Baal. He was pictured as a warrior holding a thunderbolt spear in one hand and a shield in the other. His helmet was decorated with bull horns.

In worship, the Canaanite priests cut themselves with knives. Even children were sacrificed to Baal. And in the temples, evil sexual practices were carried on.

The Hebrews were often tempted to worship Baal. Many prophets warned them against believing in false gods. Two evil queens, Jezebel and her daughter Athaliah, murdered some of the Hebrew prophets and priests for not worshiping Baal.

Finally, on Mount Carmel, the prophet Elijah called Baal's prophets to a test to show who the true God really was. Baal lost.

Baal, the pagan god of the Canaanites, was often pictured as a warrior with thunderbolt spears.

Where to find it

Athaliah promotes Baal worship   *2 Kings 11: 1-21;*
   2 Chronicles 22: 2-3
Priests of Baal cut themselves in worship   *1 Kings*
   18: 17-29
Children sacrificed to Baal   *Jeremiah 19: 5*
Elijah puts Baal to a test   *1 Kings 18: 17-40*

BAAL-BERITH *(bale-buh-REET)* was one of the Canaanite gods whose name means "lord of the covenant." Baal-berith was supposed to guard the covenant (or agreement) the Canaanites made with their gods.

Where to find it: *Judges 8: 33*

BAAL-PEOR *(bale-PEE-or)* was a god worshiped on Mount Peor by people from Moab. When the Hebrews camped near the town of Shittim, the Moabite women persuaded the Hebrews to worship Baal-Peor. But in his love, God punished the Hebrews to bring them back to himself.

Where to find it: *Numbers 25: 1-18*

BAAL-ZEBUB *(bale-ZEE-bub)* was one of the gods the Philistines worshiped. In the New Testament, Baal-zebub is spelled "Beel-zebub." Jesus said Beelzebub is Satan, the prince of demons.

Where to find it: *2 Kings 1: 2-18; Matthew 12: 22-27*

BAASHA *(BAY-uh-shuh)* killed King Nadab, son of Jeroboam, and crowned himself the third king of Israel about 914 B.C. He also killed all of Nadab's family and relatives so no one could challenge him.

During the 24 years he ruled, Baasha often fought against the country of Judah. Baasha also encouraged calf worship among his people. For that reason, the prophet Jehu told Baasha his family would be destroyed because the Lord was angry. After Baasha died, his son Elah became king. Elah reigned only two years before he was murdered along with the rest of Baasha's family and friends.

Where to find it: *1 Kings 15: 25–16: 13*

BABEL *(BAY-bul)*, **TOWER OF,** was a place where people began speaking different languages after God was displeased with them.

The Tower of Babel was probably a ziggurat like this.

The people tried to build a tower with "its top in the heavens." Scholars think their idea was to make a ziggurat—a series of levels, one on top of the other, each smaller than the one below it. At the top of such ziggurats was usually a shrine to a god.

But God "confused their languages" so they could no longer understand one another. The people had no choice but to stop working on the tower.

Many scholars believe the tower of Babel was in Babylon, located in what is now the country of Iraq.

Where to find it: *Genesis 11: 1-9*

BABYLON *(BAB-uh-lun)*, the capital city of Babylonia, built near the Euphrates River, was probably the largest and richest city in the ancient world. It's first mentioned in Genesis 11 as the place where the tower of Babel was built.

Babylon reached its full glory when Nebuchadnezzar was king (605-562 B.C.). The people of Judah were captured and taken to live in Babylon during this time. Daniel and his three friends lived in Nebuchadnezzar's courts.

Babylon was attacked, destroyed, and rebuilt again and again throughout its history. Now Babylon is only a series of mounds near the Euphrates River.

In the New Testament, *Babylon* is used as a word picture for a government that is an enemy of God. When *Babylon* is used in 1 Peter and Revelation, it probably refers to the city of Rome, the capital of the Roman Empire. Some scholars believe the word also refers to a final world empire like Rome.

Babylon today is only a field of ruins.

Where to find it

People of Judah exiled to Babylon   *2 Kings 24:10-16*
Daniel and his friend in Babylon   *Daniel 1:1-16*
Word picture of enemy of God   *Revelation 16:19; 17:5; 18:10, 21*

BACKSLIDING *(back-SLY-ding)* describes Israel's turning away from God to other gods or religions. Though the word *backsliding* isn't used in the New Testament, the idea is present. Christians, too, can slip back into old habits or sins, not caring about God.

Where to find it

The Israelites backslide   *Isaiah 57:17; Jeremiah 8:5; Hosea 11:7*
Backsliding among Christians   *Mark 4:16-17; Galatians 1:6-7; 1 Timothy 5:15*

BAG in the Bible was a sack made of leather, animal skins, or cloth. It was used for carrying food, money, treasures, weights and measures, and other things.

Where to find it: *Deuteronomy 25:13; Matthew 10:10; Luke 10:4*

BAKING was done over an open fire or in a clay oven. To heat the clay ovens, grass, straw, dung (see *Dung),* or thorns were set on fire inside the oven or under it. Then bread dough or other foods were laid inside the oven until cooked.

Where to find it: *Isaiah 44:15, 19; Ezekiel 4:12*

BALAAM *(BAY-lum)* was a Midianite prophet in the land of Moab (now called Jordan). When the Israelites camped near that country, King Balak of Moab offered Balaam a reward if he would curse the Israelites.

On the way to King Balak's city, an angel of the Lord blocked Balaam's path. This caused Balaam's frightened donkey to speak out loud. The angel warned Balaam to speak nothing but the Lord's words.

To King Balak's surprise, Balaam didn't curse Israel, but blessed Israel three times. Balaam went home to Peor. But there he helped cause the Israelites to sin. When Israel went to war against Moab and Midian, Balaam was killed.

In the New Testament, Balaam is an example of a false teacher who tries to lead Christians away from the truth.

Where to find it

King Balak's offer   *Numbers 22–24*
Balaam is killed   *Numbers 31:8, 16*
A New Testament example   *2 Peter 2:15-16*

BALM is a sticky, sweet-smelling sap that oozes from a small tree that once grew in a place called Gilead. Balm was used as a medicine to heal wounds.

Where to find it: *Genesis 37:25; Jeremiah 8:22; 46:11; 51:8*

BANISHMENT *(BAN-ish-ment)* means being thrown out of the country. It was a punishment for doing wrong. The Israelites never used banishment as a penalty, because it would force a person away from Israel, where God's house, the Temple, and the sacrifices were. Some men, however, were afraid of their enemies and ran to other countries to be safe. David did this when he ran to Gath to get away from Saul.

Where to find it

Jacob's banishment   *Genesis 27:43*
Moses' banishment   *Exodus 2:15*
David's banishment   *1 Samuel 27:1-4*
Elijah's banishment   *1 Kings 17:9*
Separation from Israel   *Hosea 9:3-6*

BANQUET *(BAN-kwit)* is a big party or feast (like our Thanksgiving) with much to eat and wine to drink. The Hebrews held banquets for religious sacrifices, marriages, birthdays, funerals, and many other occasions. People wore bright-colored robes and strings of flowers. Singers, dancers, musicians, and jesters entertained the guests, who sat or lounged at long tables. The most important people sat at the head of the table. The not-

Jesus showed how important baptism is by being baptized himself.

so-important people sat farther down.

When Jesus taught, he often used stories about banquets. Sometimes he used *banquet* as a word picture of the Kingdom of God.

Where to find it

Old Testament banquets   *1 Samuel 9: 22-24; Esther 1: 3, 5, 9*
Jesus' parables about banquets   *Matthew 22: 2-14; Luke 14: 7-24*

BAPTISM *(BAP-tiz-um).* In Moses' day, baptism simply meant washing. But when John the Baptist called the crowds to be baptized, he was asking them to be washed inside and outside. The outside washing showed that the person wanted to be changed on the inside. Baptism meant he was asking God to forgive his sins.

Jesus was baptized in the Jordan River by John. He had not done anything wrong, but he wanted to show that his work of preaching, teaching, healing, and saving had begun.

Today baptism is a way to show that we are followers of Jesus. Being baptized is a picture of Jesus dying, being buried, and rising again to life. Paul says the sinful part of us has died and been buried with Jesus. Christians begin a new life by expressing faith in Christ.

Where to find it

Baptism in Moses' day   *Exodus 30: 17-21*
John the Baptist   *Matthew 3: 1-6*
Jesus is baptized   *Matthew 3: 13-17; John 1: 29-34*
Baptism and the Christian   *Romans 6: 3-5; Galatians 3: 26-29; Titus 3: 5; 1 Peter 3: 21-22*

BARABBAS *(buh-RAB-us)* was a robber who was in prison for murder and rioting when Jesus was arrested. At the Jewish feast of Passover, the Roman governor Pilate usually set one prisoner free. Pilate asked the people if they would rather have Jesus or Barabbas. Priests standing in the crowd began screaming, "Barabbas! Barabbas!" Pilate asked the crowd what he should do with Jesus, who had done nothing wrong. The crowd yelled, "Crucify him!" So Barabbas, the criminal, was set free.

Where to find it: *Matthew 27: 15-26; Mark 15: 6-15; Luke 23: 18-25; John 18: 39-40*

BARAK *(BEAR-uk)* was a military leader of the Israelites. When Deborah was judge of Israel, the people were being oppressed by the Canaanites, who robbed their farms. Deborah told Barak that God wanted him to bring together an army of 10,000 men to fight the Canaanites. Barak said he would do it only if Deborah went along into battle with him. She agreed to go.

Although the Canaanites had 900 war chariots and the Israelites had none, the Canaanites were defeated. Their commander, Sisera, ran from the battle, and Barak followed him. Sisera hid in the tent of a woman named Jael, but while he slept, she killed him. When Barak reached the tent, Sisera was already dead.

After the great victory, Deborah and Barak sang a song of victory that is recorded in Judges 5. Barak is mentioned among the

Barnabas traveled by ship several times while preaching the gospel.

people of faith in Hebrews 11.

Where to find it: *Judges 4–5; Hebrews 11:32*

BARBARIAN *(bar-BARE-ee-un)* was any person in New Testament times who did not speak Greek, the language of the educated people in the Roman Empire.

Where to find it: *Acts 28:2, 4; Romans 1:14; 1 Corinthians 14:11; Colossians 3:11*

BAR-JESUS (see *Elymas*)

BARLEY (see *Plants*)

BARNABAS *(BAR-nuh-bus)* was the nickname of a follower of Jesus. His real name was Joseph, but the apostles called him Barnabas, which means "son of encouragement." He was always helping people as a preacher, teacher, and missionary. When the new Christians at Jerusalem needed food, Barnabas sold a field and gave the money to the apostles.

Barnabas and Paul were good friends. It was Barnabas who spoke up for Paul when the apostles still feared him. He and Paul together taught the Christians in Antioch. When a famine struck Jerusalem, the new Christians at Antioch sent money with Paul and Barnabas to help the Christians who were without food in Jerusalem.

Soon after coming back to Antioch, Paul and Barnabas went on a missionary trip. Barnabas's young cousin, John Mark, went with them. At Iconium, some people tried to kill them. At Lystra, the townspeople tried to worship them as gods when they healed a crippled man.

Paul and Barnabas disagreed when planning their second missionary trip. Barnabas wanted to take John Mark along again. Paul didn't, because John Mark had not finished the first trip. He had gone home. Finally, Paul and Barnabas chose separate trips. Barnabas took John Mark and sailed to Cyprus (Barnabas's old home). Paul chose another companion, Silas, and went to Asia Minor (now called Turkey).

Some scholars think Barnabas wrote Hebrews, though no one knows for sure.

Where to find it

Barnabas helps new churches *Acts 4:36-37; 11:22-26; 13:2-3; 14:14*
Barnabas and Paul *Acts 9:27; 11:27-30; 13:3–14:28; 15:22-41*

BARRENNESS *(BEAR-un-ness)* means that a man and wife cannot have any children. In Bible times, most men and women were very sad and ashamed when this happened. They thought God was punishing them.

Rachel, for example, didn't have any children, and her sister had many. Rachel was so jealous she cried, "Give me children or I shall die!" This was how many barren women felt.

If the Lord healed barrenness, there was much rejoicing.

Where to find it: *Genesis 30: 1; 1 Samuel 1: 5; Psalm 113: 9; Luke 1: 25*

BARTHOLOMEW (bar-THOL-uh-mew) was one of the twelve apostles, but nothing else is written in the Bible about him. We do not know what work he did or what kind of person he was.

Some people think Bartholomew and Nathanael are the same person, but the Bible does not say for sure.

Where to find it: *Matthew 10: 3; Mark 3: 18; Luke 6: 14; John 1: 45-46; Acts 1: 13*

BARTIMAEUS (bar-tuh-MAY-us) was a blind man who sat along the road outside of Jericho begging for money. When Jesus and his disciples walked by, Bartimaeus called Jesus' name.

When Jesus asked what he wanted, Bartimaeus said, "My sight."

Jesus answered, "Go. Your faith has healed you." Immediately, Bartimaeus could see, so he joined the crowd and followed Jesus.

Where to find it: *Mark 10: 46-52*

BARUCH (BEAR-uk) came from a noble family in Jerusalem. He could have been a powerful friend of the king. Instead he chose to be the friend and assistant of the prophet Jeremiah. He wrote down Jeremiah's words and read them to the people.

Together, Baruch and Jeremiah faced lots of trouble. Once King Jehoiakim threw Jeremiah's writings in the fire. He ordered Baruch and Jeremiah arrested, but they escaped. Baruch rewrote the burned prophecy and added more of Jeremiah's words. They were thrown into prison, accused of being traitors. Both Jeremiah and Baruch went to Egypt when Jerusalem was taken over (586 B.C.). And they probably died there.

Where to find it

Baruch and Jeremiah   *Jeremiah 32: 12, 16*
Baruch rewrites the prophecies   *Jeremiah 36: 27-32*
Journey to Egypt   *Jeremiah 43: 6, 7*

BASINS (BAY-suns) are like today's bowls. Made in many sizes, they were used for wash-

ing, serving foods, and in ceremonies in the Temple.

Where to find it: *Exodus 12: 22; 24: 6; John 13: 5*

BASKETS (BASS-kets) in the Old Testament were made from reeds, twigs, or ropes. They were used for carrying fruit, bread, or clay. They were carried by hand, on the head or shoulders, or attached to a pole, depending on their size.

In the New Testament, two kinds of baskets are mentioned. One was like a small backpack. The other was a large, sturdy basket that could hold a person.

Where to find it

Baskets in the Old Testament   *Genesis 40: 17; Exodus 29: 2-3; Deuteronomy 26: 2*
Baskets in the New Testament   *Matthew 16: 9-10; John 6: 13; Acts 9: 25*

BAT (see *Animals*)

BATHING (see *Washing*)

BATHSHEBA (bath-SHE-buh) was a beautiful woman. She and her husband, Uriah the Hittite, lived near King David's palace. Uriah was a soldier in David's army.

One spring afternoon, when all of his army was off fighting, King David wandered up on his palace roof. From there he saw Bathsheba bathing. Sending for her, he committed adultery with her. Bathsheba later told David she was pregnant.

David sent for Uriah and gave him a vacation. David hoped he would go home and have sexual relations with his wife, so he would think the child was his. When Uriah didn't go home, David gave orders that in the next battle Uriah was to fight where the danger was greatest. Uriah was killed.

After Uriah's death, David made Bathsheba one of his wives. Her first child died, but she and David had four more sons, one of whom was Solomon.

When David grew old, another of his sons, Adonijah, decided to claim kingship. Bathsheba and the prophet Nathan defeated Adonijah's plot, reminding David of his promise to make Solomon the next king.

Solomon was one of Jesus' ancestors.

Where to find it

David, Bathsheba, and Uriah   *2 Samuel 11*
Bathsheba's children   *1 Chronicles 3:5*
Adonijah's plot   *1 Kings 1*
Solomon and Jesus   *Matthew 1:6*

BATTLEMENT *(BAT-tul-ment)* was a stone fence on top of city walls. From the openings in it, stones, arrows, and spears were hurled down on attacking enemy soldiers. Since homes had flat rooftops for relaxing or for sleeping in hot weather, many homes also had battlements for safety.

Where to find it: *Deuteronomy 22:8*

BEAR (see *Animals*)

BEARDS were a sign of manhood to the Jews. The Egyptians shaved their faces and their heads, but if a Jew was shaved, it was considered shameful. The Israelites were forbidden to shave the "corners of their beards." Some people think the "corners" were sideburns.

A man plucked out his beard to show great sorrow. During times of extreme trouble, the Jews let their beards get uneven and ratty.

Like a handshake today, a beard was used in greeting. One man grasped another man's beard to pull him gently forward for a kiss or hug.

Where to find it: *Leviticus 17:27; 21:5; 2 Samuel 19:24; 20:9; Jeremiah 48:37*

BEAST is a wild animal.

A beast is also a symbol of something or someone who is powerful, evil, and against God. In Daniel 7, four empires (Babylon, Media-Persia, Greece, and Rome) are symbolized by four beasts.

Revelation 13:1-18 describes two beasts of the end times. The first one rises powerfully from the sea and demands that people worship him as God. He is the final version of antichrist. The other beast rises from the earth and also is called the false prophet in Revelation 19:20. These evil beasts live by Satan's power, and they fight against God. They will be destroyed in the end. The term *beast* in the Book of Revelation refers both to evil rulers and to the kingdoms or powers they rule.

Where to find it

A wild animal   *Leviticus 26:22; Mark 1:13*
The destruction of the end time beasts   *Revelation 19:20; 20:7-10*
Both rulers and kingdoms   *Revelation 17*

BEATITUDES *(bee-AT-uh-toods)* are short sayings beginning with the word *blessed* or *happy* that describe actions or thoughts that will give a person joy and peace. In the Old Testament, beatitudes were written by psalmists and prophets. Psalm 1:1-3 gives a beatitude: "Blessed is the man who walks not in the counsel of the wicked . . . but his delight is in the law of the Lord. . . . In all that he does, he prospers." The Old Testament beatitudes often promise blessings for this life: health, peace, prosperity, a family. But most of all they promise that God will be near to a righteous person.

The beatitudes in the New Testament have one big difference from those in the Old Testament. They stress the joy of belonging to God's Kingdom. In the Sermon on the Mount Jesus says the poor in spirit, those who weep, and those who are persecuted are blessed because they belong to God and enjoy being close to him.

Where to find it

Old Testament beatitudes   *Psalm 41:1; 65:4; 84:5; 106:3; Proverbs 8:32, 34; Isaiah 32:20*
New Testament beatitudes   *Matthew 5:1-11; Luke 6:20-22*

BEATEN GOLD

BEATEN GOLD is gold hammered into a thin sheet for covering wooden or metal objects. Solomon had shields overlaid with gold. In the Tabernacle the ark, lampstands, cherubim, and other pieces were covered with beaten gold.

BEATEN OIL was made by crushing fully ripe olives in a bowl. The pure oil was used in daily sacrifices as well as to keep the lamp in the Tabernacle burning.

BEATEN SILVER was silver hammered into thin sheets. It was used, like beaten gold, to cover and decorate holy objects.

Where to find it

Gold   *Exodus 25:10-18; 1 Kings 10:16-17*
Oil   *Exodus 27:20; Numbers 28:4-5*
Silver   *Jeremiah 10:9*

BEATING (see *Scourging*)

BEAUTIFUL GATE was probably the eastern gate to the Temple in Jerusalem. It was beautifully crafted of Corinthian bronze, and it opened into the Temple's Court of Women. Peter and John healed a paralyzed man outside the Beautiful Gate.

Where to find it: *Acts 3:2-10*

BED was sometimes nothing more than the ground, for those who were very poor. They would use their thin coats as blankets.

Most people used a mat or rug in the house. But the rich had beds made of ivory, iron, gold, or silver.

Where to find it: *Deuteronomy 3:11; Esther 1:6; Amos 6:4*

BEELZEBUL or **BEELZEBUB** (see *Baal-zebub*)

BEERSHEBA *(beer-SHE-buh)* is the town farthest south in Judah. The phrase *from Dan to Beersheba* meant the entire country of Israel and Judah from north to south.

The history of Beersheba's name, "well of the oath," is told in Genesis 21:22-34. Jacob

At Abraham's well in Beersheba, you can still see the grooves worn into the rock by ropes lowering and raising water buckets for many centuries of time.

had a wonderful vision at Beersheba as he traveled to Egypt to join his son Joseph.

Where to find it: *Genesis 46:1-2; 2 Samuel 3:10*

BEGGAR (see *Alms*)

BEHEMOTH (see *Animals*)

BELIEF (see *Faith*)

BELOVED *(bee-LUV-ed)* means to be greatly loved by someone. The lovers in the Song of Solomon called each other "beloved." In Isaiah 5:1-2, God was beloved. Israel was also beloved by God.

In the New Testament, at Jesus' baptism, God the Father called Jesus "my beloved Son" (Matthew 3:17).

The entire Church is beloved by God, and so is each congregation and each person. Jesus said that Christians are to love each other greatly.

Where to find it: *Psalm 108:6; Song of Solomon 1:16; 2:3, 8, 16; 6:3; Mark 1:11; 9:7; John 13:34; Romans 1:7; Colossians 3:12; 1 Peter 2:11*

BELOVED DISCIPLE (see *John, the Apostle*)

BELSHAZZAR *(bell-SHAZ-ur)* was the last king of Babylon. He was a descendant of King Nebuchadnezzar (see *Nebuchadnezzar*).

Belshazzar did not worship God. At one of his feasts in 539 B.C., he praised the idols of gold, silver, bronze, and iron because he was drinking from cups made of those materials. The cups had been stolen from the Jerusalem Temple.

As Belshazzar drank with his thousand guests, a hand appeared on the wall and wrote strange words. Belshazzar was afraid and cried for his wise men to explain the writing. No one could.

Finally, Daniel was called. His explanation is found in Daniel 5:24-28.

That very night, the writing came true. Belshazzar was killed, and his kingdom was taken over by the Medes and Persians.

Where to find it: *Daniel 5*

BENAIAH *(bee-NAY-uh)* was a strong warrior who commanded David's bodyguard. His courage is shown in 2 Samuel 23:20-21, when he killed a lion.

When Adonijah tried to become king (see *Adonijah*), Benaiah followed King David's orders and helped crown Solomon. King Solomon then made him commander of his army.

Where to find it

Benaiah protects David   *2 Samuel 23:22-23*
Benaiah helps Solomon   *1 Kings 1:38*
He becomes head of the army   *1 Kings 2:35*

When Benjamin was brought to see his older brother Joseph in Egypt, it was a happy reunion.

BENJAMIN *(BEN-juh-min)* was the youngest son of Jacob. His mother, Rachel, died when he was born. Her last word was "Benoni" ("son of my sorrow") which became his name. Later Jacob changed his name to Benjamin, meaning "son of the right hand." Jacob loved him as dearly as he had loved Rachel.

When the entire family came to live in Egypt with Joseph, the 12 sons of Jacob and their families became the 12 tribes of Israel.

In Canaan, the tribe of Benjamin was given land 26 miles long by 12 miles wide. The tribe of Judah was to the south, and the tribe of Ephraim to the north. When the country split, the tribe of Benjamin joined the Southern Kingdom of Judah.

King Saul and the apostle Paul were both from the tribe of Benjamin.

Where to find it

Benjamin's birth   *Genesis 35:16-21*
Goes to Egypt   *Genesis 42:1-45:15*
Paul from the tribe of Benjamin   *Philippians 3:5*

BERNICE *(bur-NEESS)* was the oldest daughter of Herod Agrippa I. She was an evil woman, married first to her uncle, Herod, king of Chalcis. When he died (A.D. 48), she lived with

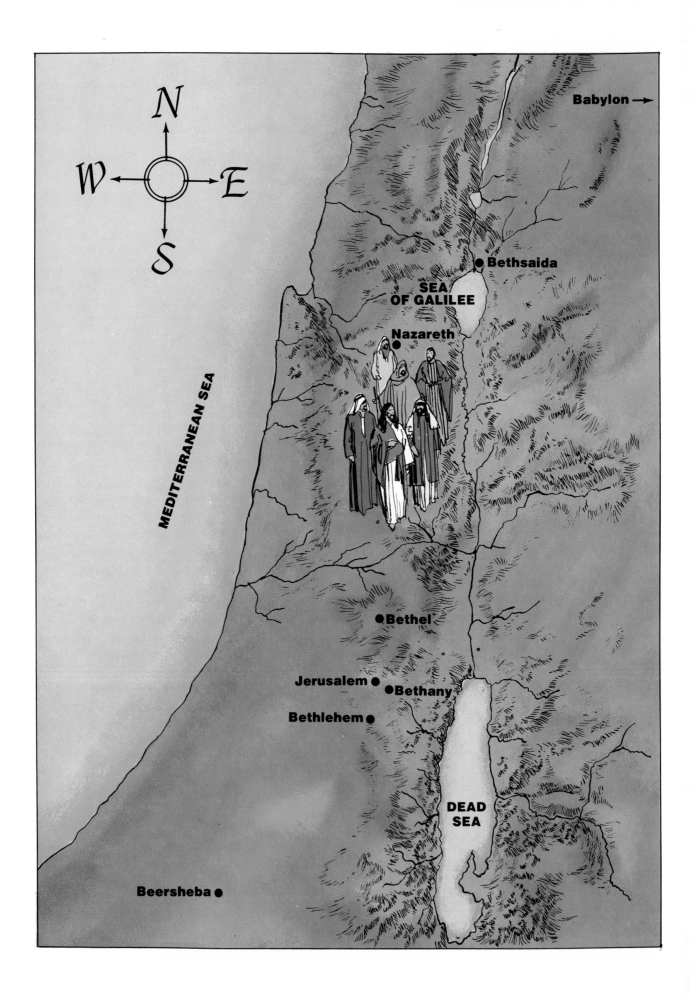

Babylon →

Bethsaida

SEA
OF GALILEE

Nazareth

MEDITERRANEAN SEA

Bethel

Jerusalem ●Bethany

Bethlehem ●

DEAD
SEA

Beersheba ●

her brother Agrippa II and had sexual relations with him. They heard the apostle Paul preach, but did not believe his gospel message about Jesus.

Where to find it: *Acts 25: 13–26: 32*

BETHANY *(BETH-uh-nee)* was a village two miles southeast of Jerusalem, near the Mount of Olives. Jesus' friends Simon the leper, Martha, Mary, and Lazarus (whom Jesus raised from the dead) lived in Bethany. Jesus rose into heaven near Bethany. A town is still there today.

Where to find it

Residents of Bethany *Matthew 26: 6-13; John 11: 1-44*
Lazarus is raised *John 11*
Jesus goes back to heaven *Luke 24: 50-51*

BETHEL *(BETH-ul)* was a town 12 miles north of Jerusalem. When Jacob was traveling to find a wife, he camped for the night near a Canaanite town called Luz. He slept on the ground with his head on a rock.

There, Jacob had an amazing dream. When he awoke, he called the place Bethel, which means "house of God," because he had met with God. He later built an altar there.

After the Israelites entered Canaan, the ark of the Covenant was kept at Bethel.

When the country split into the Northern and Southern kingdoms, wicked King Jeroboam chose Bethel as a place to set up his golden calves. The wickedness in Bethel caused the prophet Hosea to call it Bethaven, which means "house of idols." King Josiah finally destroyed the idols.

Where to find it

Jacob's dream *Genesis 28: 10-19*
The ark of the Covenant *Judges 20: 26-28*
Golden calves kept there *1 Kings 12: 26-30*
The idols destroyed *2 Kings 23: 15-23*

BETHESDA (see *Pool of Bethesda*)

BETHLEHEM *(BETH-luh-hem)* is best known as the place of Jesus' birth. The Old Testament prophet Micah predicted the Messiah would be born in Bethlehem. The angels announced Jesus' birth to the shepherds outside the town. All of the male babies two years old or younger around Bethlehem were sentenced to death by jealous King Herod, who wanted

to kill the new king of the Jews.

Bethlehem is called the "city of David" in Luke 2: 11 because David grew up there. His father Jesse, his grandfather Obed, and his great-grandparents Boaz and Ruth all lived in Bethlehem.

Where to find it

Old Testament prophecy *Micah 5: 2*
The angels' announcement *Luke 2: 8-15*
The babies are killed *Matthew 2: 16-18*

BETHSAIDA *(beth-SAY-uh-duh)* was a fishing village on the northwestern shores of Lake Galilee. Andrew, Peter, and Philip were from Bethsaida. Jesus healed a blind man there, but he also scolded the people of Bethsaida for their unbelief.

Where to find it

Hometown of some apostles *John 1: 44; 12: 21*
Jesus scolds its citizens *Matthew 11: 20-24*

BINDING AND LOOSING is the power Jesus promised Peter in Matthew 16: 19. He spoke of this power as a symbolic set of keys to the Kingdom of Heaven. Peter's "keys" could open God's Kingdom to people who wanted to belong to it. Matthew 18: 18 says this power was also given to all of the other apostles. Peter and the apostles could speak for God and tell how those who belong to God's Kingdom should act. A similar idea is mentioned in John 20: 23.

At Pentecost, Peter preached his first sermon, and thousands of Jewish people believed in Jesus Christ. By believing, they entered the Kingdom of God. Peter also preached to Samaritans (see *Samaritan*) and to the Gentiles (see *Gentile*). Acts 8: 14-17 and 10: 44-48 tell about this.

BIRDS. Of the 360 to 400 kinds of birds that live in Israel, 26 kinds can be found only in Israel and nowhere else. The Bible mentions about 50 kinds altogether.

Chickens are like our barnyard chickens. The male, called a cock or rooster, crows at dawn. This signal reminded Peter of Jesus' words that he would deny he knew his Lord. Jesus once said he wanted to care for the people of Jerusalem as a hen gathers her chicks under her wings.

Where to find it: *Matthew 23: 37; 26: 74*

BIRDS

Cocks are the male of any bird. At the time of Jesus' trial, he said Peter would deny him three times before the cock crowed. The term "cock crow" in Mark 13:35 refers to the hours between midnight and 3:00 A.M.

Doves look like the pigeons we see today in parks and city streets. Noah sent out a dove to find dry land. A dove's soft cooing often sounds like crying. Jesus told his disciples to be harmless as doves. The Spirit of God descended on Jesus like a dove. Doves were sold in the Temple for purification rituals.

Where to find it: *Genesis 8:8-12; Matthew 3:16; 10:16; 21:12*

Eagles were called unclean by God. They were unfit for the Jews to eat. The eagle is large and hawklike with powerful wings and a wingspread of four feet. Many word pictures about eagles appear in the Bible. The Lord renews a person's spiritual strength, so they mount up with wings strong like eagles. An eagle is swift in flight, like death and life. Riches are said to be like eagles, which swiftly disappear or fly away.

Where to find it: *Leviticus 11:13; 2 Samuel 1:23; Job 9:26; Proverbs 23:4, 5; Isaiah 40:31*

Falcons are hawks, with long, pointed wings and tail. They could not be eaten, as commanded in Leviticus 11:16.

Fowl is a name for all flying birds and bats. Many fowls were used as sacrifices. In God's eyes, people are worth more than many fowls.

Where to find it: *Genesis 1:20; Leviticus 1:14; 11:13-19; Luke 12:24*

Kite is probably a different name for the vulture or falcon. A kite is called unclean in Leviticus 11:13-19.

Night Hawks are small-beaked and eat winged insects; they are called unclean in Leviticus 11:16.

Ospreys *(AH-sprees)* are fish-eating hawks that have rough pads on their feet to hold slippery fish. Ospreys are said to be unclean.

Ostriches *(AH-strich-es)* are the largest living birds. Job 39:13-18 describes ostriches. They can run as fast as 40 miles per hour. Lamentations 4:3 says they are cruel.

Ossifrage (see *Vulture*)

Owls—little owl and great owl—were unfit to eat. They hunt at night for rats and other animals. They reminded the Israelites of ruined cities. The great owl is similar to the American great horned owl, about 22 inches long.

Where to find it: *Leviticus 11:17; Deuteronomy 14:16; Psalm 102:6; Isaiah 34:15*

Partridges are good for eating. David said he felt like a hunted partridge when Saul was

VULTURE

RAVEN

PEACOCK

TURTLEDOVE

QUAIL

PARTRIDGE

after him. Partridges supposedly steal other birds' eggs and hatch them—a good example of getting rich dishonestly.

Where to find it: *1 Samuel 26: 20; Jeremiah 17: 11*

Peacocks are beautiful birds that strutted about Solomon's courts.

Pelicans have webs between their toes for swimming while catching fish. Leviticus 11: 18 calls them unclean.

Pigeons were common rock doves (see *Doves*). They were used by the poor for sacrifices since they were so numerous.

Where to find it: *Genesis 15: 9; Luke 2: 24*

Quail are good for eating. They live on the ground and scratch for food. In Bible lands, quail migrate in huge flocks, flying only a few feet off the ground.

Where to find it: *Exodus 16: 13; Numbers 11: 31; Psalm 105: 40*

Ravens look like large crows. They were unclean because they sometimes eat dead bodies. But ravens also brought Elijah food during a drought.

Where to find it: *Leviticus 11: 15; 1 Kings 17: 4; Job 38: 41*

Sea gulls are web-footed birds who eat fish, worms, insects, bird eggs, and young birds. Their noisy calls are heard on the Mediterranean coasts and on the Sea of Galilee. Deuteronomy 14: 15 and Leviticus 11: 16 include sea gulls in the list of birds not to be eaten.

Sparrows are small, seed-eating birds like American sparrows. They busily flit about and chirp constantly. Sparrows were so cheap that when four were sold, a fifth sparrow was added free. But Jesus said that God knows about each one.

Where to find it: *Psalm 84: 3; Matthew 10: 29-31*

Storks feed in the marshes but nest in the trees (as Psalm 104: 17 points out). They have powerful wings, and they migrate each year.

Where to find it: *Jeremiah 8: 7; Zechariah 5: 9*

Swallows are quick fliers and have a piercing call. In Isaiah 38: 14, Hezekiah said he was as uneasy as a swallow during his illness.

Turtledoves are wild pigeons, which often sing early in the spring. Since turtledoves were cheap and plentiful, the poor used them for sacrifices.

Where to find it: *Genesis 15: 9; Song of Solomon 2: 12; Luke 2: 24*

Vultures are birds that feed on dead animals and even dead people. Leviticus 11: 13 calls them unclean or unfit to eat. Vultures fly high and far, but God knows paths they haven't seen. The ossifrage is called "the bearded vulture." Like other vultures, it is not to be eaten.

Where to find it: *Job 28: 7; Isaiah 34: 15*

Water hens could have been horned owls. Leviticus 11: 17 calls them unclean, so they probably ate flesh.

BIRTHRIGHT *(BURTH-rite)* was the blessing and double share of wealth a father gave to his oldest son. Esau carelessly sold his birthright for a bowl of soup.

Where to find it: *Genesis 25: 29-34; Hebrews 12: 16*

BISHOP *(BISH-up)* is a title used in some translations for leaders in the small New Testament churches. A bishop served the church people by encouraging them and sometimes teaching them. Other translations use *elder, leader,* or *overseer* instead of *bishop.*

Where to find it: *1 Timothy 3: 1-7; Titus 1: 7-9*

BITHYNIA *(buh-THIN-ee-uh)* was a region in what is now northwestern Turkey. Paul and his companions intended to go there to preach the gospel on their second missionary trip, but the Holy Spirit led them to Europe instead. We do not know how or when the gospel came to Bithynia, but 1 Peter 1: 1 mentions that Christians were there.

Where to find it: *Acts 16: 6-10*

BLASPHEMY *(BLAS-fuh-me)* means speaking against God, using careless, dirty, or wicked words. Exodus 20: 7 says blasphemy is a sin. The Jews punished blasphemers by stoning them to death. Jesus and Stephen were falsely accused of blasphemy.

BLESSEDNESS

When people said Jesus' miracles were done by Satan's power, they blasphemed against the Holy Spirit.

Where to find it

Laws against it *Leviticus 24:10-16*
Jesus accused *Matthew 9:3; 26:65-66*
Stephen accused *Acts 6:11*
Blasphemy against the Holy Spirit *Mark 3:28-30*

BLESSEDNESS *(BLESS-ed-ness)* comes from the verb *to bless*, which means literally "to bend the knee" or "to worship, adore, and praise." God is worshiped and adored, therefore he is blessed. In Psalm 28:6 the words "Blessed be the Lord" could mean "Let the Lord be worshiped!"

Often the reasons God should be praised are stated too. In Psalm 28:6 God had heard the psalm writer's prayers and had become his strength. Therefore the psalmist wanted everyone to praise God.

The word *blessed* is used of people, too, but its meaning is different. If people are blessed, they are happy or fortunate. This is a gift from God. In the Old Testament, a blessed person is righteous, and God often rewards him with wealth or long life. In the New Testament, faithful Christians are blessed because they will be rewarded by being with Christ.

Where to find it: *Psalm 34:8-10; 144:12-15; Matthew 5:11-12*

BLESSING *(BLESS-ing)* in the Old Testament meant a gift of something good, given by God. A blessing was usually something material, such as more cattle, sheep, children, or wealth.

A father often announced a blessing for his sons. An example of this is Isaac's blessing to Jacob, "May God give you . . . the fatness of the earth, and plenty of grain and wine."

In the New Testament, Jesus brought a different blessing from God to people. He brought them forgiveness, freedom, and salvation.

Where to find it

Material blessings *Proverbs 3:16*
Isaac's blessing of Jacob *Genesis 27:28-29*
Spiritual blessings *Ephesians 1:3*

BLINDNESS means not being able to see. A person may be born blind. Diseases like

When Jesus healed one blind man, he sent him first to wash his eyes in the pool of Siloam.

smallpox can cause blindness. Old age sometimes brings partial or complete blindness.

The Philistines, Assyrians, Babylonians, and other evil people often blinded the captives they took in war. Samson lost his eyesight this way.

Since a blind person had to beg for money to live, the Law instructed the Jews to lovingly care for the blind.

A special sign of the Messiah was that he would "open the eyes of the blind." Jesus healed many blind people (also see *Diseases*).

Where to find it

People born blind *John 9:1*
Old age causes blindness *Genesis 27:1; 1 Kings 14:4*
Samson's blindness *Judges 16:20-22*
Laws for blind people *Leviticus 19:14; Deuteronomy 27:18*
Blind people healed *Isaiah 29:18*

BLOOD in the Bible is considered to be the basis of life, both in people and in animals. Therefore God commanded the Israelites: "No person among you shall eat blood." Meat was to be drained of its blood before it could be cooked or eaten.

Blood represented life, according to Leviticus 17:11, and therefore it was needed for forgiveness. The Israelites offered animal sacrifices to God as he commanded. But when Jesus Christ died, he became the final sacrifice for our sins. Jesus said, "This is my blood of the covenant, which is poured out . . . for the forgiveness of sins."

The phrases *blood of Jesus, blood of Christ,* and *blood of the Lamb* all refer to Christ giving his life so that our sins can be forgiven and we can be saved (also see *Offerings*).

Where to find it

Laws against eating blood   *Leviticus 17:10-14*
Blood and forgiveness   *Hebrews 9:18-28*
Jesus' blood and our forgiveness   *Matthew 26:28; 1 Corinthians 10:16; Ephesians 2:13; 1 Peter 1:2, 19; 1 John 1:7*

BLOOD, ISSUE OF, was probably an excessive menstrual flow caused by a tumor in a woman's womb, making her very weak. The woman in Luke 8:43-48 suffered from this.

Today, surgery corrects this problem. But in Jesus' day, doctors were unable to help her. Jesus said the woman's own faith was what healed her.

BODY in the Old Testament was not considered separate from a person's soul or spirit. Later, the Greek idea of a person being three different things—body, soul, and spirit—became common. Many Greeks believed the body was evil and was a prison for the soul. But the Bible does not say that.

Even after death, Christians will have a permanent dwelling place. Paul says that when Christ returns, each person will have a new body. It will be a "spiritual" body—different from our present physical body.

Where to find it: *1 Corinthians 15:29-57*

BODY OF CHRIST has three meanings in the New Testament:

1. It means Christ's human body. He became a man with flesh and blood like other people. His physical body actually died. This was part of his offering of himself for us. Hebrews 10:10 says, "We have been sanctified through the offering of the body of Jesus Christ once for all." People who said Jesus didn't have a human body were called antichrists in 1 John 4:2-3.

2. Another meaning is found in Jesus' words at the last supper. He took bread, broke it in pieces, blessed it, and gave it to his disciples. He said, "Take, eat; this is my body." This is a word picture of Jesus' death on the cross. His body was "broken" on the cross to bring forgiveness and salvation.

3. The Body of Christ also refers to the total Church. All true believers everywhere and through all time are members of Jesus Christ. The Church is called "his Body," and Jesus Christ is called "the head." This shows how much Christians and Christ are a part of each other.

Where to find it

Jesus had a real human body   *1 John 4:2-3*
The last supper   *Matthew 26:26; Mark 14:22; Luke 22:19; 1 Corinthians 11:24*
The Body of Christ is the Church   *Ephesians 1:22-23; 4:15-16; Colossians 1:18*

BONDAGE *(BON-dij)* means being in slavery. In the Old Testament, the Hebrews were in bondage under the Egyptians for many years. Moses led them out of bondage.

In the New Testament, bondage means slavery to sin. But because Jesus' death and resurrection set people free, Christians are no longer slaves to sin. Now they can offer themselves to God as bondmen to do his work. (Also see *Slavery*.)

Where to find it

Bondage in Egypt   *Exodus 1:13; 3:7*
Bondage to sin   *John 8:34*
Slaves or servants of sin become slaves of God   *Romans 6:16-20*

BORROWING and **LOANING** were much the same in Bible times as they are now. In the Old Testament, the Hebrews could lend money to foreigners with interest—an extra amount of money the borrower paid to be able to use the money. But they could not charge each other interest. Though there were many guidelines for lending and borrowing, the people who owed money were often treated badly.

In the New Testament, the Jews lived under the Roman system of banking, which included tax collectors, bankers, and the money lenders who charged interest. Jesus said to show mercy to people who owed money. He even said his followers should lend without expecting interest. Another Bible word for interest is *usury.*

Where to find it

Guidelines for lending and borrowing   *Deuteronomy 15:1-6; 23:19-20; 24:10-13*
The oppressed debtor   *Proverbs 22:7*
Jesus' teaching of mercy and generosity   *Matthew 18:23-35; Luke 6:34-36*

BOWELS

BOWELS is a word with three meanings—the intestines of a person; the womb; and the emotions. Today we say the emotions come from the heart rather than the bowels.

Where to find it

Intestines   *Acts 1:18*
Womb   *Psalm 71:6*
Emotions   *Lamentations 1:20; Philippians 1:8*

BRACELETS were worn on the wrist or arm by both men and women. Armlets were signs of royalty. Necklaces, brooches, and gold jewelry were also called bracelets.

Where to find it

Descriptions of bracelets   *Genesis 38:18; Exodus 35:22; 2 Samuel 1:19; Isaiah 3:19*

BRAMBLE (see *Plants*)

BRANCH is a name the prophets Jeremiah and Zechariah gave to the coming Messiah, because he would be part of David's family tree. The Messiah would be a king, peace-bringer, and savior.

Where to find it: *Jeremiah 23:5-6; 33:15; Zechariah 3:8; 6:12*

BREAD in Bible times was made from wheat flour that was leavened (raised by yeast). Then the dough was shaped into loaves and baked.

The night of the Passover, the Israelites ate unleavened bread because of their hurry to leave Egypt. Unleavened bread has no yeast, doesn't have to rise, and comes out hard and flat. Many churches today use it in Communion.

Poor people made their bread from barley. The boy with five barley loaves in John 6:9 was probably from a poor family. Times of famine caused everyone to eat barley bread. Ezekiel 4:9-17 describes baking in famine times.

Jesus called himself "the Bread of Life." Bread symbolizes the food all people need to live. Just as people need food to live a healthy physical life, so Jesus said he was the source of spiritual life.

Where to find it

Passover meal   *Exodus 12*
The bread we need   *Genesis 3:19; Matthew 6:11*
"The Bread of Life"   *John 6:35-59*

BREAD OF THE PRESENCE (see *Showbread*)

BREASTPIECE or **BREASTPLATE** was a special square of cloth worn by the high priest in the Tabernacle and the Temple. Made of beautiful colored linen, the breastpiece was nine inches square when folded. It was decorated with 12 jewels, each engraved with the name of one of the tribes of Israel. When the high priest wore this breastpiece, he represented all the Hebrew people before God.

Where to find it: *Exodus 28:15-30*

For a while God gave his people miracle food to gather each morning, called manna.

BROTHERS OF OUR LORD. Matthew 1:25 says that Jesus was born when Mary was a virgin. Since God, not Joseph, was Jesus' father, the other sons born later to Mary and Joseph were Jesus' half brothers. Mark 6:3 gives their names: James, Joses, Juda, and Simon.

During the first part of Jesus' ministry, his brothers didn't believe in him, but later some of them did. James became a leader of the first church in Jerusalem. Most likely, the letters of James and Jude in the New Testament were written by two brothers of Jesus. Nothing is known about Joses and Simon.

Where to find it

The brothers' disbelief *John 7:1-10*
James becomes a leader in the church *Acts 15:13; 21:18*

BRICKS and BRICKMAKING (see *Occupations*)

BROTHERS or **BRETHREN** can describe several different relationships. The most common meaning of *brother* is the relationship of a son to other sons or daughters of the same parents. *Brother* can also mean a man from the same country, a member of the same tribe, an ally, or any member of the human race.

In the New Testament, the Christians called each other "brother" because they were all in God's family and they deeply loved one another. Christians are even called brothers of Jesus.

Where to find it

Brothers in a family *Genesis 27:6; 28:2; Judges 8:19*
Men from the same country *Exodus 2:11*
Men from the same tribe *2 Samuel 19:12*
An ally *Amos 1:9*
Members of the human race *Matthew 7:3-5*
Christian "brothers" *Matthew 23:8; Romans 1:13*
Christ and his brothers *Hebrews 2:10-13*

BUCKLER (see *Weapons*)

BUGLE (see *Musical Instruments–Trumpet*)

BULL, BULLOCK (see *Animals*)

BULRUSH (see *Plants*)

BULWARK *(BULL-werk)* means a strong wall or foundation. The Bible sometimes uses *bulwark* as a word picture of God protecting his

Jesus once stopped a funeral procession– so he could raise the dead man back to life!

people. I Timothy 3:15 speaks of the church as the "bulwark" of the truth.

BURIAL *(BEAR-ee-ul)* is placing a dead body in a grave or tomb. The Israelites usually buried their dead in caves, for two reasons: first, Palestine has a lot of caves; and second, the ground there is mostly rock with only a small layer of soil, so digging is difficult.

Long before the Israelites took over the land of Canaan, Sarah, Jacob, Joseph, and others were buried in a cave at Hebron.

The Egyptians embalmed their dead by treating the bodies with chemicals to keep them from decaying. Some of their bodies have been preserved to this day. But the Israelites quickly buried their dead.

In Jesus' day, dead bodies were wrapped in clean linen with fragrant spices and ointments. When a death occurred, friends (usually women) hurried to the house and cried loudly. Mourners were often hired to add to the noise.

Wicked rulers sometimes didn't get a natural burial. Dogs ate Jezebel, Uzziah was buried in a field (instead of the kings' tombs), and Jehoiakim was buried like a donkey.

Where to find it

Sarah's burial *Genesis 23*
Jacob's burial *Genesis 49:29-32*
Joseph's burial *Joshua 24:32-33*
Burial ceremonial rules *Numbers 19:11-22*
King Saul's death and burial *1 Samuel 31:8-13*
Jesus' burial *Matthew 27:57-61; Luke 23:53-56*
Mourners *Jeremiah 9:17; Mark 5:38*
Burials of the wicked *2 Kings 9:10; 2 Chronicles 26:23; Jeremiah 22:18-19*

BURNT OFFERINGS (see *Offerings*)

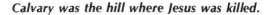

Calvary was the hill where Jesus was killed.

CAESAR *(SEE-zur)* was at first the family name of Julius Caesar (see *Julius Caesar)*. Later the name *Caesar* was added to the name of each of the Roman emperors, so it became a title like *emperor* or *king*. Instead of "Emperor Tiberius," he was called "Tiberius Caesar." "Caesar Augustus" meant the same as Emperor Augustus.

CAESAREA *(SES-uh-REE-uh)* was a city on the Mediterranean Sea named in honor of Caesar Augustus. It was about 65 miles northwest of Jerusalem (see map). During the time of Christ and the early church, it was the official capital of Palestine. It had beautiful palaces, an open-air stadium, a large arena, and a temple dedicated to Caesar.

Caesarea was the military headquarters for the Roman army in the area. The first time Peter preached to Gentiles was in Caesarea in the house of Cornelius, a Roman soldier.

Caesarea was also the home of Philip the evangelist and his four daughters who prophesied. Paul stayed in Philip's home on his third missionary journey.

After Paul had been arrested in Jerusalem, he spent two years in Caesarea as a prisoner. While a prisoner, Paul preached to three Roman officials: Felix, Festus, and King Agrippa.

Where to find it

Peter preaches to Cornelius *Acts 10*
Home of Philip *Acts 21:8-9*
Paul in prison *Acts 23:23–26:32*

CAESAREA PHILIPPI *(SES-uh-REE-uh FILL-uh-pie)* was an ancient town in northern Palestine (see map). There Herod the Great built a temple in honor of Augustus Caesar. Herod's son, Philip, enlarged the town and named it Caesarea Philippi so it would not be confused with another Caesarea, the larger city on the coast.

At a quiet place near Caesarea Philippi, Jesus Christ began to tell his disciples about his coming suffering and death. There Jesus asked his disciples, "Who do you say that I am?"

Peter answered with his famous statement, "You are the Christ, the Son of the living God."

Where to find it: *Matthew 16:13-28; Mark 8:27-37*

CAESAR'S HOUSEHOLD probably refers to the servants in the palace of the Caesars (emperors). It also means Caesar's political advisers and the soldiers responsible for guarding him.

When Paul wrote, "All the saints greet you, especially those of Caesar's household," it showed that some of the employees of Caesar were Christians.

Where to find it: *Philippians 4:22*

CAIAPHAS *(KAY-uh-fuss)* was high priest from about A.D. 18 to 36, during the life and death of Christ and the beginning of the early church. He was the son-in-law of Annas and seemed to work closely with him.

After Jesus raised Lazarus from the dead, Caiaphas and others were eager to kill Jesus. They said he was "stirring up the people." Caiaphas was involved in the trial of Jesus. He

is also mentioned in the later arrest of Peter and John.

Where to find it

Wants Jesus put to death *John 11:45-53*
Involved in trial of Jesus *John 18:13-28*
Trial of Peter and John *Acts 4:5-22*

CAIN was the first son of Adam and Eve—the first person born by a natural birth. He was a farmer who brought an offering of vegetables to God. His brother Abel brought a lamb. God was not pleased with Cain's offering. The Bible does not explain why, but 1 John 3:12 does say that Cain "was of the evil one."

Cain was so jealous of his brother that he killed him. When the Lord asked Cain where Abel was, Cain answered, "I do not know; am I my brother's keeper?"

Cain was punished by having to leave his parents and become a wanderer. He always lived in fear of being killed. God promised to give him a mark to protect him from being killed by his enemies.

Cain went to a country east of Eden where he married and had a son, Enoch.

Where to find it: *Genesis 4:1-17*

Caleb and the others brought back huge clusters of grapes from Canaan.

CALEB *(KAY-lub)* was one of the twelve men sent by Moses to spy out the land of Canaan.

Caleb and 11 other men spent 40 days in Canaan, observing the land, the cities, the crops, the people and their way of life. When the spies returned, they had samples of the juicy grapes, figs, and pomegranates that grew in the land. The spies told the people it was a rich land, but it also had walled cities and people who were big like giants.

The Israelites were unhappy. They were sure they would all be killed if they tried to conquer the land.

Caleb and another spy named Joshua did not agree. They told the people, "Let us go up at once and occupy it, for we are well able to overcome it." But the ten other spies said, "We are not able to go up against the people; for they are stronger than we."

The people of Israel wept and said they wanted to go back to Egypt. Caleb and Joshua tried to calm them. "If the Lord delights in us, he will bring us into this land and give it to us, a land which flows with milk and honey. Only do not rebel against the Lord; and do not fear the people of the land for . . . the Lord is with us."

The Israelites wanted to kill Caleb and Joshua for giving that advice. The Lord was angry at the way the people acted. He said that none of the adults except Caleb and Joshua would ever be permitted to enter Canaan. They would have to wander in the wilderness until all the adults were dead.

Forty years later, their sons and daughters did enter Canaan, led by Joshua, who replaced Moses. Caleb was the only other man of the original group still alive. He asked to settle near Hebron, the same part of the country where the giantlike people lived who had frightened the other spies! Even though Caleb was now an old man, he directed the battle against these people and drove them out.

Where to find it

Spies out the land *Numbers 13:1–14:38*
Conquers Hebron *Joshua 14:6-15; 15:13-14*

CALENDARS *(CAL-un-ders)* have been based since Bible times on the appearance and disappearance of the moon in cycles of 29-30 days. The first day of a new month on the Jewish calendar began when the thin sliver of the new moon could be seen at sunset. The Jews had two separate calendars—the sacred calendar that began in the spring, and the government calendar that began in the fall.

Usually, the months were spoken of by number ("the third day of the second month") but sometimes by name. The names changed over the years. In Exodus 13:4, the first month is called Abib; in Esther 3:7, the first month is called Nisan. The same is true of other months. We do not know the early names of all the months.

The months of the Jewish calendar didn't begin on the same days that ours do today. The biblical months overlapped parts of two of our months. See chart on page 59.

CALF (see *Animals*)

CALF, GOLDEN (see *Golden Calf*)

CALL is used in several ways in the Bible:
1. It sometimes means belonging to God's family. "And all the peoples of the earth shall see that you are called by the name of the Lord" (Deuteronomy 28:10).
2. It sometimes means to pray and give yourself to God. "Whoever calls on the name of the Lord shall be saved" (Acts 2:21).
3. It sometimes means to give a name to. "And whatever the man called every living creature, that was its name" (Genesis 2:19).

CALLING often refers to God's choosing a person to become a Christian. It can also mean each person's way of serving God.

Where to find it: *1 Corinthians 1:26; 2 Timothy 1:9*

CALVARY *(KAL-vuh-ree)* is where Jesus was crucified. The name comes from a Latin word meaning "skull." It may have been called that because it was a place where criminals were executed and skulls were found there, or because the hill itself looked like a skull.

We don't know the exact location of Calvary. Two places have been suggested. One is where the Church of the Holy Sepulchre now stands in Jerusalem; the other is a hill known as "Gordon's Calvary." On Gordon's Calvary there are holes in the rocky side of the hill that resemble the eyes and nose of a skull.

The Bible says nothing about location except that it was near Jerusalem and that it was near a garden with a new tomb.

Where to find it: *Matthew 27:33; Luke 23:33; John 19:41*

JEWISH CALENDAR

The months of the Jewish calendar didn't begin on the same days that ours do today.
The biblical months overlapped parts of two of our months.

MONTH SACRED	MONTH GOV'T	EARLY NAME	LATER NAME	MENTIONED IN BIBLE	OUR CALENDAR	FESTIVALS
1	7	Abib	Nisan	Exodus 12:2 Esther 3:7	March-April	Passover Unleavened Bread First Fruits
2	8	Ziv	Iyyar	1 Kings 6:1, 37	April-May	Later Passover
3	9		Sivan	Esther 8:9	May-June	Pentecost Feast of Weeks
4	10		Tammuz		June-July	
5	11		Ab		July-August	
6	12		Elul	Nehemiah 6:15	August-Sept.	
7	1	Ethanim	Tishri	1 Kings 8:2	Sept.-Oct.	Trumpets Day of Atonement Tabernacles Solemn Assembly
8	2	Bul	Heshvan	1 Kings 6:38	Oct.-Nov.	
9	3		Chislev	Nehemiah 1:1	Nov.-Dec.	Dedication
10	4		Tebeth	Esther 2:16	Dec.-Jan.	
11	5		Shebat	Zechariah 1:7	Jan.-Feb.	
12	6		Adar	Ezra 6:15	Feb.-March	

CAMEL

CAMEL (see *Animals*)

CAMEL'S HAIR is what John the Baptist's cloak (see *Cloak*) was made of. Today, some Bedouin tribesmen in Israel and surrounding areas still wear clothing made of camel's hair.

Where to find it: *Matthew 3:4; Mark 1:6*

CAMP refers to a group of tents set up for temporary living.

The Israelites camped for forty years in the wilderness. They moved from one site to another, waiting for the time they could enter the Promised Land. God gave exact instructions about how their camp was to be set up—the Tabernacle in the center, the tents of the priests and the Levites around the sides, and further back those of the twelve tribes—each assigned a certain position.

After the Israelites entered Canaan, armies camped when they were at war. During battles, often some warriors remained behind to guard the camp.

Where to find it

How Israelites camped   *Numbers 2–3*
Armies camping   *1 Samuel 25:13*

CANA (*KAY-nuh*) was a village in Galilee mentioned four times in the Gospel of John. We don't know its exact location, but it was probably west of the lake of Galilee.

Jesus performed his first miracle in this town—turning the water at a wedding into wine. It is also the place where Jesus met the nobleman whose son was dying, and Jesus told him his son would live.

Where to find it

Jesus turns water into wine   *John 2:1-11*
Jesus meets a nobleman   *John 4:46-54*

CANAAN (*KAY-nun*) was the name of a man and the name of a place.

1. Canaan was the grandson of Noah and the son of Ham. He was the ancestor of the people who later lived in the land of Canaan, which was named after him.

2. Canaan was one of the old names for Palestine (now Israel). The people who lived there before the Israelites conquered it were called Canaanites.

Where to find it: *Genesis 9:18; Exodus 6:4*

CANAANITES (*KAY-nuh-nites*) were the people living in Canaan when the Israelites came into the land after wandering forty years in the wilderness.

They were descendants of Canaan, the son of Ham. We aren't sure exactly when these people began to live in Palestine, but they probably lived there about 800 years before the Israelites moved in. The Canaanites included tribes of the Hittites, Jebusites, Amorites, Hivites, and others. They lived in well-developed cities, each with its own king, army, and taxes. The city-kingdoms often battled each other.

The Canaanites had many gods and goddesses. The main ones were Baal, Dagon, Astarte, and Asherah. Many temples to these gods have been found by archaeologists.

The Israelites had to conquer the Canaanites before they could live in peace in the Promised Land. But the Israelites never completely conquered them.

CANDACE (*KAN-duh-see*) was the title of the queens of Ethiopia. One of these queens had a treasurer who became a Christian after he met Philip the evangelist.

Where to find it: *Acts 8:26-40*

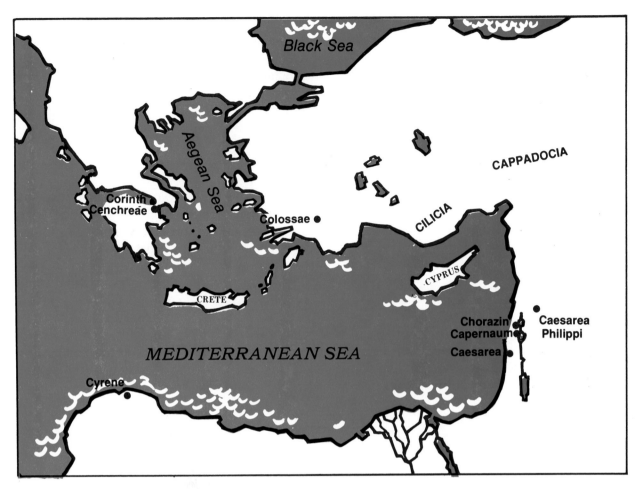

CANON *(KAN-un)* is the set of books that make up the Bible. Christians believe each of these books was inspired by God and is therefore God's Word. The canon is the basis for what Christians believe and the way they act.

The Old Testament canon is 39 books. It was accepted by the Jews before the time of Christ, although the books were not in the same order as we have them today. The Dead Sea Scrolls, copied between 150 B.C. and A.D. 100, include parts of most of the Old Testament books (see *Dead Sea Scrolls).*

The Protestant Old Testament is the same as the Jewish Bible. The Roman Catholic Old Testament has some additional ancient writings not included in the Jewish or Protestant Old Testament (see *Apocrypha).*

In the New Testament, Protestants and Roman Catholics agree that the same 27 books have authority for the Church.

During the early years of the Christian church, the various books of the New Testament were copied by hand and passed from group to group to be read and studied. After a while, Christians came to agree about which books were teaching the truth of God.

All of the books were written by apostles (including Paul) or by those who had close contact with the apostles.

Although the books of the New Testament were officially listed by the church council at Carthage in A.D. 397, Christians had agreed long before on which writings were to rule the Church. This is how the canon was determined.

CAPERNAUM *(kuh-PURR-nay-um)* was a large town on the northwest shore of the Sea of Galilee (see map). Jesus made this town his headquarters during his work in Galilee. He performed many miracles at Capernaum, including the healings of a centurion's servant and a nobleman's son. Many of his important teachings were spoken there. Because the people did not respond, Jesus predicted the city would be destroyed.

His prediction was so completely fulfilled that today no one is sure where the town was.

Where to find it

Jesus' miracles in Capernaum *Matthew 8: 5-13; Luke 7: 1-10; John 4: 46-54*
Jesus predicts its fall *Matthew 11: 23-24*

CAPPADOCIA *(kap-uh-DOH-shee-uh)* was an eastern section of Asia Minor (now Turkey; see map). Jews from Cappadocia were among those who heard Peter's sermon in Jerusalem on the Day of Pentecost. Peter wrote his first letter to Christians living in Cappadocia and other parts of northern Asia Minor.

Where to find it

Among those at Pentecost *Acts 2: 9*
Peter writes to them *1 Peter 1: 1*

CAPTAIN *(KAP-tun)*, when used in the Bible, does *not* refer to a specific rank in the army or police force. It is a general term meaning leader or someone with authority.

Where to find it: *2 Kings 7: 2*

CAPTAIN OF THE TEMPLE was a priest who was second in authority to the high priest. He was in charge of the Levites, who were organized into groups with a captain over each group. When Luke 22: 52 speaks of the "captains of the temple," it probably refers to these lower captains or leaders (see *Captain*).

CAPTIVITY (see *Exile*)

CARAVAN *(CARE-uh-van)* is a group of people traveling together for protection. In Bible times, travelers in the deserts or foreign lands went in groups to protect each other from robbers, wild animals, or accidents. When families moved, they went in caravans; traders also traveled in caravans.

CARNAL *(KAR-null)* usually means living under the control of sin rather than under the control of God. People living for themselves are said to live carnal, selfish lives.

Where to find it: *Romans 7: 14; 1 Corinthians 3: 1-3*

Even today in the Middle East, caravans of camels move across the deserts.

CASEMENT (see *Lattice*)

CASTLE *(CASS-ul)* is a building or group of buildings made strong enough to keep out enemies. Although castles were sometimes used by kings as places to live, they were more like forts than palaces. The castle where Paul was taken when he was rescued from the mob was the fortresslike Tower of Antonia.

Where to find it: *Acts 21: 34-37*

CATHOLIC *(KATH-lick)* means "universal." When the Apostles' Creed speaks of "the holy catholic church," it refers to Christians everywhere—the Body of Christ, those who belong to him. Today we use *Catholic* to refer to the Roman Catholic Church, but in the early church *catholic* meant "universal"—all over the world.

Some New Testament letters, such as James, 1 and 2 Peter, and Jude, are occasionally called "catholic letters." This means they were general letters addressed to all Christians rather than to specific churches.

CATTLE (see *Animals*)

CAVES are openings in the earth. In Palestine, where the hills are largely limestone or chalk, there are many large caves that are quite safe from cave-ins. Some are large enough to be used for homes. Lot and his two daughters lived in a cave after Sodom and Gomorrah were destroyed. Some of the prophets hid in caves when Jezebel was trying to kill them.

Caves were also used for storage and as burial places.

Where to find it

Lot and his daughters   *Genesis 19: 30*
Prophets hid from Jezebel   *1 Kings 18: 4*

CEDAR (see *Plants*)

CELESTIAL BODIES *(suh-LESS-jull BOD-eez)* means the sun, moon, and stars.

Where to find it: *1 Corinthians 15: 40-41*

CENCHREAE *(sen-KREE-uh)* was a harbor city just southeast of Corinth in what is now Greece (see map). Phoebe was a leader in the church in Cenchreae. The church there may have been started by Paul on his second missionary journey. Paul stopped in Cenchreae and had his head shaved to fulfill a vow.

Where to find it

Phoebe a leader   *Romans 16: 1*
Paul shaves his head   *Acts 18: 18*

CENSER *(SEN-ser)* was a copper pan shaped somewhat like a small shovel. Priests used censers in the Tabernacle and in the Temple to carry burning coals. They would also burn incense in censers.

CENSUS *(SEN-sus)* is the counting of the number of people in an area. A census was taken soon after the Israelites left Egypt. Another was taken near the end of the forty years in the wilderness. David also made a census when he was king, and the Bible says that David displeased God by doing it.

These census reports counted only men twenty years and older so they could find out how strong the army could be.

The New Testament says Caesar Augustus once ordered a census. Because each person had to be counted in the place of his birth, Joseph and Mary had to go to Bethlehem. While they were there, Jesus was born.

Where to find it

Old Testament censuses   *Numbers 1: 2; 26: 2; 1 Chronicles 21: 1-7*
Census at Jesus' birth   *Luke 2: 1-7*

CENTURION (see *Occupations*)

CEREAL OFFERINGS (see *Offerings*)

CEPHAS *(SEE-fus)* means rock or stone. It was the name Jesus gave to the apostle Peter (see *Peter*).

Where to find it: *John 1: 42; 1 Corinthians 1: 12; Galatians 1: 18*

CHAFF is the dry, worthless parts of grain the farmers of Bible times got rid of by throwing the grain into the air on a windy day. This useless stuff blew away, and the heavier kernels of grain fell back where they could be gathered.

CHALDEA *(kal-DEE-uh)* was a country in what is now part of Iran and Iraq. Babylon was its capital, and sometimes during its history, it was part of Babylonia. Chaldea conquered Judah (the Southern Kingdom), and many of Judah's people were exiled to Babylon. The prophet Daniel was among them.

CHAMBER *(CHAYM-bur)* means a room. Sometimes it refers to a special room set aside for a particular purpose, such as a council chamber.

CHAMBERLAIN *(CHAYM-bur-lin)* in the Old Testament was the man in charge of a king's wives and concubines. In the New Testament it may refer to someone who is in a high, confidential position with the king.

CHAOS *(KAY-oss)* means confusion or without order.

Where to find it: *Isaiah 45:18*

CHARGER *(CHAR-jer)* was a large serving platter. Herodias's daughter asked to have the head of John the Baptist on a charger.

Where to find it: *Matthew 14:8; Mark 6:25*

CHARIOTS *(CHAIR-ee-uts)* were two-wheeled carts used in ancient times mainly for war, but also for races and important processions by kings or other high officials. They were pulled by horses. Usually two men rode in a chariot—a driver and a warrior. In some countries, a third man with a shield also rode along.

Joseph rode in Pharaoh's second chariot in Egypt. When the people of Israel left Egypt, Pharaoh's warriors went after them with

chariots and got bogged down in the Red Sea.

When the Israelites were trying to conquer Canaan, they had a difficult time because some of the Canaanites had chariots "with iron," and the Israelites had none. However, the chariots were not so useful in hilly areas, so the Israelites won more battles there.

When David became king, he added chariots to his army, and Solomon added many more.

Where to find it

Joseph rides in chariot *Genesis 41:43*
Chariots destroyed in Red Sea *Exodus 14:21-29*
Canaanites' iron chariots *Judges 1:19*

CHARITY (see *Love*)

CHASM *(KAZ-um)* is a deep valley or pit that separates two places. In the story of the rich man and Lazarus, Jesus said there was a great chasm between the place of Lazarus and Abraham on one side and the place of the wicked rich man on the other. This was a word picture of the separation of heaven and hell.

Where to find it: *Luke 16:26*

CHASTE, CHASTITY *(chased, CHAS-tuh-tee)* means moral purity. In the New Testament it usually refers to purity in sexual relations.

Where to find it: *2 Corinthians 11:2; Titus 2:5; 1 Peter 3:2*

CHERITH *(KEY-rith)* is the name of the brook where Elijah hid during the drought in Palestine. The ravens brought him bread and meat, and he drank from the brook. Later the brook dried up and Elijah had to move. The exact location of the stream is not known.

Where to find it: *1 Kings 17:1-7*

CHERETHITES (see *Pelethites*)

CHERUBIM *(CHAIR-uh-bim)* are heavenly creatures described in Ezekiel 10 as having wings and also some human features. Each cherub had four faces: man, lion, ox, eagle. Cherubim and a flaming sword were placed east of the Garden of Eden to keep Adam and Eve from coming back after they sinned.

Pictures of cherubim were embroidered on the curtains of the Tabernacle; carvings of cherubim were on the walls of the Temple.

Cherubim made of gold were on the mercy seat of the ark of the Covenant.

Where to find it

Descriptions *Ezekiel 10*
Embroidered *Exodus 26:1*
On Temple walls *1 Kings 6:23-29*
On mercy seat *Exodus 25:18-22*

CHIEF PRIEST (see *High Priest*)

CHILDREN OF GOD in the New Testament usually means those who have put their faith in God and in Jesus Christ, his Son. Believers have a special relationship with God because Christ died for them and forgave their sins. It is not simply because God has created them.

Paul says that Christians are children of God by "adoption." The apostle John also speaks of those who "receive Christ" as the "children (or sons) of God."

In the Old Testament, the words *children of God* sometimes mean the Jewish people.

Where to find it: *Deuteronomy 14:1; John 1:12; Romans 9:8*

CHLOE *(KLO-ee)* was a woman in Corinth. Either her slaves or some members of her family told the apostle Paul that there was quarreling in the church there. We do not know whether Chloe herself was a Christian.

Where to find it: *1 Corinthians 1:11*

CHORAZIN *(koh-RAY-zin)* was a city about two miles north of Capernaum (see map). The people there rejected Jesus, and he said they would be judged. The city is now only a field of ruins.

Where to find it: *Matthew 11:21; Luke 10:13*

CHRIST (see *Jesus Christ*)

CHRISTIANS *(KRIS-chuns)* means "Christ's ones." The term was first used by non-Christians in Antioch to point out those who were following Jesus Christ's teachings.

The word appears only three times in the New Testament. The believers in New Testament times usually spoke of themselves as *brethren, believers, saints, disciples,* or *the church.*

Where to find it: *Acts 11:26; 26:28; 1 Peter 4:16*

CHRONICLES, 1 and 2 *(KRON-uh-culls)* are two books in the Old Testament that tell the history of Israel. They cover some of the same things as 2 Samuel and 1 and 2 Kings. But the Chronicles concentrate more on the Southern Kingdom, Judah, than on the Northern Kingdom, Israel.

The books do not tell who wrote them, but many scholars think they were written by Ezra, the priest and scribe. The people of Judah had been taken into Babylonia when the Southern Kingdom was conquered in 586 B.C. Ezra wanted the people to know about their own history and the importance of the reign of David and Solomon. He wanted them to understand Temple worship so that when Cyrus, king of Persia, allowed them to return home, they could rebuild the city of Jerusalem and begin worshiping again in the Temple.

The first nine chapters of 1 Chronicles is almost all "begats." It tells who was the father of whom—all the way from Adam to King Saul.

1 Chronicles 10—29 is about the kingdom of David and how it developed.

2 Chronicles 1—9 tells about Solomon, the Temple he built, and the worship there.

2 Chronicles 10—36 gives the history of the Southern Kingdom, Judah, and points out its religious reforms and its military victories.

Chronicles was originally written as one book. It was divided into 1 and 2 Chronicles about 150 B.C. In the Jewish Bible, the Chronicles are the last books in the Old Testament.

When Jesus spoke in Luke 11:50-51 of the "blood of all the prophets . . . from Abel to Zechariah" he was speaking of the first martyr, Abel, and Zechariah, the last one in the Jewish Old Testament. His story appears in 2 Chronicles 24—the last book of the Jewish Bible.

CHURCH is a group of believers in Jesus Christ. The "local church" means the believers in a certain city or area.

The word *Church* also refers to believers anywhere in the world, from the time of Christ to the present. This is the "universal church." Every local church is part of the universal Church because it is a part of Christ.

Jesus said the Church was "his Church." He is the head of the Church, the one who brought the Church and all creation into being (Colossians 1:18-20).

The Church began to grow rapidly soon after the resurrection of Christ and the Day of Pentecost. New Jewish believers in Jerusalem gathered to pray, sing, and encourage each other. Later, in other cities, many non-Jews became Christians and met together to form fellowships or churches, usually meeting in the homes of Christians.

Paul formed many new churches on his missionary journeys to the countries now known as Greece and Turkey. Some of what they did in their meetings can be seen in Ephesians 5:19-20:

"Addressing one another in psalms and hymns and spiritual songs, singing and making melody to the Lord with all your heart, always and for everything giving thanks in the name of our Lord Jesus Christ to God the Father." 1 Corinthians 12—14 also explains some of the practices of the early church.

Paul knew it was important for the new churches to understand how much they were tied to other churches. This is one reason he suggested that some churches mostly made up of Gentiles send money to the church at Jerusalem (mostly Jews), where members were very poor. Paul risked his life by personally carrying the gifts of money to Jerusalem (see *Paul*).

Many of the books of the New Testament are letters written by Paul or other apostles to the young churches.

Where to find it
Money for Jerusalem church *1 Corinthians 16:1-4*

CILICIA *(suh-LISH-ee-uh)* was a province in Asia Minor (now Turkey; see map). Paul was born in one of its cities, Tarsus. Paul probably first brought the gospel to Cilicia. Churches had already begun in Cilicia at the time of Paul's second missionary journey—he stopped there to encourage the Christians.

Where to find it: *Acts 15:41*

CIRCUMCISION *(SIR-kum-SIH-zhun)* is an operation to cut away the foreskin, an unneeded flap of skin on the penis. It is usually done when the baby boy is only a few days old.

Among the Hebrews this was a sign of their covenant (or agreement) with God that they had a special relationship with him. If they faithfully worshiped God and obeyed him, he would be their God and they would be a special nation.

In the early church, some people thought that all Christians had to be circumcised to become a part of God's people. The apostle Paul argued against this idea, and the leaders of the early church agreed with Paul.

Where to find it
Old Testament commandment   *Genesis 17:9-14*
New Testament decision   *Acts 15:1-35*

CISTERN *(SIS-turn)* is a covered tank or hole dug in the earth or hollowed out of rock to collect and store water. There were many cisterns in Palestine, because the summers were usually long and dry and water was scarce. The water in cisterns usually came from rainwater collected through gutters and pipes. Some cisterns were 100 feet deep.

Empty cisterns were sometimes used as prisons. Jeremiah was kept in one for a while.

Where to find it: *Jeremiah 38:6*

CITIZENSHIP *(SIT-uh-zen-ship)* means belonging to a certain country and having certain rights and responsibilities. For example, Paul was a citizen of Rome and also a citizen of Tarsus, where he was born. To be a citizen of Rome was a special privilege not given to everyone who lived in lands ruled by Rome.

A Roman citizen could not be punished without a trial, he was not to be tied up or beaten, and he had the right to "appeal to Caesar"—to have his trial moved to Rome. Paul's Roman citizenship helped him in his work as a special messenger of the gospel to Gentiles (non-Jews).

Where to find it: *Acts 16:37-39*

CITY. Ancient cities were different from modern cities.

1. A city always had a high wall around it several feet thick and made of rocks. The wall protected the people from enemy armies and from robbers.

2. Cities had gates. Some cities had only one gate; large cities might have up to 12. The gates were closed and barred at night.

3. The marketplace was an open area just inside the main gate. Here the people carried on business, held court, assembled for meetings, and visited one another.

4. The tower was an inner fort usually just inside the wall. People could run there for protection if the rest of the city was conquered by an enemy.

5. Streets in the city were narrow and winding, without any fixed plan.

Ancient cities were usually built to give protection to the farmers who worked in surrounding fields. The people went out to their fields in the daytime and returned at night to sleep. Most cities were built on hills because the people could see approaching enemies better. Cities were often built around a spring or a well because water was scarce in Palestine.

Sometimes small villages were built outside the city, but the people in the villages knew they could go to the city for protection.

CITY GATES were important in ancient times. The gates were the opening in the walls of the city that were always closed and barred at night (see *City*).

The gates were usually double doors plated with metal. Most of the important functions of a city took place in the broad, open area just inside the city gates. People bought and sold things there, listened to reading of the Law, and held courts of justice.

When enemies conquered a city, they were said to "possess the gates."

Where to find it: *Ruth 4:1-12; Psalm 107:16*

CITY OF DAVID has three meanings.

1. Bethlehem was called "the city of David" because it was his hometown.

2. A part of the city of Jerusalem was known as "the city of David." It was captured by David from the Jebusites. David later made this part his royal home when he became king.

3. The entire city of Jerusalem. Later writers often used the term *city of David* to refer to the entire walled city of Jerusalem.

Where to find it

Bethlehem   *1 Samuel 17:12-15; Luke 2:4*
Part of Jerusalem   *2 Samuel 5:5-7*
All Jerusalem   *Isaiah 22:9*

CITIES OF REFUGE were named by Moses for accidental killers. In Old Testament times, if someone killed accidentally or intentionally, his relatives felt they had to kill the person who caused the death.

The purpose of the cities of refuge was to protect the killer until his case could be properly judged. He could stay in the city of refuge until his trial was held. If he was found innocent, he could go on living protected in the city of refuge for quite a long time, so everyone's anger could cool off. Then he was to return to his own home.

There were three cities of refuge on the east side of the Jordan River and three cities on the west side. So there was a city of refuge within 30 miles (one day's walking distance) of any place in Palestine.

Where to find it: *Numbers 35; Deuteronomy 19:1-13; Joshua 20*

Jesus called Matthew from his tax booth in the city gate.

CLAUDIUS *(CLAW-dee-us)* was the emperor of Rome from A.D. 41 to 54. He was an evil man who was finally poisoned by his fourth wife, who wanted her son to be king.

While he was emperor, Claudius gave all Jews in the Roman Empire the right to worship as they chose. But later, he made all Jews leave Rome for a while because of trouble in the Jewish section of the city. There was also a famine during his reign.

Where to find it: *Acts 11:28; 18:2*

CLEAN AND UNCLEAN (see *Unclean*)

CLEMENT *(KLEH-ment)* was a Christian man who worked with Paul at Philippi.

Where to find it: *Philippians 4:3*

CLEOPAS *(KLEE-uh-pus)* was one of the two men who saw Jesus on the afternoon of his resurrection. Cleopas and his friend were walking home to Emmaus when Jesus joined them along the road. They did not recognize him. We don't know why. When Jesus asked what they were talking about, Cleopas said, "Are you the only person in Jerusalem who does not know the things that have happened there?"

Cleopas and his friend told about the death and disappearance of Jesus, and how they had hoped that he was the redeemer of Israel. Jesus told them that all the happenings were predicted in the Old Testament. Later, when the three got to Emmaus and ate together, they suddenly recognized Jesus when he blessed the food. Just as suddenly, Jesus disappeared.

Cleopas and his friend immediately walked back to Jerusalem to find the eleven apostles and to tell them what happened. While telling their story, Jesus again appeared to the group.

Where to find it: *Luke 24:13-53*

CLOAK *(cloke)* was a loose-fitting robe that men in biblical times wore over their other clothing.

Men in high positions had fancy, sometimes embroidered cloaks made of silk, linen, or velvet, with fringes and other decorations.

The cloaks worn by common men were

usually of wool, goat hair, camel hair, or burlap. Cloaks were worn during the day except when doing hard work. At night men wrapped themselves in their cloaks to keep warm. That is why the Old Testament Law said that if a person took another man's robe as a guarantee that the man would pay a debt, he had to return it before sundown.

Usually cloaks were made of two large pieces of cloth sewed together at the shoulders. Sometimes a cloak was woven as one piece of cloth with no seams. This is the kind of cloak Jesus wore.

Where to find it

Robe returned before sundown   *Exodus 22:26*
Jesus' robe with no seams   *John 19:23*

CLOTH in Bible times was made mostly of wool, linen, goat hair, or camel hair. It was often dyed blue, red, and purple.

CLOTHING in Bible times was quite different from ours. Men and women dressed somewhat alike except for colors and differences in embroidery or needlework. Women's garments were usually more colorful than men's.

Except in hot weather, both men and women wore long white cotton undershirts that might reach to the knees or even to the ankles.

In hot weather, men and women wore rather close-fitting tunics, with either short or long sleeves. They were usually made of wool and often lined with white cotton material so they wouldn't scratch the skin when the undershirt was not worn. Although the tunic usually came to the ankles, hard-working men sometimes wore shorter tunics.

People tied their tunics at the waist with a wide sash called a girdle. The girdle was usually a square yard of woolen, linen, or silk cloth. It was folded first into a triangle and then folded into a sashlike belt five to eight inches wide. This girdle not only held the tunic in place but also formed pockets in the folds where men and women could carry small articles or money. When a person was "girded," he was ready to work or travel.

The outer garment was a cloak or mantle. This was used as a coat during the colder seasons of the year and also as a blanket to wrap up in at night. The cloaks were usually made of wool, goat hair, or camel hair.

Men used three kinds of headwear.

1. Cotton or wool caps, similar to skullcaps, were worn by poor men.

2. Turbans were also common. These were long pieces of thick linen material wound around the head with the ends tucked under.

Arab men still wear headscarves today.

3. Headscarves were a square yard of colored cotton, wool, or silk folded into a triangle and draped around the man's head with the point of the triangle falling down the middle of the back. The man held it in place with silk or woolen cord coiled around his head.

Women wore headscarves or shawls. These were often pinned over a cap made of stiff material and decorated with pearls, silver, or other ornaments. Sometimes they were used to form a veil that covered at least part of a woman's face and upper body.

Both men and women wore jewelry including earrings, nose rings, and rings on toes, ankles, and wrists.

Where to find it: *Isaiah 3: 18-24*

COAT usually refers to the long shirtlike undergarment made of linen or cotton that men wore when the weather was cold (see *Clothing*).

COAT OF MAIL was a kind of armor covering the body from the neck to the waist. In Bible times it was probably formed from two pieces of leather joined beneath the arms.

Goliath had a coat of mail that was covered with bronze. When David was going to fight Goliath, Saul's coat of mail was put on David. But David refused it because he was not used to it (see *Weapons*).

Where to find it: *1 Samuel 17: 5, 38-39*

COCK (see *Birds*)

COHORT (*COE-hort*) was a military word that normally meant a group of 600 soldiers. However, the cohorts in Palestine included 760 foot soldiers and 240 soldiers on horses. In the King James Version, a cohort is called a "band."

Where to find it: *Acts 10:1; 21:31; 27:1*

COLONY (see *Roman Colony*)

COLOSSAE (*kuh-LAH-see*) was an important city for more than a thousand years—from 500 B.C. to A.D. 600. It was located in the southwestern part of what is now Turkey (see map).

Originally it was on the main road from Ephesus to the east, but the Romans changed the main road so that it no longer went through Colossae, and the city became less important.

The little that was left of the city was destroyed by the Turks in the twelfth century A.D. No one lives there now, but archaeologists have uncovered some of its ruins.

The church at Colossae probably was begun by Epaphras, a friend of Paul's, while Paul was living at Ephesus during his third missionary journey. Probably Philemon and Onesimus were also members of the church at Colossae, and it apparently met in Philemon's home. Most of the Christians at Colossae were Gentiles.

Paul probably wrote his famous letter to this church while he was in prison in Rome, near the end of his life.

Where to find it

Epaphras at Colossae   *Colossians 1:7; 4:12-13*
Meets in home of Philemon   *Philemon 1-2*

COLOSSIANS (*kuh-LAH-shuns*) is a letter written by the apostle Paul to the church in Colossae (see *Colossae*), a city in the southwestern part of what is now Turkey. Paul was probably

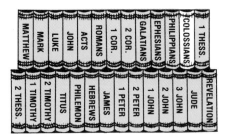

in prison in Rome when he wrote this letter about A.D. 61.

Epaphras, who had helped begin the church at Colossae, had visited Paul and told him of some of the wrong ideas being taught there. Paul wrote this letter to help the Christians at Colossae get their ideas straightened out.

He sent the letter with two men. One was Tychicus and the other was Onesimus, a runaway slave who had become a Christian through Paul. Onesimus lived in Colossae, and Paul sent another letter along with him to his owner, Philemon.

The letter to the Colossians shows that some of the Christians there were letting wrong ideas interfere with their worship of Christ.

1. They were worshiping angels—giving more importance to angels than to Christ. Paul reminded them that Christ is the Creator of the universe, the Lord of heaven and earth, stronger than any other powers.

2. They were worrying too much about certain things they should do and should not do—observing holy days, fasting, not eating certain foods, or touching certain things. Paul reminded them that becoming strong Christians did not depend nearly so much on these things as on loving Christ and trying to do what pleases him.

3. They were too impressed with the fancy language and knowledge of some false teachers. Paul said that real knowledge about Christ comes to every person who truly gives himself to Christ.

Paul included practical advice in this letter to the Christians about how to live for Christ in the society of their day. He also added many greetings to individuals he knew in the church.

COLT (see *Animals*)

COMFORT (*KUM-furt*) in the Bible means much more than to relieve pain or to make someone comfortable. The word appears often in the King James Version, where it really means to encourage, to strengthen, or to help.

In the newer translations, different words have been used where the King James Version

70

uses *comfort* so that these broader meanings can be seen.

COMFORTER *(KUM-furt-er)* is a term sometimes used in the King James Version for the Holy Spirit. Other translations use *counselor, advocate, helper,* or *intercessor.* The Greek word means "someone who pleads another's cause."

Where to find it: *John 14: 16 (KJV)*

COMMANDMENT *(kuh-MAND-ment)* means a rule, a teaching that has authority. Jesus summarized the commandments of God as being "to love God" and "to love your neighbor as yourself."

Where to find it: *Matthew 22: 35-40*

COMMON has several meanings. In the Old Testament, it often means "not holy," as in Leviticus 10: 10. In 1 Samuel 21, David asked the priest for some loaves of bread. The priest answered, "I have no common bread . . . but there is holy bread." Here *common* means "not consecrated for use in the Tabernacle."

In the New Testament, *common* sometimes means "unclean," referring to food Jews were not permitted to eat (see *Unclean*).

In Acts 2: 44, *common* means "shared." "All who believed were together and had all things in common."

Occasionally it means ordinary, as in Acts 4: 13—"They were uneducated, common men."

Where to find it

Common bread   *1 Samuel 21: 4*
Unclean food   *Acts 10: 14-15*
Shared   *Acts 2: 44; Titus 1: 4; Jude 3*
Ordinary   *Acts 4: 13*

COMMONWEALTH *(KAH-mun-welth)* means a nation or the citizens of a nation. Paul says Gentiles were "alienated from the commonwealth of Israel," meaning they were not part of the Jewish nation.

Paul also says "our commonwealth is in heaven," meaning the Christian is a citizen of heaven, even though he is now living on earth.

Where to find it: *Ephesians 2: 12; Philippians 3: 20*

COMMUNION *(kuh-MEWN-yun)* means sharing fellowship, having a close relationship, or being a part of something. The word is also used by the Church to mean the Lord's Supper (see *Lord's Supper*). When we eat the bread and wine, we commune with Christ and show our close relationship with him.

Where to find it: *1 Corinthians 10: 14-22*

COMPASSION *(kum-PASH-un)* means love, care, and the desire to help. The Bible says God has compassion on people. Jesus had compassion on those who came for healing or to hear him teach. The good Samaritan had compassion on the man who had been robbed and beaten. The father of the son who left home had compassion on his son when he returned.

Where to find it

God's compassion   *Lamentations 3: 22*
Christ's compassion   *Matthew 9: 36*
Good Samaritan   *Luke 10: 33*
Father of prodigal son   *Luke 15: 20*

CONCISION *(kun-SIH-zhun)* is a word that appears in the King James Version in Philippians 3: 2. It refers to those who believed that a person becomes acceptable to God simply by being circumcised.

CONCUBINES *(KON-kyu-bines)* were usually slave girls who belonged to a Hebrew family and had children by the father of the family. These women were sometimes captured in war, purchased from poor Hebrew families, or taken instead of money to pay off a debt. Such women did not have the same rights as regular wives. But they still had to be given food, clothing, shelter, and one day of rest each week.

Hebrew men in Old Testament times often had children by concubines when their wives could not have children.

By New Testament times, the practice of having more than one wife, or of having concubines, had largely disappeared. Jesus taught that a man should have only one wife.

Where to find it: *Matthew 19: 3-6*

CONCUPISCENCE *(kon-KYU-pih-sents)* is a word that appears only in the King James Version. In the Revised Standard Version it is translated "evil desire." It means to want something very much that God has forbidden.

Where to find it: *Romans 7: 8 (KJV); Colossians 3: 5 (KJV)*

CONDEMN, CONDEMNATION *(kun-DEM, kon-dem-NAY-shun)* are words that refer to judging something wrong, or judging someone guilty of doing wrong and pronouncing punishment.

In the Old Testament, God often condemns those who do wrong, but he will not condemn those who trust him.

The New Testament says that all of us are sinners and therefore are under the judgment or condemnation of God. However, there is "no condemnation for those who are in Christ Jesus." The Gospel of John states that God did not send Christ into the world to condemn the world, but that the world through him might be saved.

Final condemnation is a judgment that will not be changed.

Where to find it: *Psalm 34: 21-22; John 3: 17-18; Romans 8: 1*

CONGREGATION *(kong-gruh-GAY-shun)* in the Old Testament usually refers to the Jewish people gathering for a religious meeting.

In the New Testament, *congregation* refers to a group of people who have gathered for a specific purpose. It usually means local Christians who come together for a church service.

Where to find it: *Psalm 22: 22; Acts 15: 30*

CONFESSION *(kun-FEH-shun)* means to admit or declare something. Confession sometimes means telling God our sins. Confession also may mean to state publicly our faith in Christ. We "confess Christ."

Confessing our sins to God and confessing our faith to others are both important for Christians.

Where to find it: *Romans 10: 9; 1 John 1: 9*

CONSCIENCE *(KON-shuns)* is an inner sense of what is right or wrong. Our conscience seems to depend on what we understand to be right or wrong. It reminds us when we don't live the way we think we should. The

Bible says that all people have consciences and that each Christian should be sure he or she has a clear conscience.

Where to find it: *Romans 2: 15; 1 Timothy 1: 19*

CONSECRATE, CONSECRATION *(KON-see-krate, kon-see-KRAY-shun)* means setting apart someone or something to serve God in a special way. Aaron and his sons were consecrated as priests. Christians are told to consecrate themselves to God.

Where to find it

Aaron is consecrated   *Exodus 28: 41*
Christians are to be consecrated   *2 Timothy 2: 21*

CONSOLATION *(kon-so-LAY-shun)* means to help a person overcome grief or misery. God consoles us, and Christians can bring consolation to each other.

Where to find it: *Psalm 94: 19; 1 Corinthians 14: 3*

CONTENT, CONTENTMENT *(kun-TENT, kun-TENT-ment)* means being satisfied with what we have. The New Testament says Christians are not to constantly desire more money, but to trust God to supply their needs.

The apostle Paul said he had learned "in whatever state I am, to be content."

Where to find it: *Philippians 4: 11; 1 Timothy 6: 6-10*

CONTRIBUTION FOR THE SAINTS *(kon-trib-YOU-shun)* refers to money given to poor Christians in Jerusalem during a famine. Paul, in his missionary travels, encouraged all the other churches to give generously to help the Jewish believers in Jerusalem. Paul himself took the money to Jerusalem at the end of his third missionary journey. He considered this important to show that Christians who were Gentiles and Christians who were Jews were part of the same Body of Christ and should love and help each other.

Where to find it: *Romans 15: 25-31; 1 Corinthians 16: 1-4*

CONTRITE *(KON-trite)* means "crushed." In the Bible it is always used to refer to the inner spirit of a person. It means humility and being sorry for our sins. Isaiah 57: 15 says that God dwells "with him who is of a contrite and humble spirit."

CONVERSATION *(kon-ver-SAY-shun),* when used in the King James Version, does not mean "talking." This word appears many times meaning "way of life" or "behavior," as in 1 Peter 1:15.

In Philippians 3:20 *conversation* means "citizenship" or "homeland," and it is translated that way in most of the newer versions.

CONVERSION *(kun-VER-zhun)* means "turning," and usually describes a person turning away from sin and self-love to worship and serve the true God.

There are many examples of conversion in the Bible. The most dramatic is that of Paul on the road to Damascus (see *Paul),* when he was struck by a bright light as he was going to persecute Christians. The Philippian jailer also had a dramatic turning to God.

Other examples in the Bible tell of more gradual conversions. Timothy apparently came to know and trust God over a period of time. The disciples learned little by little what it meant to be followers of Christ.

Whether a person turns from sin to faith in God in a sudden, emotional experience, or whether he turns in a more gradual process is not important in the Scriptures. Either way, the believer gives himself fully to God and is changed from being a selfish person to being a person who is growing in his understanding of Christ and desire to serve him.

Where to find it

Paul's conversion   *Acts 9:1-20*
Philippian jailer   *Acts 16:25-34*
Timothy   *Acts 16:1-3; 2 Timothy 3:15*

CONVERT *(KON-vert)* is a person who has experienced conversion (see *Conversion)* or a turning to God. In Romans 16:5, it says Epaenetus was the first convert in the province of Asia.

CONVERT *(kun-VERT)* means the process of conversion or turning. Peter told the crowd on the Day of Pentecost, "Repent ye therefore and be converted."

Where to find it: *Acts 3:19; Romans 16:5*

CONVOCATIONS, HOLY *(KON-voe-KAY-shuns)* were Hebrew religious festivals (also

see *Feasts).* No work was allowed during a holy convocation. The list of convocations is found in Leviticus 23. It includes:

1. All sabbaths—Leviticus 23:3.
2. Pentecost—Leviticus 23:15-21.
3. The first and seventh day of the Feast of Unleavened Bread—Leviticus 23:6-7.
4. The first and tenth day of the seventh month—Leviticus 23:23-28. The tenth day was the Day of Atonement.
5. The first and eighth day of the Feast of Tabernacles—Leviticus 23:34-36.

COOKING AND COOKING UTENSILS. Women did most of the cooking in Bible times except in wealthy homes, where servants did it. The evening meal was the most important meal of the day. For poor people, it was the only meal.

Bread was the most important food. Poor people made their bread of barley. The rich made theirs of wheat. Each family ground its own grain and baked its own bread, although some large cities had public bakeries where women could take their bread to be baked.

Families also used wheat or barley to eat as hot cereal. They grew and stored dried beans and lentils to eat. Many people ate locusts. Food was seasoned with salt, onions, garlic, and sometimes with dill, anise, coriander, mint, and thyme. Nuts of all kinds were important in the diet of the Hebrews.

Cooking meant a lot more work in Bible times.

COOKING

Martha's cooking may have been served like this.

Most Hebrews ate very little meat—it was too expensive. On special occasions when common people ate meat, they usually had lamb or goat. Since there was no way to preserve meat or keep it cold, a family had to cook and eat the whole animal the same day they killed it. They cooked meat over an open fire on a spit, or boiled it in water, or cooked it in oil. They broiled fish over coals.

Ovens were usually outside to protect the house from fire. They were made of clay mixed with stones or pottery fragments. Often ovens were shaped like huge bowls two or three feet wide and turned upside down with the bottom missing. The cook placed large stones in the oven among the charcoal. When the fire was only embers, the women brushed off the stones and placed the food on the stones or around the walls of the oven. Most people used cooking utensils made of pottery, although some wealthy people had kettles and pans made of copper.

Families usually cooked with wide shallow pots. Most families had a small-mouthed piece of pottery for heating water. They stored grain, flour, and oil in pottery designed especially for these foods.

CORBAN *(KOR-bun)* means something dedicated to God. The word appears in Mark 7:11, where Jesus says that some of his listeners used Corban to excuse themselves from caring for their parents. A man could say that certain money or valuables he owned were Corban (dedicated to God) and therefore could not be used for anything else—even to care for his needy, aged parents. Jesus said this was wrong.

Where to find it: *Mark 7:9-13*

CORINTH *(KORE-inth)* was the capital of Achaia (now southern Greece) and an important seaport in New Testament times (see map). It was known for its luxury but also for its low morals.

Most of the 700,000 people who lived in Corinth were Greeks or Romans, but there were also some Jews. More than half the people in Corinth were slaves.

One reason for the low moral standards of the Corinthians was their worship of Aphrodite, the goddess of love. In the large and magnificent temple to this goddess, worship included immoral acts.

When Paul visited Corinth on his second missionary journey, he began, as usual, by preaching in the synagogue to Jews. When the Jews refused his message about Christ, another man, Titus Justus, invited Paul to use his house next door to the synagogue.

Justus and many others who heard Paul preach became Christians. Paul stayed in Corinth for a while with Aquila and Priscilla, a Jewish couple who were Christians.

The new church included Jewish Christians, slaves who had been converted to Christ, pagans who used to worship the goddess of Corinth, and some people from the upper social classes. It was hard for this group of people to understand each other and to live in harmony together. Paul's two letters to this church show some of the problems the church faced.

In the years after the New Testament period, Corinth was destroyed and rebuilt several times. In 1858 an earthquake destroyed most of the city, so another city named Corinth was built a few miles away from the old location. The new Corinth had a destructive earthquake in 1928. But the city was rebuilt.

CORINTHIANS, 1 and 2, are two New Testament letters that the apostle Paul wrote to the church at Corinth (in what is now southern Greece). Paul wrote the letters during his third missionary journey around A.D. 55 or 56.

In the first letter, Paul answered some questions he had received in a letter from the Christians in Corinth. 1 Corinthians 7:1 begins, "Now concerning the matters about which you wrote."

74

The church at Corinth had many problems. The Christians were divided into groups, each favoring a different teacher. Some said they were followers of Paul, others of Apollos (who had been a teacher at Corinth), others of Cephas (Peter), and still others of Christ!

Paul reminded the Corinthians that Christ alone was their Master and that the other teachers were all servants of Christ.

Paul then took up, one by one, some of the problems disturbing the church. He discussed immorality among the Corinthian Christians, the practice of suing each other in the courts, problems of sex and marriage, and eating meat offered to idols.

In chapters 11 to 14, Paul discussed what they did in public worship and told them how they should worship. He reminded them of the gifts God had given them and that all gifts should be used to glorify God.

In chapter 15, Paul said the truth of the resurrection of Christ is the basis for the future resurrection of believers.

The second letter to the Corinthians was written later, during Paul's third missionary journey, after Titus brought him a report about the church. Earlier, many in the church had turned against Paul and said he wasn't even an apostle of Jesus Christ. Titus had visited the church and helped to straighten things out, and the church was again loyal to Paul. Paul defended his right to speak as an apostle, and he promised to visit the church again soon.

This second letter was a very personal message to the church. Paul shared some of the trials he had been facing. He told them about his illness and how he accepted the fact that God did not heal him. He also told them about some of his God-given visions.

He reminded the people of their responsibility to contribute to the gift of money he was collecting for poor Christians in Jerusalem.

CORN is used frequently in the King James Version to mean seeds of grasses, such as barley or wheat. Newer versions use the more correct term *grain*. The word *corn,* as used in the King James Version, is not what we know as corn. For example, John 12:24 says, "Except a corn of wheat fall into the ground . . ." (KJV). It should read, "Except a grain of wheat falls into the ground . . ."

CORNELIUS *(kor-NEEL-yus)* was a centurion (commander of 100 men) in the Roman army. He was stationed at Caesarea, Palestine (see *Caesarea).* He was a Gentile who had become interested in the Jewish religion. He prayed to God and gave money to the poor.

God told Cornelius in a vision to send men to the house of Simon the tanner in the city of Joppa and to ask for a man named Peter.

Cornelius did as he was told. Meanwhile, God sent a vision to Peter. A sheet seemed to come down from heaven holding animals that Jews were not permitted to eat. In the vision, Peter was told to kill and eat them. Peter refused, saying that they were "unclean" (see *Unclean).* But God told him that what God had cleansed, Peter must not call unclean.

God gave Peter a rather shocking vision.

While Peter was trying to figure out what the vision meant, the men from Cornelius came to the door. They told him their master, a God-fearing Gentile, wanted Peter to come and visit him.

Until that time, Peter had not tried to preach the gospel to anyone but Jews, and he had lived and eaten only with Jewish people who ate "clean" (permitted) foods.

Peter went with the men to Cornelius's house. He and Cornelius told each other about their visions. Peter understood, probably for the first time, that the good news about Jesus Christ was not only for Jewish people but for the whole world.

He told Cornelius and his family and servants how Christ had come to earth to die for their sins so they could be forgiven. While Peter was still preaching, the Holy Spirit came to those who were listening. Peter saw that God was at work, and he said they should be baptized as believers. Peter stayed with them for several days.

All this was important to the early church because it showed clearly that Gentiles did not have to keep the Jewish laws in order to become Christians.

Where to find it: *Acts 10:1–11:18*

CORNERSTONE is usually the large stone at the corner of the foundation of two walls. It holds the two walls together. It is the first and most important stone in the building.

Sometimes, in the Bible, the word refers instead to the top stone in a defense tower.

When the word *cornerstone* is used in the Bible, it stands for strength and stability. When *cornerstone* is used in the New Testament, it also refers to Christ.

Where to find it: *Psalm 118:22; Isaiah 28:16; Ephesians 2:20-21; 1 Peter 2:6-7*

CORRUPTION *(kor-RUP-shun)* usually means "decay." It is sometimes used in the Bible to show that our physical bodies eventually return to dust. It sometimes refers to all the things in the world that eventually fade or break down.

Where to find it: *Acts 13:35; 2 Peter 1:4*

COUNCIL *(KOWN-sul)* is a group of persons who have been given certain responsibilities to govern or give advice. In ancient times there were religious councils and also government councils.

In the New Testament, the word *council* often refers to the Sanhedrin, the ruling group of Jews in Palestine. It had 70 members (see *Sanhedrin*).

Where to find it

Sanhedrin   *Matthew 10:17; Acts 5:34*
Roman council   *Acts 25:12*

COUNCIL OF JERUSALEM was a meeting held in A.D. 48 by leaders of the churches in Jerusalem and Antioch. The apostles and a few others met to discuss the problems they faced because so many Gentiles were becoming Christians.

During the first few years of the early church, nearly all converts were Jewish, and they kept on following the Old Testament Jewish laws while they worshiped Christ as Savior. The few Gentiles who were converted did the same as the Jewish Christians.

In Antioch, however, and in the new churches outside Palestine, almost all the new converts were Gentiles. Did the Christian gospel require that they follow the Old Testament Jewish Law? If not, how could Jewish Christians eat and be friends with these Christians, since they would then become "unclean" (see *Unclean*) in the eyes of Jews? It was a serious problem.

When the council met, both groups presented their ideas. Some Jewish believers felt that the Gentile converts should keep the Jewish Law.

Peter explained how Cornelius (a Gentile) and others in his house had received the Holy Spirit—a sign that God had accepted them—without keeping the Jewish Law. Paul and Barnabas explained that many Gentiles were becoming Christians in this way.

The group finally agreed that Gentile believers should not be asked to keep the Jewish Law. But, to keep harmony in the church, they should not do certain things to offend Jewish Christians such as eating certain foods. They should also avoid sexual immorality.

This made it possible for Jewish and Gentile believers to fellowship together at meals and in the church.

Where to find it: *Acts 15:2-29*

COUNSELOR *(KOWN-sell-or)* means one who gives advice or help. God gives counsel to those who serve him.

In the Old Testament, kings often had counselors to help them make hard decisions.

In the New Testament, the Holy Spirit is called the counselor of the Christian.

Where to find it: *2 Chronicles 25:16; Psalm 16:7; 33:11; John 14:16 (RSV)*

COURT OF THE WOMEN

COURT OF THE GENTILES

COURT OF THE PRIESTS

COURT OF ISRAEL

COURT, COURTYARD *(KORT-yard)* was an enclosed place in a building. It had no roof, but it was surrounded by other parts of the house and was therefore private. Homes in Palestine often had enclosed courts.

The Temple of Solomon and the Temple of the New Testament (Herod's Temple) had four courts. (See *Court of the Gentiles, Court of Israel, Court of the Priests, Court of the Women,* and *Temple.)*

COURT OF THE GENTILES *(JEN-tiles)* was the largest open area in Herod's Temple. Anyone could enter this section, and people often used it as a shortcut across the Temple (instead of going around the outside). It was larger than a football field. In this area, scribes debated each other and held schools. Merchants sold animals for sacrifices and changed money from Roman coins to the required Temple money. It was in this court that Jesus drove out the money changers and overturned their tables (see *Temple).*

Where to find it: *Matthew 21:12; Mark 11:15-17*

COURT OF ISRAEL was the inner court in the Temple where only Jewish males were permitted.

COURT OF THE PRIESTS was the part of the Temple to which only priests were allowed— except during the Feast of Tabernacles, when all Jewish men could enter. The altar for burnt offerings was in this section.

COURT OF THE WOMEN was a small court in the inner section of the Temple. Both Jewish men and Jewish women could enter the women's court, but women were not permitted in the men's court, called the Court of Israel. Jesus often taught in the Court of Women.

In the women's court were 13 chests shaped like trumpets. Offerings were placed in them.

Where to find it: *Mark 12:41-44*

COVENANT *(KUV-uh-nunt)* means an agreement. The word appears often in the Bible, especially in the Old Testament.

Sometimes covenants are made between people; both sides decide what the agreement shall be. This was the kind of friendship covenant Jonathan and David made in 1 Samuel 18:3.

More often, *covenant* means an agreement between God and people. However, in God's covenants, God decides what shall be done, and people accept and live by the covenant.

Some of the covenants of God mentioned in the Old Testament include:

1. God's covenant never again to destroy the earth by flood.

2. God's covenant with Abraham to make his family into a great nation.

3. God's covenant with Israel to make them his special people. This covenant demanded that the people show they accepted the covenant by doing certain things. One of these acts was circumcision. Another was to serve

only God and not idols.

The New Testament speaks of a "new covenant" that came through Jesus Christ. Christ said his blood was the "blood of the covenant, which is poured out for many for the forgiveness of sins" (Matthew 26: 28).

In Hebrews 9, the writer compares the New Covenant with a will that a person makes before he dies, telling what he wants done with his belongings. Christ is compared to a person who makes a will that does not take effect until he dies. Thus, the New Covenant that Christ made could not take effect until Christ died.

The New Covenant makes it possible for every person who believes in Christ to become a member of the family of God.

Where to find it

God's covenant after the flood   *Genesis 9: 12-17*
God's covenant with Abraham   *Genesis 17: 2-7*
God's covenant with Israel   *Exodus 6: 4-7; 24: 7-8*
God's New Covenant in Christ   *Matthew 26: 28;*
   Hebrews 9: 15-22; 8: 8-13; 10: 15-18

COVET, COVETOUSNESS *(KUV-et, KUV-et-us-nus)* means wanting very much to have something that belongs to someone else. Both the Old Testament and the New Testament say that covetousness is sin.

Where to find it: *Exodus 20: 17; Deuteronomy 5: 21; Luke 12: 15-21; Ephesians 5: 3-7; Colossians 3: 5-6*

CRAFTSMAN (see *Occupations*)

CREATION *(KREE-ay-shun)* is God's work of beginning all new things. Usually *creation* refers to the beginning of the universe and life on earth.

Genesis 1 and 2 tell that God created everything. They do not tell us how God created. God said, "Let there be light;" "Let the waters under the heavens be gathered together into one place, and let the dry land appear;" "Let the earth put forth vegetation." And after every statement like that, it says, "And it was so."

The Genesis story seems to center about a plan of telling rather than exactly recording what followed what. For example, the writer says that in the first three days, God "formed"—in the last three days, God "filled" those things he had formed.

God formed	God filled with
Day 1 Light	Day 4 Sun, moon, stars
Day 2 Firmament (sky)	Day 5 Birds
Day 3 Seas, land, vegetation	Day 6 Fish, animals, and people

Genesis says that animals, birds, and people were all formed "from the ground."

The story in Genesis talks of "days." The word *day* has several meanings in the Bible. Sometimes it means a 24-hour period; other times it means a long period of time; sometimes it means a time of judgment. Some people believe that the days in Genesis are 24-hour periods; others think they represent periods of time, or that the pattern of days shows that God created everything in an orderly way. The story of creation in Genesis does not emphasize *how* God created the world, but that he *did*. The important thing is that God did the creating.

Genesis shows that God is not the same as nature. God is different from the things he made. People who know this do not worship trees, animals, or other people.

The creation account in Genesis also shows that men and women are supposed to manage the universe for its owner—God. They are to be responsible caretakers of the world that belongs to God.

The Bible says God made both men and women "in the image of God" and that men and women need each other. They are to work together to manage the universe.

God did not make the world and everything in it, and then leave. God is still active in the world and is concerned with everything he has made.

Where to find it: *Genesis 1–2; Hebrews 11:3*

CREATURES, LIVING (see *Living Creatures*)

CRETE *(kreet)* is a mountainous island in the Mediterranean Sea (see map). It is about 156 miles long and varies from 7 to 35 miles wide. Paul's ship stopped there when he was on his way to Rome as a prisoner. After he was released from prison in Rome, Paul visited Crete again and left Titus, one of his helpers, to be in charge of the believers.

The people in Crete (Cretans) had a reputation for being lazy and for telling lies. The Letter to Titus was written by Paul while Titus was working in Crete.

Where to find it: *Acts 27:7-13; Titus 1:5, 12*

CRISPUS *(KRIS-pus)* was a Jewish man who was a synagogue leader at Corinth. When the apostle Paul came to Corinth, he began preaching in the synagogue. Many of the Jewish people opposed him, so Paul began teaching in the house next door. Crispus and his family became Christians. He was one of the few in Corinth whom Paul personally baptized.

Where to find it: *Acts 18:4-8; 1 Corinthians 1:14*

CROSS in the Bible has three meanings.

1. The wooden frame for torturing criminals to death. Jesus was crucified on a Roman cross. Four kinds of crosses were used (see diagram). Christ probably died on a cross shaped like the one on the left.

2. The word *cross* in the New Testament also stands for the gospel of salvation through Christ.

3. Jesus used *cross* as a word picture of obedience to him that could include trials, suffering, and death. Jesus told his disciples they must take up their cross and follow him.

Where to find it: *Matthew 10:38; Luke 14:27; 1 Corinthians 1:18*

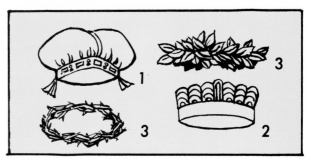

CROWN is a band that goes around the head. There are four kinds of crowns mentioned in the Bible.

1. The high priest's crown was a turban. Fastened to it was a gold piece across the forehead with the words *Holy unto the Lord.* The crown was a symbol of the priest's consecration to God.

2. Kings wore crowns, usually made of gold, as a mark of their royal position.

3. In the New Testament, *crown* sometimes refers to a head wreath worn by athletes as a sign of victory. This is the kind that Paul referred to in 1 Corinthians 9:25 where he spoke of an athlete who receives a "perishable wreath" (RSV) or a "corruptible crown" (KJV).

Christ's crown of thorns was no doubt made like an athlete's crown of victory, but it was to mock him.

4. *Crown* sometimes stands for the future reward and blessings that Christians will receive from Christ. This is the meaning in 1 Peter 5:4 and James 1:12.

CROWN OF THORNS was the circle made of briars that the soldiers pushed down on Jesus' head after Pilate had sentenced him to death. It was done to make fun of him while they spit on him and knelt before him saying, "Hail, King of the Jews."

Where to find it: *Matthew 27:29; Mark 15:17-20; John 19:2-3*

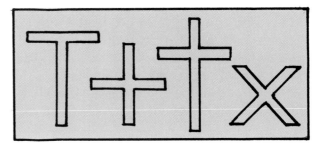

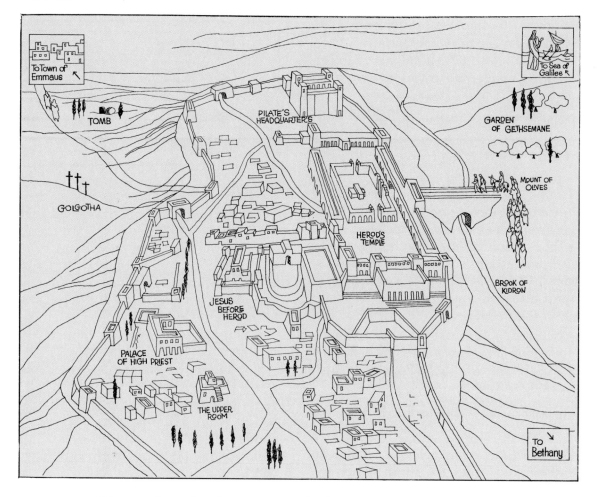

This map shows the places Jesus was in the hours before his crucifixion.

Labels on map: To Town of Emmaus · To Sea of Galilee · TOMB · PILATE'S HEADQUARTERS · GARDEN OF GETHSEMANE · GOLGOTHA · MOUNT OF OLIVES · HEROD'S TEMPLE · BROOK OF KIDRON · JESUS BEFORE HEROD · PALACE OF HIGH PRIEST · THE UPPER ROOM · TO Bethany

CRUCIFIXION *(kroo-suh-FIK-shun)* was the kind of death Jesus suffered to make salvation possible for us. It was a terribly painful way to die.

Romans used crucifixion to execute criminals who were not citizens of Rome. Hands and feet were nailed to the wood, and the person was left to hang there until he died of fever and infection. Death usually took two to eight days, but Jesus died in a few hours—perhaps because he had been so badly beaten before the crucifixion.

CRUSE *(crews)* is a small jug made of baked clay, used to store olive oil. In the story of Elijah's visit to the widow, the prophet told her, "The cruse of oil shall not fail until the day that the Lord sends rain upon the earth." And although she kept on cooking with the oil, the cruse never became empty.

Where to find it: *1 Kings 17: 8-16*

CUBIT (see *Measures*)

CUCUMBER (see *Plants*)

CUMMIN (see *Plants*)

CUPS in Bible times were made of clay, pottery, copper, bronze, porcelain, gold, or silver.

Cups had two common shapes. One shape was similar to our cups. Some had handles; some did not. A cup with a handle was often used as a dipper.

Other cups were shaped like shallow bowls. This was probably the kind of cup used at the last supper of Jesus and his disciples.

Throughout the Bible *cup* is often used as a word picture of people sharing blessings or troubles. When Jesus said to the disciples, "The cup that I drink you will drink," he meant that he was going to suffer and they would, too. The cup in the Lord's Supper is a symbol of sharing in the life and death of Christ.

Where to find it: *Mark 10:35-45*

CUPBEARER was a palace official who served wine to the king. Only a man of proven loyalty and trust was chosen as a cupbearer. Nehemiah was a cupbearer to the king of Persia.

Where to find it: *Nehemiah 1:11; 2:1*

CURSE, CURSING in the Bible does *not* mean profanity or swearing. When God curses something or someone, it means he pronounces judgment. When a person curses something, he wishes harm upon it. Christ said his followers should "bless those who curse you, pray for those who abuse you" (Luke 6:27).

CURTAIN OF THE TABERNACLE (see *Tabernacle*)

CURTAIN OF THE TEMPLE (see *Veil of Temple*)

CUSTODIAN *(kuss-TOE-dee-un)* was a slave in New Testament times who walked with a young boy to school and looked after him. Sometimes, a custodian would help the boy with his schoolwork. In Galatians 3:24-25, Paul said the Old Testament Law was our "custodian"—the one who looked after us and brought us to Christ. Now that Christ has come, we are no longer under the Old Testament Law that way.

CUSTOM has two meanings in the Bible:
1. Habit, tradition, or the expected way of doing things (Luke 1:9).
2. Tax. Matthew, who became one of the disciples of Jesus, was a tax collector; he "sat at the receipt of custom" (Matthew 9:9, KJV).

CYPRESS (see *Plants*)

CYPRUS *(SY-prus)* is an island in the eastern Mediterranean Sea (see map). It is 148 miles long and about 40 miles across.

Paul and Barnabas visited Cyprus on their first missionary journey. On the island, a government official named Sergius Paulus heard the message of Christ and believed.

Barnabas and John Mark later came back to Cyprus to preach.

Where to find it: *Acts 13:4-12; 15:36-39*

CYRENE *(sy-REE-nee)* was a city in North Africa (see map). A man named Simon from this city was in Jerusalem when Jesus was crucified. The soldiers made him carry Jesus' cross.

There were many Jews in Cyrene, and some of them were in Jerusalem at Pentecost. Some of them became Christians and later went to Antioch to tell about Christ.

Where to find it

Simon carried the cross   *Luke 23:26*
Cyrene people at Pentecost   *Acts 2:10*
Cyrene Christians go to Antioch   *Acts 11:20*

CYRUS *(SY-rus)* was the founder of the Persian Empire. When Cyrus came to power, most of the Jews had been forced out of their own land and sent to Babylonia. Cyrus allowed the Jews to return to their land and to rebuild the Temple that had been destroyed.

Where to find it: *Ezra 1:1-11; 5:1–6:15; Isaiah 45:1*

D

DAGON *(DAY-gun)* was the chief god of the Philistines. Scholars are not sure whether Dagon was a fish-god or a god of agriculture, but the people built many temples to honor this god.

When Samson was blinded by the Philistines, they brought him to a temple of Dagon to make fun of him. Samson prayed for strength, put his arm around two pillars, and pulled down the whole temple.

Another time when the Philistines were fighting the Israelites, they captured the ark of God in a battle and took it to a temple of Dagon. The next day they found the image of Dagon face down in front of the ark. The Philistines put it back, but the next day it had fallen again and its head and hands had broken off.

David was thirty years old when he became king.

Many years later, the Philistines took the head of King Saul after he had been killed in battle and placed it in one of their temples of Dagon.

Where to find it

Samson pulls down Dagon's temple *Judges 16:23-30*
Ark is placed in Dagon's temple *1 Samuel 5:1-5*
King Saul's head in Dagon's temple *1 Chronicles 10:10*

DAMARIS *(DAM-uh-ris)* was an important woman in Athens who became a Christian after the apostle Paul preached on Mars' Hill.

Where to find it: *Acts 17:34*

DAMASCUS *(duh-MAS-kus)* is still an important city today; it is the capital of modern Syria. On our maps it is sometimes called Dimashq. It is at least 4,000 years old—probably the oldest continually inhabited city in the world.

It is mentioned in Genesis 15:2 as the city from which Abraham's servant came. David once captured Damascus, but usually it belonged to Israel's or Judah's enemies.

In the New Testament, Saul was going to Damascus when Christ appeared to him in a vision. Saul lost his sight, and was taken to Damascus, where it was restored. Disciples in Damascus taught Saul about Christ, and he

began preaching in the synagogue there. Eventually, he had to escape by being let down over the walls in a basket.

Where to find it

David captures Damascus *2 Samuel 8:5-6*
Saul goes to Damascus *Acts 9:1-22*

DAMNATION (see *Condemnation*)

DAN was the name of one of the tribes of Israel and also the name of a city.

The tribe was named for the fifth son of Jacob. They settled in the northern area and called their main city Dan. The city was in the extreme northern part of Israel. Jeroboam, king of Israel, once made a golden calf and set it in Dan as a place for the Israelites to worship.

Where to find it: *1 Kings 12:28-30*

DANCING was part of the cultural life of the Israelites and the nations around them. Both children and adults danced, but men and women did not dance together. Dancing usually involved rhythmic body movements accompanied by music.

Dancing was often a part of celebrating a military victory or a religious festival. Psalm 149:3 shows that dancing was sometimes part of Hebrew worship. It was also a part of weddings or other times of rejoicing.

Where to find it

Dancing as part of worship *Psalm 149:3; 2 Samuel 6:14*
Dancing to rejoice in victory *1 Samuel 18:6*
Part of merrymaking *Luke 15:25*

DANIEL *(DAN-yull)* is best known for being thrown into a den of lions when he refused to stop worshiping God. But Daniel was more than a brave man—he was a prophet and a high government official.

In 605 B.C., Daniel was a young man when Babylon defeated his nation, Judah. Daniel and many other Hebrews were taken from Judah to Babylon. It was the custom for the winners in war to take the leaders and the most promising young people away from the defeated country so they could not begin a rebellion against the new rulers.

In Babylon, Daniel and three of his friends were trained to serve in the court of King

Daniel spent one whole night with the lions.

Nebuchadnezzar. They were treated well and given the same food as the king. However, some of the food was "unclean" (see *Unclean*) to the Hebrews. So Daniel asked that, as an experiment, they be fed simple food—vegetables and water. They became so healthy and strong on this diet that they were allowed to continue eating that food.

During Daniel's second year in the court, Nebuchadnezzar had a troubling dream, but he could not remember what it was. Daniel was the only wise man in the court who could tell Nebuchadnezzar what his dream was and also what it meant. The king rewarded him by making him chief of his wise men and ruler over the province of Babylon. However, Daniel did not want to be ruler. He asked the king to appoint his three friends to that work instead.

Later, Daniel had to interpret another dream, which showed that Nebuchadnezzar would become mentally ill for a while but then recover. The prophecy came true.

A few years after Nebuchadnezzar's reign, Belshazzar became king. During a fancy banquet, handwriting mysteriously appeared on the wall. Daniel was the only person who could read it. He told the king that it said his kingdom would be destroyed. Belshazzar died that same night as Persia conquered Babylon.

The new ruler was Darius. He recognized Daniel's abilities and made him one of the three top officials of the country. Other officials were jealous and plotted to get rid of Daniel. They persuaded Darius to make a law that no one could make any requests to any god or man, except to Darius. If any person broke the law during the next thirty days, he would be thrown into a den of lions.

Daniel kept on praying to God three times a day. He was thrown to the lions, but God protected him and the lions did not hurt him. The next day he was taken out and returned to power.

Although Daniel was an important government leader, he was also a great prophet. His prophetic visions are recorded in Daniel 7—12.

Where to find it

Is permitted his own food *Daniel 1*
Interprets king's dream *Daniel 2*
Foretells king's illness *Daniel 4*
Reads handwriting on wall *Daniel 5*
Thrown into den of lions *Daniel 6*

DANIEL, BOOK OF, tells in the first six chapters about the life of Daniel and the dreams he interpreted (see *Daniel*, above). The second half of the book, chapters 7—12, tells about the visions Daniel had. Bible scholars do not agree about what the visions mean, but they do agree that the writings helped bring confidence in God to the Jewish people who had been forced away from their land.

The vision in chapter 7 centers around four beasts representing world empires. The vi-

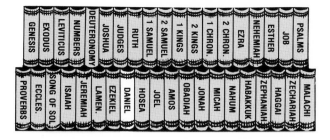

sions in chapters 8—12 tell about various rulers. Some scholars think these prophecies were fulfilled in the events leading up to the birth, death, and resurrection of Christ. Others think some parts will be fulfilled near the time when Christ returns to earth.

DARIUS *(duh-RYE-us)* was the name of several rulers of the Medo-Persian Empire. One Darius is mentioned in the story of Daniel. He was the king who made Daniel a ruler. Some officials were jealous and planned to get rid of Daniel. They had Darius sign an unchangeable law that no one could pray to any god or man except Darius for thirty days. Anyone who disobeyed would be thrown into a den of hungry lions.

Daniel kept on praying to God, was caught and thrown to the lions. The next morning Darius went to the lion den and called, "O Daniel . . . has your God, whom you serve continually, been able to deliver you from the lions?"

When Darius found that Daniel was unhurt, he ordered the men who had accused him to be thrown to the lions. Darius then wrote a law that his people were to fear the God of Daniel, "for he is the living God, enduring for ever."

Another King Darius appears later in the Book of Ezra. During the reign of this Darius, some people tried to stop the rebuilding of the Temple in Jerusalem. Darius looked through old records and found a decree from Cyrus, king of Persia, saying that the Jews were free to rebuild the Temple. Darius ordered that the rebuilding could continue.

Where to find it

Daniel thrown to lions *Daniel 6*
Darius permits Temple rebuilding *Ezra 6: 1-15*

DAVID, king during Israel's time of greatest glory, had many talents. He was a great ruler, a poet, a fine musician, a skillful military commander, and intensely loyal to his friends.

He had deep feelings that showed in his poetry. He was often discouraged; he often wept. He was tempted and did some wicked things. But he was not afraid to repent and show sorrow for his sin.

The story of David begins in 1 Samuel 16, and continues through all of 2 Samuel.

David was born in 1040 B.C., the youngest son in a family of shepherds. Saul, who was king before him, often had times of nervousness that could be calmed with music. David became his musician. In the palace, David also became a close friend to Saul's son Jonathan.

David first became known for using his sling and a stone to kill Goliath, a Philistine giant. Because of his bravery, David became popular, and Saul grew jealous of him.

Even after David married Michal, one of Saul's daughters, Saul was so jealous of David he tried to kill him. Finally David had to flee to the hills, where he could hide in the caves. Others joined him. They included many men who, like David, were hiding from enemies. This group grew into a small army.

Saul tried to find David and kill him, but he could not. Twice David could easily have killed Saul, but he refused to do so.

The story of David and his sling is one of the Bible's highlights.

David's men couldn't understand why he wouldn't kill the sleeping King Saul.

David stayed away from Israel until he learned that Jonathan and Saul had died during battle with the Philistines. When David returned to Judah, the people quickly proclaimed him king.

At first, David was king only of Judah (the southern portion of Canaan). After seven years, the northern tribes also accepted him as their king.

The Israelites gradually defeated the Philistines and forced them out of the country. At that time, the city of Jerusalem belonged to a group called the Jebusites. David captured the city and made it the capital of Israel. He built a simple Tabernacle there and brought the ark of the Covenant to the Tabernacle.

David and his army then conquered neighboring kingdoms to the east and the north until Israel became the strongest nation in the area.

With all these people to govern, David set up a large central government and appointed officials over the conquered lands. He also carefully organized his army.

Even though David was a skillful leader, his own family life was sad. He had many wives, among them Bathsheba, whom he took from another man. Some of his own children killed each other, and two sons led rebellions against him.

Near the end of his life, David ordered that the people be counted. This was against the will of God, and God sent a plague that killed 70,000 people. It was miraculously stopped at a place just north of Jerusalem. David purchased that land and built an altar to God there. Later Solomon built the Temple there.

David's name is in the title of 73 of the Psalms—the most famous being the 23rd, which begins, "The Lord is my shepherd; I shall not want."

Where to find it

Samuel anoints David king   *1 Samuel 16: 1-13*
David kills the giant   *1 Samuel 17*
Captures Jerusalem   *2 Samuel 5: 6-10*
Takes Bathsheba   *2 Samuel 11–12*
Sons lead rebellions   *2 Samuel 15: 1–18: 15; 1 Kings 1: 5-53*
Numbers the people   *2 Samuel 24: 10-25*

DAY OF ATONEMENT (*uh-TONE-ment*) is the most solemn and important day of the Jewish religious calendar. It is in September, ten days after the Jewish New Year. Jews today observe it by not eating and not working.

In Bible times, the Day of Atonement included a series of ceremonies and sacrifices by the priests. It was the only time of the year the high priest entered the Holy of Holies—the most sacred part of the Tabernacle or Temple.

As part of the ceremony for the Day of Atonement, the high priest purified himself by a ceremonial bath and put on white garments. Then he sacrificed a bull as a sin offering for himself and the other priests. He took some of the blood of the bull into the Holy of Holies and sprinkled it on the ark of the Covenant.

Then two goats were brought to the Tabernacle or Temple. One was sacrificed as a sin offering for the people, and some of its blood was sprinkled in the Holy of Holies. The high priest confessed the sins of the people over the head of the other goat and then sent it into the wilderness as a symbol of sin being removed.

Toward the end of the day, other sacrifices were made.

After the Jerusalem Temple was destroyed in A.D. 70, the sacrifices described in the Old Testament stopped.

Christians see the Day of Atonement as a symbol of the sacrifice of Christ for the sins of the world.

Where to find it: *Leviticus 16*

DAY OF CHRIST, DAY OF JESUS CHRIST, and **DAY OF THE LORD** mean the same thing in the New Testament. They refer to the time of triumph when Christ will reign over everyone. For those who do not believe in Christ, it will be a time of judgment.

Day of the Lord appears often in the Old Testament. When the prophets talked of the Day of the Lord, they usually referred to a time when God would punish the sins of the nation. Sometimes this punishment came through an enemy invasion, but other times the words refer to a final judgment.

Where to find it

Old Testament use *Isaiah 13: 6-19; Joel 1: 15; 2: 1-2*

New Testament use *Philippians 1: 6, 10; 2: 16; 1 Thessalonians 5: 2; 2 Thessalonians 2: 1-3; 1 Corinthians 1: 7-8*

DAY'S JOURNEY was usually the distance a person could walk in seven or eight hours—about 20 to 30 miles.

DEACON *(DEE-kun)* comes from a Greek word that means "servant" or "minister." House-

hold servants and those who waited on tables were called deacons. Paul called himself a deacon or servant in 1 Corinthians 3: 5.

In 1 Timothy 3: 8-12, *deacon* seems to apply to certain persons in the church who had particular responsibilities. We are not sure exactly what those responsibilities were, but they seemed to be important to the church.

DEACONESS *(DEE-kuh-ness)* is our English-language female form of the Greek word for *deacon.* Romans 16: 1 says that Phoebe was a deacon or leader in the church at Cenchreae.

DEAD SEA, in southern Israel, has four times as much salt as the ocean. It is called "dead" because nothing lives in it. Even a nonswimmer can float on the Dead Sea because it is so salty. Its surface is 1,300 feet below sea level, and in some places the water is more than 1,000 feet deep. The Dead Sea is forty-seven miles long and about seven miles across—the largest body of water in Israel. Sodom and Gomorrah were somewhere near the Dead Sea.

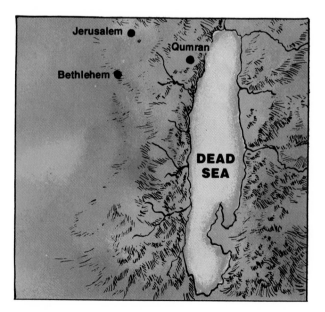

DEAD SEA SCROLLS are a group of ancient writings discovered in 1947 by Arab shepherds who were exploring some caves near the Dead Sea.

Archaeologists recognized the value of the scrolls and began to search other caves in the area near the ruins of a small village called

Our oldest copies of parts of the Bible were found in these caves near the Dead Sea.

Qumran *(KOOM-ron).* Many other scrolls were found. They included parts of every book in the Old Testament except Esther. Written in ancient Hebrew and Aramaic, these are the oldest Old Testament scrolls ever found. They help translators of the Bible know more accurately what the original writings said.

Many other scrolls at Qumran were writings about the history of the Qumran people, their religious beliefs, and how they lived. The Dead Sea Scrolls reveal that about 100 B.C. or earlier, a few hundred Jews from Jerusalem built this small village, far from other cities, as a place to study the Old Testament Law and wait for God to send a strong new leader. The community apparently died out about A.D. 70.

DEATH has two meanings in the Bible. Death is the end of physical life. For example, in Deuteronomy 34: 5 the Bible says flatly, "So Moses the servant of the Lord died." In other places the Bible speaks of death as "sleeping with his fathers," as in 2 Kings 13: 9, "So Jehoahaz slept with his fathers, and they buried him in Samaria."

But the Bible also speaks of death as a spiritual separation from God. Romans 6: 23 says, "The wages of sin is death, but the gift of God is eternal life." This "new life" of fellowship with God shows itself in the way we live. "We know that we have passed out of death into life, because we love the brethren," ac-

cording to 1 John 3: 14.

Those who are forever separated from God are said to experience the "second death" (Revelation 20: 6, 14).

DEATH OF CHRIST is one of the central events in the Christian faith. The Bible says that Christ died to show God's love for people. He did not die for us because we are good, but because we are sinful. We deserved to die, but his death became a *substitute* for our death.

Christ was put to death by the cruel method of crucifixion (see *Crucifixion*). He had been accused of blasphemy because he said he was the Son of God.

Even as Jesus was dying in great pain, he thought of others. He saw his mother, Mary, and asked one of his followers to care for her. He talked kindly to the two robbers being crucified with him. To one he said, "This day you will be with me in Paradise." He thought about the Roman soldiers and those who wanted him to die, and he said, "Father, forgive them, for they know not what they do."

Although Jesus' death was a terrible event in history, it was the way we could know God as a friend. John 3: 16 says that God gave his Son to die for us because he loved us so much.

Where to find it

Christ died for us *Romans 5: 8; 1 Peter 3: 8; 1 Peter 2: 21, 25*
Christ died because he said he was the Son of God *John 19: 7*
Christ thought of others when dying *John 19: 25-27; Luke 23: 34, 43*
Christ's death shows God's love *John 3: 16*

DEBORAH *(DEB-er-uh)* was one of the greatest judges of Israel. (During the 400 years before the Israelites asked for a king, they were ruled by judges, through whom God spoke and led his people.)

Together, the tribes of Israel had not won a war for 175 years before Deborah became ruler. She led them to victory over Jabin, king of Canaan, who had been threatening Israel for twenty years.

Deborah was also a prophetess, and God gave her instructions on how to defeat Jabin even though he had 900 iron chariots. Deborah went with her soldiers into battle as they defeated the enemy on Mount Tabor. After the victory, Deborah and Barak composed and sang a song of praise to God.

Where to find it: *Judges 4–5*

DEBT, DEBTOR *(det, DET-er).* A debt means something owed to someone else—usually money. A debtor is the one who must pay it.

The Law of Moses said that Hebrews could not charge interest on debts to another Hebrew, especially if he was poor. This law, however, was largely ignored in New Testament times.

People sometimes had to sell their children and wives as slaves to pay their debts. Jesus always showed sympathy and care for people in debt, and he often used stories about them in his parables.

The word *debt* in The Lord's Prayer, however, refers to sins that we do. *Debtors* are people who sin against us.

Where to find it

People sold wives and children to pay debts *Matthew 18:23-30*

Moses forbids interest charges *Exodus 22:25; Deuteronomy 23:19*

Jews in New Testament charged interest *Matthew 25:27*

DECALOGUE *(DEK-uh-log)* means "ten words" and refers to the Ten Commandments.

Where to find it: *Exodus 20:1-17*

DECAPOLIS *(dee-KAP-oh-lis)* was a group of about ten cities southwest of the Sea of Galilee and east of the Jordan River. (This area is now part of the country of Jordan.)

In the time of Christ, people in these cities were mostly Gentiles. They had their own money, courts, and army.

Some of the people of the Decapolis followed Christ. When Jesus landed his boat there, he healed a man, who later told throughout the Decapolis what Christ had done.

Where to find it: *Matthew 4:25; Mark 5:1-20*

DELILAH *(dee-LYE-luh)* was a wicked Philistine woman who pretended to be in love with

Samson (the strong man and judge of Israel). She wanted to find out the secret of his great strength.

Three times he misled her when she asked where he got his strength. She tried each of his suggestions, but they did not take his strength away. Finally he admitted that he was strong because of his vow to God that he would never cut his hair. While he slept, she called in his enemies to cut his hair. His strength was gone, and he was captured.

Where to find it: *Judges 16:4-22*

DEMAS *(DEE-mus)* was a helper when Paul was first imprisoned in Rome. Paul called him his "fellow-worker." Later Demas deserted Paul and went back to Thessalonica—probably his hometown.

Where to find it: *Colossians 4:14; Philemon 24; 2 Timothy 4:10*

DEMETRIUS *(duh-MEE-tree-us)* was a silversmith in Ephesus who made his living by making images of the goddess Artemis (Diana in Latin). When Paul preached in Ephesus and people began believing in Christ, Demetrius was afraid he would lose customers. He started a riot so that Paul had to leave the city.

Where to find it: *Acts 19:23-40*

DEMONS *(DEE-muns)* are evil spirits. They are often mentioned in the Bible. Sometimes they

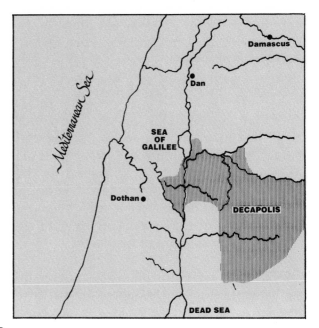

DEMONIAC

are called the devil's angels. They do not have bodies. They are servants of Satan (the devil). They are intelligent and do all they can to oppose God and those who serve God. The New Testament tells about demons who made people mentally ill, or blind, or unable to speak. The King James Version says that Mary Magdalene had seven devils, but the newer translations have the more correct term, *demons*.

The New Testament teaches that Jesus has power over demons and protects his followers from them. At the end of the world, all demons will be destroyed with Satan, their master.

Where to find it: *Luke 8: 2, 26-39; Matthew 12: 22; 25: 41*

DEMONIAC *(dee-MOAN-ee-ak)* is a person controlled by demons. Jesus healed many persons from demon control.

Where to find it: *Matthew 4: 24; 8: 16, 28-33; 9: 32*

DENY ONESELF is a phrase used often in the New Testament. It means that a Christian should love and serve God and other people even when he doesn't feel like it and would rather do something else. Jesus Christ "denied himself" when he came to earth to live and die for people. Christians are told to deny themselves and follow Christ.

Where to find it: *Matthew 16: 24; Mark 8: 34*

DERBE *(DUR-bee)* was a city in what is now the country of Turkey. Paul visited there on his first and second missionary journeys and perhaps on his third.

Where to find it: *Acts 14: 20; 16: 1*

DESCENT INTO HADES *(de-SENT into HAY-dees)* by Christ is mentioned in the Apostles' Creed. The idea is found in 1 Peter 3: 18-21 and 4: 6, where it says Christ preached to "the spirits in prison" and to "the dead." Although the meaning is not entirely clear, these passages show that Christ was Lord over all creation even at the time of his death.

DESERT *(DEZ-ert)* in the Bible does not mean a sandy wasteland like the Sahara. It usually refers to an area where grass grew but that

needed more rain to make it good farmland. A Palestine desert (or wilderness) was often a place where sheep grazed.

DESOLATING SACRILEGE (see *Abomination of Desolation*)

DEUTERONOMY *(DOO-ter-ON-uh-mee)* is the fifth book in the Old Testament. It begins by telling how the Israelites arrived at the Jordan River after forty years of wandering in the wilderness. They were now ready to enter the Promised Land.

As the thousands of Hebrews gathered at the edge of the Jordan, Moses reminded them of God's Covenant (or agreement) with them. He told them why they had not been able to enter Canaan forty years before—their unbelief had kept them out until all of the older people from Egypt were dead. He repeated many of the stories of their years in the wilderness.

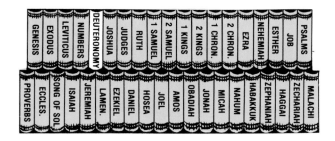

Then, Moses declared again all of the laws of God that they were to obey. The Ten Commandments were repeated, and then Moses included the laws about feast days and offerings to God (Deuteronomy 12: 5—16: 17).

Chapters 22 to 26 review the laws about taking care of property and of each other. They tell how disagreements were to be settled. Then Moses reminded the people what would happen if they disobeyed God.

The closing chapters of Deuteronomy tell how Moses chose Joshua to lead the Israelites in their conquest of Canaan. Then Moses went to the top of Mount Nebo, where he looked across the Jordan River to the Promised Land. There Moses died.

Deuteronomy is the last of the five books of Moses known among the Jews as "The Law."

DEVIL is one of the common names for Satan

(see *Satan*). Other names are Beelzebub, Abaddon, the great dragon, the ancient serpent, and the deceiver.

Where to find it: *Matthew 12:24; Revelation 9:11; 12:9; 20:2*

DEVOTED THING *(dee-VOTE-ed)* means something that has been set aside for God or for a heathen god. It is not to be used for common purposes. In the Old Testament, the Israelites were told that as they conquered cities, they should always destroy the "devoted things." Achan's sin at Jericho was more serious than stealing, because he had taken "devoted things" (consecrated to false gods) and brought them into the Israelites' camp.

Where to find it: *Leviticus 27:28; Deuteronomy 13:17; Joshua 6:18; 7:1*

DIANA *(die-ANN-uh)* is the Latin name of the Greek goddess called Artemis (see *Artemis*).

DIADEM *(DIE-uh-dem)* is a symbol for a ruler. It is usually a crown. Christ is said to wear diadems in Revelation 19:12.

DIASPORA *(die-ASS-por-uh)* is the name for Jews who lived outside of Palestine but who continued to follow the Jewish religion.

Twice in the Old Testament, many Israelites were sent away from Palestine after they lost a war. Most of them stayed in these foreign lands and became loyal citizens. Except for the rabbis, most forgot how to speak Hebrew or Aramaic.

In New Testament times, many Jews moved away from Palestine to other countries where there were more job opportunities. They usually built synagogues wherever they went. Paul preached in many of these synagogues of the Diaspora when he was on his missionary journeys. During Paul's life, there were more Jews living outside of Palestine than in it.

Gentiles were often attracted by the life and faith of the Jews and became "proselyte Jews." Some of these later became Christians.

DIDRACHMA *(die-DRAHK-muh)* was a silver Greek coin worth about half a day's wages. It was the amount Jews had to pay for an annual Temple tax. In the Revised Standard Version it is called a "half-shekel." When Jesus was told to pay the tax, he sent Peter to fish, saying he should open the mouth of the first fish he caught and he would find a shekel. That would pay the tax for them both (see *Money*).

Where to find it: *Matthew 17:24-27*

DIDYMUS *(DID-ee-mus)* means "a twin" and was the Greek name for Thomas, the doubting disciple of Jesus.

Where to find it: *John 11:16; 20:24; 21:2*

DINAH *(DIE-nuh)* was the only daughter of Jacob and Leah. She was the sister or half sister of the twelve sons of Jacob, who became founders of the twelve tribes of Israel. She was raped by a man named Shechem who later wanted to marry her. Dinah's brothers said they would agree to the marriage if all the men of Shechem's village would agree to be circumcised. They agreed, but while the men were weak and recovering from the operation, Dinah's brothers came and killed Shechem and many other men of the village.

Where to find it: *Genesis 34*

DIONYSIUS *(die-oh-NISH-ee-us)* was a member of the supreme court of Athens. He became a Christian after hearing Paul's famous sermon at Mars' Hill.

Where to find it: *Acts 17:34*

DIOTREPHES *(die-OTT-ruh-feez)* was a member of the church to which Gaius belonged. The apostle John wrote his third letter to Gaius and talked about Diotrephes, who caused trouble in the church by trying to run everything. Diotrephes refused to welcome anyone who did not agree with him. He spread false stories about John and tried to put people out of the church who would not do as he said.

Where to find it: *3 John 9-10*

DISCIPLE *(dih-SY-pul)* means "learner" and refers to someone who accepts and follows the ideas and practices of a certain teacher. John the Baptist had disciples, and so did the Pharisees.

In the New Testament, *disciples* usually refers to those who were followers of Jesus. Sometimes it means the twelve apostles. Other times it refers to all those who believe in Christ. In the Book of Acts, it always means believers in Christ who live according to his teachings.

Where to find it

John's disciples   *Matthew 9:14*
Pharisees' disciples   *Matthew 22:16*
Jesus' disciples   *Matthew 10:1; Luke 6:17; John 8:31*
Believers in Christ   *Matthew 28:19-20; Acts 6:1*

DISCIPLINE *(DIH-suh-plin)* is related to training and learning. In the Old Testament, that training often involved punishment. It also involved teaching by example.

The New Testament has more emphasis on training by example and word. Ephesians 6:4 says, "Fathers, do not provoke your children to anger, but bring them up in the discipline and instruction of the Lord."

Where to find it

Old Testament discipline   *Proverbs 22:15; 13:24; Deuteronomy 8:5-6*
New Testament discipline   *Ephesians 6:4; Hebrews 12:5-11*

DISEASES or sicknesses were common in Bible times. They are usually described rather than named. For example, Matthew 8:14 says Peter's mother-in-law was sick with a fever. We don't know what disease caused the fever. It may have been due to malaria (quite likely) or to typhus, typhoid, or some other infection.

People and animals are described as having "boils" or "sores." There are many reasons for boils and sores, but the Bible writers did not name the diseases causing them. The writers recognized that how people think affects their health and feelings. Proverbs 16:24 says, "Pleasant words are like a honeycomb, sweetness to the soul and health to the body."

Sometimes a general term is used to describe a whole family of diseases. *Pestilence* could mean cholera, dysentery, or other diseases that spread easily and are caused by poor diet, crowding, and unsanitary habits.

When names of diseases are used, the Bible names are sometimes not the same ones we use today. For example, the Bible mentions "scurvy." We know scurvy today as a disease caused by lack of Vitamin C. Fresh fruits and vegetables were the main diet of the people in Bible times, so they would not have had our kind of scurvy. Their "scurvy" was some kind of fungus disease.

Here are some of the diseases the Bible mentions.

Blindness is not being able to see. Some blindnesses were caused by eye infections; others were the result of gonorrhea, cataracts, or glaucoma. Moses gave special instructions to provide for the blind and the deaf. Jesus healed several blind people. These are mentioned in John 9:1-7; Matthew 20:30-34; Mark 8:22-25.

Sometimes blindness is used as a word picture of a person who refuses to see what God wants him to do. Jesus spoke of the Pharisees as "blind guides" (Matthew 15:14).

Boils were red, inflamed swellings of the skin that could be caused by several different diseases. Some scholars think that Job's boils may have been smallpox. The "boils" of the cattle in Exodus 9:9 may have been anthrax.

The boil of Hezekiah in 2 Kings 20:7 was probably a carbuncle—a large, aggravated boil. The prophet Isaiah prescribed a fig poultice for his boil.

Dropsy *(DROP-see)* is involved in several diseases. It means that too much watery fluid collects in the body, the feet, or the legs (Luke 14:2). It is often present in diseases of the heart or kidneys.

92

When Naaman asked to be healed of his leprosy, he was told to go bathe in the Jordan River.

Dysentery *(DIS-in-tare-ee)* is a serious, painful infection and inflammation of the colon. It can cause death if not properly treated (Acts 28:8).

Epilepsy *(EP-uh-lep-see)* is a disorder of the central nervous system that brings occasional seizures or convulsions. Jesus healed epilepsy (Matthew 4:24). In Matthew 17:14-18, Jesus healed a boy who was demon possessed and who also had epilepsy.

Fever is a symptom of many diseases, including typhus, malaria, dysentery, and cholera. Peter's mother-in-law, who was healed by Jesus in Matthew 8:14-16, may have had malaria. In Acts 28:8, Publius's father had both fever and dysentery—the fever probably caused by the dysentery.

Itch in Deuteronomy 28:27 was probably either ringworm or scabies, a disease caused by a tiny insect that burrows under the skin and causes intense itching. It easily spreads to other people.

Leprosy is caused by a microorganism that attacks the skin. Today it's called Hansen's disease. In the Bible, *leprosy* may also have meant some other skin diseases. Leviticus 13 tells what people were to do about skin diseases and leprosy. A person with these kinds of disease was to stay away from other people

for certain periods of time until the disease showed signs of healing.

Lunatic (see *Madness,* below).

Madness is mental illness. It was common in Bible times. King Saul apparently became more and more unbalanced. He was moody and suspicious. He became more and more unable to perform his duties as king.

Nebuchadnezzar suffered from a mental illness that made him think he was an animal. It is called *boanthropy.* Other times madness was caused by demon possession (Luke 8:26-33).

Palsy *(PALL-zee)* is a general term used in the King James Version to mean paralyzed in some way (see *Paralysis,* below).

Paralysis *(puh-RAL-uh-sis)* means some part of the body is crippled or won't work. The paralysis may have been due to polio, birth injuries, or other illnesses.

Pestilence *(PEST-uh-lunss)* usually refers to a disease that spreads rapidly. Pestilences probably included cholera, undulant fever, typhoid, dysentery, and other diseases that often go with poor diet, crowding, and unsanitary habits (Deuteronomy 28:21). The difference between pestilence and plague is not always clear.

Plague can include any serious epidemic,

but in 1 Samuel 5—6 it probably referred to the dread bubonic plague. Bubonic plague brings high fever, swellings of glands in the groin ("tumors"), and swift death. It is usually spread by rats. When the plague broke out among the Philistines, they thought it was because they had captured the ark of God from the Israelites. When they sent the ark back, they included a "guilt offering" of "five golden tumors and five golden mice." They recognized some connection between the tumors and the mice.

Scab and **scurvy** are skin diseases probably related to eczema, psoriasis, or impetigo. Scurvy in the Bible is not the scurvy of our day caused by a lack of Vitamin C. The year-round diet of fresh fruit and vegetables would make that unlikely. The diseases are mentioned in Leviticus 21:20; 22:22.

Scabies (SKAY-beez) (see Itch, above).

Sores or skin ulcers are infections on the skin, often developing around wounds, bruises, or skin eruptions that become infected. Lazarus had sores (Luke 16:20-21).

Tumors (TOO-murs) are mentioned in 1 Samuel 5—6 in connection with the plague sent on the Philistines after they captured the ark of God. They were probably swollen glands in the groin that came with bubonic plague.

Ulcers (UL-sers) or sores were wounds or skin openings that would not heal. They often appeared with bubonic plague or with leprosy.

Withered hand was some form of paralysis that affected the hand only. It may have been caused by polio. Withered hand is mentioned in Matthew 12:9-14; Mark 3:1-6; and Luke 6:6-11.

Worms caused the death of Herod Agrippa in Acts 12:21-23. They were probably intestinal roundworms. They are common in lands where sanitation is poor. These worms form a tight ball and block the intestine, causing death.

DIVINATION (div-in-AY-shun) was the fortune-telling of Bible times—the attempt to get secret knowledge, especially of the future. Whenever it is mentioned in the Bible, it is condemned. Paul healed a young girl of "the spirit of divination."

Where to find it: *Deuteronomy 18:10-14; Acts 16:16-18*

DIVINE (dih-VINE) is used both as a verb and as an adjective in the Bible.

1. *Divine* as a verb means to try to get information or knowledge not available through normal human channels. This is condemned, because it is related to fortune-telling (see *Divination*).

2. *Divine* as an adjective means "godly." 2 Peter 1:3-4 says, "His *divine* power has granted to us all things . . . that through these . . . you may become partakers of the *divine* nature."

DIVORCE (dih-VORSE) is the dissolving of a legal marriage. In Deuteronomy 24:1-4 Moses discussed a bill of divorce, so we know divorce was permitted among the Israelites. Jesus said, "For your hardness of heart, he [Moses] wrote you this commandment." Jesus' teachings showed that marriage was intended to be permanent (see *Marriage*).

Where to find it

Moses' law of divorce   *Deuteronomy 24:1-4*
Jesus' teaching about marriage   *Mark 10:2-12; Luke 16:18; Matthew 19:3-12*

DOCTOR means "teacher of the Law." The word appears only in the King James Version. Other translations use *teacher*.

Where to find it: *Luke 2:46; 5:17; Acts 5:34*

DOCTRINE (DOK-trin) means teachings recommended to others. Jesus said that the Pharisees taught "as doctrines the precepts of men" (Matthew 15:9). Paul told Christians to so live that "in everything they may adorn the doctrine of God our Savior" (Titus 2:10).

DOEG (DOE-eg) was the chief herdsman for King Saul when Saul was trying to kill David. He was in the Tabernacle at Nob when David came there to ask the priest for bread for himself and his men and for a sword for himself. Doeg told Saul that the priest had given these things to David. Saul was so mad with jealousy that he called the priest and his relatives and ordered Doeg to kill them all—85 people.

Where to find it: *1 Samuel 21:3-9; 22:6-19*

Dorcas was a Christian woman who often made clothes for needy people. She died—and was raised to life again through Peter's prayers.

DOG (see *Animals*)

DOMINION (*doe-MIN-yon*) means to have power or authority. The Bible speaks often of God's dominion. In creation God gave to men and women dominion over other living things. Nations are sometimes said to have dominion over other nations because they have won a war.

Where to find it: *Genesis 1: 27-28; Judges 14: 4; Psalm 22: 28; 1 Timothy 6: 16*

DOORKEEPER is one who guards a door in a public building, temple, or walled city. In the Bible this person is also called a porter. Doorkeepers could be either men or women. The psalmist said, "I would rather be a doorkeeper in the house of my God than dwell in the tents of wickedness."

Where to find it: *2 Samuel 4: 6; Psalm 84: 10; John 18: 16-17*

DORCAS (*DOR-kus*) was a woman disciple who lived at Joppa (on the Mediterranean coast). She showed her love for Christ by making clothing for those in need and helping in other ways. When she became ill and died, other Christians learned that Peter was in a nearby town and sent for him.

When Peter arrived, he was surrounded by weeping women who showed him the clothing Dorcas had made for them. He sent everyone out of the room, then knelt and prayed beside Dorcas's body. Finally he said, "Tabitha [the Aramaic word for Dorcas], arise." Dorcas opened her eyes, sat up, and was well.

Where to find it: *Acts 9: 36-42*

DOTHAN (*DOE-thun*) was an ancient city located in what is now about the middle of Israel. It was where Joseph was thrown into a pit by his brothers, who were jealous of him.

Nearly a thousand years later, the prophet Elisha was living at Dothan when the king of Syria sent an army to capture him. The army surrounded the city of Dothan. Elisha prayed, and God sent temporary blindness on the army so Elisha could lead them to the city where Israel had its army! However, Elisha told Joram, king of Israel, that the enemy soldiers were not to be killed but were to be fed and sent home. Joram followed Elisha's orders.

Where to find it

Joseph in the pit *Genesis 37: 24*
Elisha surprises the Syrian army *2 Kings 6: 12-23*

DOUBLE-MINDED describes the person who sometimes believes God and sometimes

95

DOUGH

doubts, or who tries both to follow God's ways and to do as he pleases.

Where to find it: *Psalm 119:113; James 1:7-8; 4:8*

DOUGH *(doe)* is a mixture of flour, water, and leavening from which bread is made. The flour was usually made of wheat, rye, oats, or barley (see *Bread)*. In Romans 11:16, *dough* is used as a word picture to represent the nation Israel.

DOVE (see *Birds)*

DOWRY *(DOW-ree)* was the gift a father gave his daughter when she was about to be married. Sometimes it was property such as a field or a spring of water or even a city. Often the dowry included a maidservant, over whom the husband never had control. The dowry seems to have belonged permanently to the wife, and it served as a kind of insurance in case her husband died or divorced her (see *Marriage)*.

Where to find it

Property as a dowry *Joshua 15:18-19; 1 Kings 9:16*
Maidservant as a dowry *Genesis 16:1; 29:24, 29*

DRACHMA *(DRAHK-muh)* was a Greek silver coin, worth about one day's wages (see *Money)*.

Where to find it: *Luke 15:8-10*

DRAGON *(DRAG-un)* in the King James Version may refer to jackals, sea monsters, or serpents. In the Revised Standard Version, when *dragon* is used in the Old Testament, it is a word picture for Egypt. In the New Testament it appears only in Revelation as a word picture for Satan.

Where to find it

Old Testament, meaning Egypt *Isaiah 27:1; 51:9; Ezekiel 29:3; 32:2*
New Testament, meaning Satan *Revelation 12:3-4, 7, 9, 13; 13:2-4, 11; 16:13; 20:2*

DREAMS were sometimes used by God to communicate with people. However, Ecclesiastes 5:3 says, "A dream comes with much business," showing that people in Bible times realized that dreams were usually related to their activities.

Jacob set up a stone to mark the place where God spoke to him in a dream.

The Bible has many examples of God speaking to people through dreams—both to people who worshiped him and to those who did not. Pharaoh had a dream of seven fat cows and seven thin ones. Joseph interpreted the dream as showing there would be seven years of very good crops followed by seven years of famine. Joseph also interpreted the dreams of a butler and a baker in prison.

In Deuteronomy 13:1-5, the Israelites were told that any prophet or dreamer who told them to serve other gods should be put to death.

The New Testament also has examples of God speaking to people through dreams or visions. God spoke to Joseph twice through dreams; once before the birth of Jesus, and again before he fled with Mary and Jesus to Egypt.

Dreams and visions are not the same. In a dream, the person is in a natural sleep. In a vision, such as Paul's vision on the road to Damascus, the individual is clearly awake (see *Visions)*.

Joseph interprets dreams *Genesis 40: 1-20; 41: 14-36*

Joseph, husband of Mary, has dreams *Matthew 1: 20-24; 2: 13-14*

DROSS is the waste matter or scum that rises to the surface when metals are melted. The pure metal, such as silver, stays below the surface. *Dross* is usually used in the Bible as a word picture meaning "worthless," as in Psalm 119: 119.

DRUNKENNESS is condemned in the Bible. Wine was common among the Israelites and their neighbors, and too much drinking was often a problem. Proverbs 23: 29-34 shows the foolishness of drinking too much. Amos 4: 1 shows that women also had problems with drink in Bible times. Ephesians 5: 18 says, "Do not get drunk with wine, for that is debauchery, but be filled with the Spirit."

DRUSILLA (see *Felix* and *Drusilla*)

DUNG is the excrement or manure of people, animals, or birds. In the Old Testament sacrifices, priests were told to burn the dung and certain other parts of the sacrificial animals outside the camp.

Animal dung had two main uses: fuel and fertilizer. As fuel, it was often mixed with straw and dried. It could then be burned in the clay or stone ovens of Palestine. Human dung was used for fuel only in cases of terrible emergency—such as a city being attacked in war. Such a case is described in Ezekiel 4: 12-15.

Animal dung was used as fertilizer in much the same way it is used today.

In Bible times, as now, dung was considered offensive. In Philippians 3: 8 (KJV), Paul said, "I have suffered the loss of all things, and do count them but dung, that I may win Christ." In this passage, the word also means other kinds of garbage or rubbish.

DUNG-GATE was one of the eleven gates to Jerusalem. The refuse of the city was taken out the dung-gate.

Where to find it: *Nehemiah 2: 13; 3: 13-14; 12: 31*

DUST in the Bible generally refers to tiny pieces of earth or soil. Man was made from dust, and he returns to dust after death. *Dust* is also often used in word pictures to mean uncountable numbers. Abraham was told, "I will make your descendants as the dust of the earth; so that if one can count the dust of the earth, your descendants also can be counted." Other times dust pictures destruction, or being made into nothing. The phrase *dust and ashes* is often used to picture sorrow or smallness.

Where to find it

Man created from dust *Genesis 2: 7*
Destruction *Genesis 3: 19; 2 Kings 13: 7*

DYER (see *Occupations*)

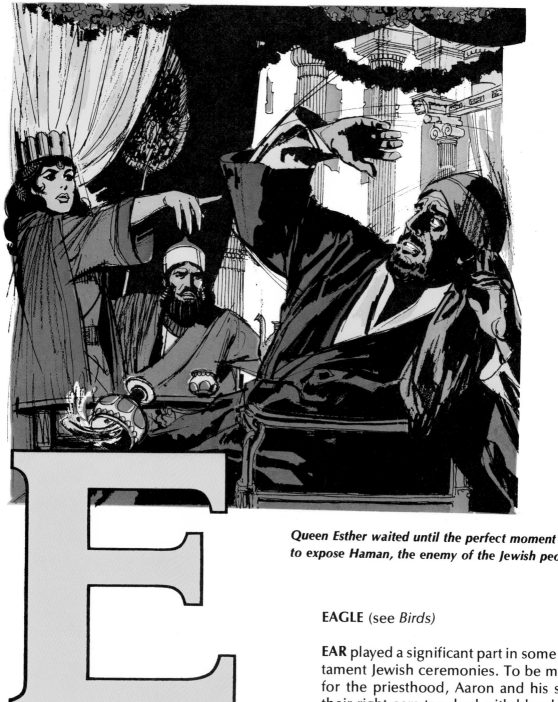

Queen Esther waited until the perfect moment to expose Haman, the enemy of the Jewish people.

EAGLE (see *Birds*)

EAR played a significant part in some Old Testament Jewish ceremonies. To be made holy for the priesthood, Aaron and his sons had their right ears touched with blood. This action symbolized forgiveness or cleansing. The right ear of a healed leper was also touched by blood. A slave's ear was pierced to show he belonged to someone else.

Ear is often used as a word picture of understanding and obeying God. Jesus said, "He who has ears to hear, let him hear." In this verse, *hearing* means "obeying." When Jesus said, "Let those words sink into your ears," he meant, "Understand what I am saying to you."

Aaron and his sons   *Exodus 19:19-21*
Slave   *Exodus 21:6*
Healed leper   *Leviticus 14:14*
In Jesus' teachings   *Matthew 11:15; Luke 9:44*

EARLY RAIN in the Bible referred to the first rains of *autumn*–not spring. The rainy season in Palestine is from about December 1 to March 1. The early rains were the rains that came before the rainy season started. Rains that came after March were called the "latter rains."

Where to find it: *Deuteronomy 11:14; Psalm 84:6; Joel 3:23*

EARNEST *(ER-nest)*, in the Greek language, was a business word. An earnest was the down payment, which guaranteed full payment in the future.

The apostle Paul used the word *earnest* for the Holy Spirit, God's gift that guarantees the rest of the Christian's inheritance will be given. Most modern translations use "guarantee" instead of earnest.

Where to find it: *2 Corinthians 1:22; Ephesians 1:13-14*

EARTH has several meanings in the Bible. *Earth* means our world or planet in Genesis 1:1. *Earth* means the dry land as separate from the sea in Genesis 1:10. *Earth* also means the place where people live in Genesis 1:28. Psalm 104:14 speaks of the earth as soil or dirt where plants can grow.

EARTHENWARE *(ER-thun-ware)* is clay dishes, bowls, and containers. To make earthenware, a potter shaped the clay on a potter's wheel

Soft clay can be shaped while spinning on a disc.

with his hands. He then glazed the clay dish and baked it in a furnace. In the Bible the potter and his earthenware sometimes stand for God and his people.

Where to find it: *Isaiah 45:9; Jeremiah 18:4; 2 Corinthians 4:7*

EARTHQUAKE is a movement of the earth that often causes great destruction. The Bible mentions several earthquakes and describes what they did. Elijah experienced one. Another one occurred during the reign of Uzziah (786-735 B.C.). Earthquakes happened at the time of Jesus' death and resurrection. Paul and Silas were freed from prison by an earthquake.

The Book of Revelation says earthquakes will be part of God's judgment in the future.

Effects of earthquakes   *Numbers 16:31-33; Psalm 18:7; Jeremiah 4:24; Zechariah 14:4-5*
During Elijah's time   *1 Kings 19:11-12*
During Uzziah's reign   *Amos 1:1; Zechariah 14:5*
At Jesus' death and resurrection   *Matthew 27:51; 28:2*
Frees Paul and Silas   *Acts 16:26*
Part of God's judgment   *Revelation 8:5; 11:13, 19; 16:18*

EAST COUNTRY was a land southeast of Palestine in Arabia. After Sarah died, Abraham married again and had several sons. He sent these sons and their families to the east country, away from Isaac.

Where to find it: *Genesis 25:1-6*

EAST WIND was a bitter wind that blew from the deserts southeast of Palestine. This hot, dry, dusty wind blew from April to June and September to November. It withered plants and made life hard for people and animals. Today, this wind is called *sirocco* or *khamsin*.

Where to find it: *Genesis 41:6; Isaiah 27:8; Ezekiel 17:10; Jonah 4:8*

EASTER is the day when Christians celebrate Christ's resurrection. The New Testament doesn't mention an Easter celebration. Soon after Christ's death, Jewish Christians celebrated Christ's resurrection on Passover, while Gentile Christians celebrated it on a certain Sunday. In A.D. 325 the Council of Nicea ruled that Easter should be celebrated on the first Sunday after the full moon in the spring (a

No one knows exactly where Jesus was buried and rose again, but this garden tomb is a likely possibility.

Sunday between March 22 and April 25).

Easter eggs and the Easter bunny have nothing to do with the real meaning of Easter.

EBAL *(EE-bull),* **MOUNT,** is located in Samaria. The steep, rocky mountain rises 3,077 feet above the sea. Jacob dug a well at its base. A narrow, well-traveled valley separates Mount Ebal from Mount Gerizim.

Moses told the Israelites what they were to do on these mountains after they crossed the Jordan River into Canaan. Later, Joshua carried out all Moses' instructions. He built an altar on top of Mount Ebal. He put plaster on the altar stones and wrote the words of the Law on them. Some of the tribes of Israel stood on Mount Gerizim. The rest of the people stood on Mount Ebal. Then, like a huge speaking choir, those on Mount Gerizim cried out the blessings that would come to those who followed God, and those on Mount Ebal shouted the curses that would follow sin.

Where to find it: *Deuteronomy 27: 4-26; Joshua 8: 30-35; John 4: 5*

EBENEZER *(eb-un-EE-zur)* means ''stone of help.'' Samuel set up a stone near Mizpah to remind the Israelites of the victory God gave them over the Philistines.

Where to find it: *1 Samuel 7: 12*

ECCLESIASTES *(ee-klee-zee-AS-teez)* is an Old Testament book. Some scholars believe the author was Solomon, writing in his old age. Ecclesiastes 1: 1 and 1: 12 say the writer was the son of David and king over Israel.

The word *ecclesiastes* means ''preacher.'' The writer called himself ''the Preacher'' and said he had tested out many things. He tried pleasure and found it to be vanity, or emptiness. He saw that wisdom was better than foolishness; but since both wise and foolish men die, he decided wisdom was worthless, too.

The writer ended almost every section of the book with ''This also is vanity and a striving after wind.'' He also repeated, ''Vanity of vanities.'' He meant he had decided everything was useless.

This man seemed to know very little about life after death, and that may be part of the reason life looked so dark to him.

But the Preacher also gave some wise advice. He said people should enjoy their work, go to God's house, keep their promises to

EDEN *(EE-den)*, **GARDEN OF**, was the beautiful place God created for the first man and woman, Adam and Eve. In it grew many fruit trees and two special trees: the tree of life and the tree of the knowledge of good and evil. Adam and Eve lived in the garden until they sinned against God by eating the fruit of the tree of knowledge of good and evil that God had told them not to eat.

The story of the Garden of Eden shows what life would have been like if people had not sinned. In Eden there was peace between people and God, between people and nature, and between Adam and Eve. When sin came, all this peace was destroyed.

People have always wondered where the Garden of Eden was located. The only clue is Genesis 2: 10-14, which says a river in the garden divided into four rivers: Pishon, Gihon, Tigris, and Euphrates. We know where the Tigris and Euphrates rivers are. We do not know where the Pishon or Gihon rivers were. The Bible says Pishon flowed through a place called Havilah, where gold was found. This may have been India. The Gihon flowed through Cush, perhaps Ethiopia. So no one knows for sure where the Garden of Eden really was.

In the Garden of Eden, animals lived together with Adam and Eve without hurting one another.

The Old Testament sometimes speaks of Eden as the garden of God. A description of a garden somewhat like Eden (although part of

God, and be trustworthy.

Chapter 12: 1-8 is a word picture of growing old and the changes that come to the body with age.

Some scholars think the Book of Ecclesiastes shows that even the wisest person can't find out what God has planned for his life unless God tells him.

ECSTASY *(EK-stuh-see)* is the feeling or experience some people have when they meet the Holy Spirit in an unusual way. These experiences might include dreams, visions, and trances. David danced in ecstasy before the ark.

Peter was in a trance when the Lord taught him that no people were "unclean."

Paul was in ecstasy when he was caught up into heaven and heard amazing things. The Book of Revelation comes from John's experience of ecstasy.

Where to find it

David danced *2 Samuel 6: 14-16*
Peter's trance *Acts 10: 10*
Paul caught up *2 Corinthians 12: 2-4*
John's vision *Revelation 1: 9-19*

ECUMENISM *(ek-YOU-men-izm)* means unity or oneness among Christians. The word is not found in the Bible, but the idea is in the New Testament. Jesus prayed that his followers might be one, even as God the Father and God the Son are one.

Paul said there should be unity and oneness among believers. True unity exists when people agree on important beliefs, and when the power of Christ is changing their thoughts, words, and deeds so that they love and obey God more.

Today, the idea of churches cooperating in fellowship and service is called the ecumenical movement.

Where to find it: *John 17: 9-23; Ephesians 4: 3-6*

a city) is used in Revelation 22:1-2 as a word picture of heaven.

Where to find it: *Genesis 2–3; Ezekiel 28:13; Revelation 22:1-2*

EDICT *(EE-dikt)* was the written law or decree of a king. After his seal was put on it, it was read in public. To disobey a king's edict meant death. Pharaoh made an edict that all Hebrew boy babies were to be killed. In the time of Esther, the king made an edict that all Jews were to be killed.

Where to find it

Pharaoh's edict that all male Israelite babies be killed *Exodus 1:22; Hebrews 11:23*
King's edict that all Jews be killed *Esther 3:12; 8:8-9, 17; 9:1, 13*

EDIFY *(ED-if-eye)* means "to build up." Paul used this word picture to mean strengthening, encouraging, and bringing peace between Christians. In 1 Corinthians 14:26, Paul says, "Let all things be done for edification." He wanted believers to do everything they could to build up the faith of other Christians.

EDOM *(EE-dum)* was the name of the people who descended from Esau. (Esau's name was changed to Edom after he sold his birthright for a bowl of bean soup.) The country of Edom was also called Seir, named after Mount Seir. The country, 100 miles long and 40 miles wide, was located between the Dead Sea and the Gulf of Aqaba. It was ruled by a king long before Israel had a ruler. David conquered the Edomites, but they revolted successfully against King Jehoram in 847 B.C. When Jerusalem was destroyed by the Babylonians in 586 B.C., the Edomites rejoiced. God punished them because they did not help Judah.

Where to find it

Esau's name changed *Genesis 25:30; 36:8*
David conquers Edomites *2 Samuel 8:14*
Edomites revolt *2 Kings 8:20, 22*
Edomites rejoice *Psalm 137:7*
God's judgment *Ezekiel 25:12-14; Obadiah 10-14*

EDUCATION (see *Schools*)

EGLON *(EGG-lon)* was a fat, evil Moabite king who ruled over the Israelites for 18 years. Eglon was killed by Ehud, who was then able to set Israel free from the Moabites.

Where to find it: *Judges 3:12-30*

EGYPT of the Old Testament covered about the same territory as Egypt does today. It is about the size of Texas and Colorado combined. The only thing that keeps the land from being all desert is that the Nile River floods every year. The floods water the fields and deposit rich black soil.

The Pyramids and Sphinx tell us the Egyptians were an ancient, highly civilized people.

Egyptian pharaohs were buried inside the Pyramids.

The Israelites called Egypt "Mizraim." They asked Egypt for help during times of famine. The seven years of famine during the time of Joseph were probably caused by the Nile not flooding to its usual level. Interesting details of ancient Egyptian life are told in the stories of Joseph's life and the slavery of the Hebrews up to the Exodus. Egypt was at war with Israel several times in the Old Testament period.

Where to find it

Abraham goes to Egypt during famine *Genesis 12:10*
Joseph sold to an Egyptian *Genesis 37*
Joseph in charge of grain in Egypt during famine *Genesis 39–50*
Israelites slaves in Egypt *Exodus 1–15*
Egyptian king captures cities of Judah *2 Chronicles 12:1-9*
Josiah fights Egyptian king *2 Chronicles 35:20-27*

EHUD *(EE-hud)* led Israel to freedom from Eglon, a Moabite king. Ehud told the king he had a secret message for him. Then Ehud surprised him with a sword and killed him. The Israelites fought against the Moabites, won the battle, and lived in peace for 80 years.

Ehud was the son of Gera, a Benjaminite, and was left-handed.

Where to find it: *Judges 3:12-30*

EKRON *(EK-ron)* was a Philistine city on the boundary between Judah and Dan. The Israelites captured Ekron. The god of Ekron was Baal-zebub.

Where to find it: *1 Samuel 7:14; 2 Kings 1:3*

ELAM *(EE-lum)* was one of the earliest civilizations. It existed before 2350 B.C. Elam was east of the Tigris River, close to Babylonia. The Bible mentions Elam's destruction.

Where to find it: *Isaiah 21:2; 22:6; Jeremiah 25:25; 49:34-39*

ELDER *(ELL-dur)*, in the Old Testament, was an older man of a village. Elders governed the community and made major decisions. Each town had its group of elders.

The Sanhedrin at the time of Christ was a ruling body made up of elders, priests, and scribes. This group helped bring about the crucifixion of Jesus.

In the New Testament church, the idea of ruling elders was probably carried over from Jewish life. Paul appointed elders in every church. (*Elder* and *bishop* mean the same thing in the New Testament.) Elders taught the people and encouraged spiritual growth among the Christians. Because an elder's job was very important, Paul wrote about what kind of person should be appointed as an elder.

Where to find it

Group of elders   *Ruth 4:1-4; 1 Samuel 16:4; Ezra 10:14*
Sanhedrin   *Matthew 27:12*
Paul appoints elders   *Acts 14:23*
Requirements for elders   *1 Timothy 3:1-7; Titus 1:5-9*

ELEAZAR *(el-ee-AY-zur)* was the third son of Aaron. Because his two older brothers had already died, Eleazar became chief priest and the assistant to Moses when Aaron died. After Moses' death, Eleazar helped Joshua divide the Promised Land among the twelve tribes. His only son was Phinehas. Eleazar died soon after Joshua did.

Where to find it

Becomes chief priest   *Numbers 3:32*
Is Moses' assistant   *Numbers 31:13-54*
Helps Joshua divide land   *Joshua 14:1*
Dies   *Joshua 24:33*

ELECT *(ee-LEKT)* **LADY** was either a Christian woman or a Christian church to whom the short New Testament letter known as 2 John was written.

She was probably a Christian woman whom the apostle John had known for some time. He said he had met some of her children and he was glad they were following Christ. He warned the woman not to invite false teachers into her house.

Some people think that when John mentioned the lady's children, he was talking about members of a church that met in her house. Others think John's letter to the elect lady is to a church itself.

ELECTION *(ee-LEK-shun)* in the Bible means God's choice. Moses was called God's chosen one. The nation of Israel was God's chosen people. The Messiah was called God's elect. In the New Testament, those who believe in Jesus are called the elect 20 times. Twice Jesus is called God's chosen one.

Since everyone has sinned, no person can *do* anything to deserve being chosen by God. All people are trapped in sin and cannot free themselves. Because of God's great love, he chose Christ, and those who believe in him belong to him. This choice of God's is called election.

God chose people "in Christ" before the earth was made. It is God's plan that the people he has chosen will become like Jesus Christ.

Where to find it

Moses   *Psalm 106:23*
Israel   *Psalm 105:43; Isaiah 43:10, 20*
Messiah   *Isaiah 42:1*
Those who believe in Jesus   *Mark 13:20, 22, 27; John 6:44; Acts 13:48; Romans 9:23-24; 11:28; Ephesians 1:4-5, 11; Colossians 3:12; 2 Timothy 2:10; 1 Peter 1:1-2*
Jesus   *Luke 9:35; 23:35*
God chose people "in Christ"   *Ephesians 1:4*
What God has planned   *Romans 8:28-30*

ELEMENTS *(EL-uh-ments)*. During New Testament times, people believed the earth was made of four elements: earth, fire, water, and air. Later people thought stars and planets were also elements. Peter tells us that the elements—the heavens and the earth—will be destroyed in God's final judgment.

Where to find it: *2 Peter 3:10, 12*

ELI *(EE-lie)* was both judge and high priest of Israel for 40 years. He lived at Shiloh, near the Tabernacle.

While Eli was priest, Hannah came to the Tabernacle to pray for a son. Eli thought Hannah was drunk because she cried so loud as she prayed. Hannah had a son and named him Samuel. When Samuel was very young, she left him in Eli's care.

Eli had two grown sons, Phinehas and Hophni. They were irresponsible and worthless, but Eli did not correct them. A prophet warned Eli that his two sons would die on the same day.

When Eli was 98 years old, his two evil sons carried the ark of the Covenant out of the Tabernacle and into battle for the Israelites. They thought that would help Israel win. But Israel was defeated, Eli's two sons were killed, and the ark was captured by the Philistines.

When the sad news was brought to Eli, he fell off his seat and died of a broken neck.

Where to find it: *1 Samuel 1:1–4:18*

ELI, ELI, LAMA SABACHTHANI *(AA-lee, AA-lee, LAH-muh, suh-BACH-thuh-nee)* are Hebrew or Aramaic words that Jesus cried from the cross. They mean, "My God, my God, why have you forsaken me?" Jesus was quoting from Psalm 22:1. The people standing near the cross thought Jesus was calling for Elijah and waited to see if Elijah would come. But immediately after Jesus said these words, he died.

Where to find it: *Matthew 27:45-50; Mark 15:33-37*

ELIHU *(ee-LIE-hew)* was the youngest of Job's friends and the last one to speak. His words helped, encouraged, and scolded Job, but did not answer Job's questions about why he was suffering so much.

Where to find it: *Job 32–37*

ELIJAH *(ee-LIE-juh)* was an Old Testament prophet famous for his fiery words and for courageously opposing the pagan worship of wicked Queen Jezebel.

Elijah would appear without warning, wearing his leather loincloth and cloak made of woven goat hair. He would deliver a message from God to Israel's rulers—and then he would disappear again. Kings listened to his words, because they recognized that he was a prophet of God. Elijah lived during the reigns of King Ahab, his son Ahaziah, and his grandson Jehoram.

Elijah's story begins in 1 Kings 17, where he told King Ahab there would be no rain. The Lord cared for Elijah during the drought. First he sent him to the brook Cherith *(KEE-rith)*, where ravens brought food to him. After the

brook dried up, God told Elijah to go to the town of Zarephath. A widow and her only son were preparing a meal with their last grain and oil when Elijah met them. During the time Elijah stayed with them, their supplies of grain and oil never ran out. The woman's son became deathly sick, but after Elijah prayed, the boy was healed.

Meanwhile, King Ahab and his wicked wife, Queen Jezebel, kept on worshiping Baal.

After Elijah's prayer ended the three-year drought,
both he and King Ahab headed for cover.

After three years of drought, Elijah put the prophets of Ahab's pagan gods to a test.

On Mount Carmel, the 450 prophets of Baal built an altar and placed a sacrifice on it. Elijah did the same thing. They all agreed that the true God would send down fire to burn up the sacrifice offered to him. The priests and prophets of Baal prayed, chanted, cut themselves, and cried out for many hours, but no fire came.

Then Elijah's turn came. He shocked the crowd by pouring water over his sacrifice and filling up a trench that was dug around the altar. Then he prayed. The Lord sent a fire so hot it burned up not only the sacrifice but the altar and water as well.

Elijah then prayed for rain to end the three-year drought, and God sent a great rain.

Then Elijah went to Mount Horeb. This is probably the same as Mount Sinai, where God had spoken to Moses, giving him the Ten Commandments. When Elijah came to the mountain, he experienced a great wind, an earthquake, and fire. But after all that, God chose to speak to him in a still, small voice.

Elijah then returned to Israel and anointed Elisha to be a prophet after him.

When King Ahab and Queen Jezebel murdered a man named Naboth so they could steal his vineyard, Elijah told Ahab and his family that God would punish them.

King Ahaziah once sent three captains with 50 men each to capture Elijah. But Elijah prayed, and fire from heaven burned up the first two captains and their men. The third captain begged for his life, and Elijah agreed to go with him.

Elijah never did die. Instead, God took him to heaven in a whirlwind with fiery horses and a chariot.

In the New Testament, Jesus called John the Baptist "Elijah." The prophet Malachi had said God would send Elijah before the Day of the Lord would come. Jesus said that John ful-

Elijah-Elisha

Elijah was born first.

Elisha was bald.

Elijah wore rough camel's-hair clothing.

Elisha wore Elijah's mantle (cape).

Elijah prayed for fire on Mount Carmel.

Elisha raised a dead boy back to life.

Elijah went to heaven in a whirlwind.

Elisha died a natural death.

filled Malachi's prediction because John came "in the spirit and power of Elijah."

Elijah and Moses met with Jesus on the Mount of Transfiguration.

Where to find it

Elijah cared for at brook Cherith   *1 Kings 17: 3-7*
Elijah cared for at Zarephath   *1 Kings 17: 8-16*
Elijah raises the son of the widow   *1 Kings 17: 17-24*
The test on Mount Carmel   *1 Kings 18: 18-40*
Jezebel vows to kill Elijah   *1 Kings 19: 2*
Elijah under the broom tree   *1 Kings 19: 3-8*
Meeting God at Mount Horeb   *1 Kings 19: 9-13*
Elijah anoints Elisha   *1 Kings 19: 16-21*
Ahab murders Naboth   *1 Kings 21*
Three captains try to seize Elijah   *2 Kings 1: 9-16*
Elijah taken to heaven in a whirlwind   *2 Kings 2: 1-12*
Prophecy about Elijah coming before Messiah   *Malachi 4: 5-6*
John the Baptist called Elijah   *Matthew 11: 14*
Elijah meets with Jesus on Mount of Transfiguration   *Matthew 17: 1-3*

ELIM *(EE-lim)* was the second place the Israelites camped after leaving Egypt and crossing the Red Sea. Located west of the Red Sea in the Sinai Peninsula, Elim had 12 springs of water and 70 palm trees.

Where to find it: *Exodus 15: 27*

ELIPHAZ *(EL-ih-faz)* was one of Job's three friends. Eliphaz told Job that his suffering and tragedy came because he had sinned. So he told Job to repent.

However, the Lord said Eliphaz was wrong to accuse Job and wrong for not telling Job what was right about God. Eliphaz was told to prepare a sacrifice and ask Job to pray for him.

Where to find it

Job suffering because of sin   *Job 4–5*
Job should repent   *Job 22*
Eliphaz should ask Job to pray for him   *Job 42: 7-9*

ELISHA *(ee-LIE-shuh)* was an Old Testament prophet to whom God gave power to do many miracles. He was a counselor and adviser to several kings, always delivering the message God had given him.

He was anointed by Elijah, the prophet, to take his place when Elijah went to be with God. Elijah showed this choice by throwing his prophet's mantle over Elisha's shoulders. Elisha became a companion to Elijah until Elijah was taken to heaven in a fiery chariot and a whirlwind. Elisha had asked Elijah for a "double share of your spirit," and Elijah said it would be his if he saw God take him to heaven.

Elisha was a prophet during the reign of four kings of Israel—Jehoram, Jehu, Jehoahaz, and Jehoash. These were some of the miracles that God worked through Elisha:

1. Made a dry path through the Jordan River by striking the water with his mantle (2 Kings 2:13-14)
2. Made the bad waters of a spring turn good (2 Kings 2:19-22)
3. Saved a widow from losing her sons to slavery by making her oil supply keep going until she had enough to pay her debts (2 Kings 4:1-7)
4. Told the Shunammite woman she would have a son even though her husband seemed too old to have children (2 Kings 4:11-17)
5. Restored to life the son of the Shunammite woman (2 Kings 4:18-37)
6. Saved prophets from dying after eating poisonous food (2 Kings 4:38-41)
7. Healed Naaman from leprosy (2 Kings 5:1-27)
8. Made a borrowed iron axhead float (2 Kings 6:1-7)
9. Led the Syrian army, blinded, to Samaria (2 Kings 6:11-23)

Elisha was hardly afraid of the Syrians at Dothan—not with God's fiery army nearby.

He also prophesied some miraculous military victories, such as the defeat of Benhadad's army that had been besieging Samaria. He ordered Jehu to be anointed the next king of Israel, in place of Ahab's descendants.

When Elisha was old and sick, King Jehoash came to visit him. The dying prophet used the little strength he had left to do one final prophetic act. He told Jehoash to shoot an arrow through a window. The king did so, and Elisha assured him it was "the Lord's arrow" that would conquer the Syrians. The prophecy came true, but Elisha did not live to see it.

Elisha was a true spiritual leader. He trained and taught many younger prophets and destroyed the last remains of Baal worship in Israel.

Where to find it: *1 Kings 19:15–21; 2 Kings 2–13*

ELIZABETH *(ee-LIZ-uh-beth)* was the mother of John the Baptist. She was the wife of a priest named Zechariah, and she was a descendant of Aaron. Both she and her husband were faithful, godly people. But Elizabeth could not have any children.

When Zechariah and Elizabeth were too old to have children, an angel of the Lord told Zechariah that Elizabeth would have a son. When Elizabeth was six months pregnant, her cousin Mary, the virgin mother of Jesus, came to visit her. Elizabeth greeted Mary with Spirit-filled words, and Mary rejoiced by singing a song of praise to God.

Elizabeth's son was John the Baptist, who prepared the people of Israel for the coming of the Lord.

Where to find it: *Luke 1:5-57*

ELKANAH *(el-KAY-nuh)* was the father of the prophet Samuel. Elkanah had two wives, Peninnah and Hannah. Peninnah had children but Hannah did not. This made Hannah very sad. She asked God to give her a son. She promised that she would dedicate the son to serve God all his life.

God answered her prayer, and Samuel was born. Elkanah loved Hannah and their son, Samuel, but he agreed with Hannah that the child should be taken to the house of God to serve Eli the priest. Samuel was Eli's helper from the time he was very young.

Where to find it: *1 Samuel 1:1-28; 2:11*

ELYMAS *(EL-uh-mus)* was a Jewish magician and a false prophet. His real name was Bar-Jesus, which means "son of Jesus (or Joshua)." But he was called Elymas because that name is connected with magic.

Paul and Barnabas met Elymas when they came to the town of Paphos on the island of Cyprus. Elymas was with Sergius Paulus, an intelligent Roman officer. Sergius Paulus wanted to hear Paul's message about Jesus, but Elymas tried to prevent it. Paul rebuked Elymas and told him he would be blinded for a time. When Elymas stumbled away, looking for someone to lead him, Sergius Paulus believed Paul's message.

Where to find it: *Acts 13:4-12*

EMBROIDERY *(em-BROY-dur-ee)* and **NEEDLEWORK** were probably something like our fancy needlework. The instructions for the Tabernacle often mention embroidery or needlework on curtains and robes of priests. In Bible times, both men and women were often skilled in this kind of work. Exodus 38:23 mentions one man in particular, Oholiab, who was especially good at needlework.

Where to find it: *Exodus 26:36; 27:16; 28:39; 36:37; 38:18, 22-23*

EMMAUS *(ee-MAY-us)* was a village about seven miles from Jerusalem. Two of Jesus' disciples walked to Emmaus with Christ after his resurrection. They finally recognized him when he broke bread at dinner.

Where to find it: *Luke 24:13-35*

Cleopas and his friend didn't recognize Jesus until they had walked several miles.

EMPEROR *(EM-purr-er)* was the highest Roman ruler. Julius Caesar was the first Roman to call himself emperor. Rulers after him were also called emperors or caesars.

EMPEROR WORSHIP was the reverence and worship of both the dead and living emperors throughout the Roman Empire. Julius Caesar was praised as "a god . . . and the savior of the whole human race." Usually, the living emperor did not claim to be a god. But after his death, the people often called him divine and built temples to him.

Emperor worship was not intended to replace the worship of other gods. On Roman coins both the emperor and a Roman god or goddess were pictured. To burn incense before the statue of an emperor was patriotic as well as religious.

But Christians could not worship the emperor because the names commonly given to emperors—savior, son of god, god, lord—belonged to Jesus Christ alone. Because Christians would not say "Caesar is Lord," they sometimes suffered terrible persecution and death.

ENCAMPMENT (see *Camp*)

ENCHANTER *(en-CHANT-ur)* was a person who used or tried to use supernatural power to make things happen or to know what was going to happen. This is related to what we call the occult. The Bible says trying to do such things is very wrong.

Where to find it: *Leviticus 19:26; Deuteronomy 18:10-12; Daniel 2:10*

ENDOR *(EN-door)*, **WITCH OF,** lived in the town of Endor during the reign of King Saul. She was a sorceress or medium who said she could call up dead men's spirits to tell future events.

God had told the Israelites in Deuteronomy 18:10-14 and Exodus 22:18 that they should not go to mediums. Isaiah 8:19 says, "When they say to you, 'Consult the mediums . . .' should not a people consult their God? Should they consult the dead on behalf of the living?" Mediums got their information from Satan.

But when the Philistines started a war

against the Israelites, King Saul went to the medium of Endor and asked her to bring Samuel's spirit back from the dead, even though Saul had once ordered all mediums to leave the country. The medium of Endor said she saw an old man in a robe. This old man, actually a spirit, told Saul he and his sons would die the next day, and they did.

1 Chronicles 10: 13-14 says Saul died for his unfaithfulness, because he asked for guidance from a medium and not from the Lord.

Where to find it: *1 Samuel 28: 3-25*

ENDURANCE *(en-DUR-unce)* means patience or the ability to keep doing the right thing. Jesus said Christians need endurance especially when we're hurt, or people treat us badly, or try to make us do something we know is wrong.

Where to find it: *Mark 13: 13; Romans 5: 3-4; Hebrews 10: 36*

ENEMY *(EN-uh-me)* is one who hates somebody else and tries to hurt him. An enemy can be a person or a nation. Jesus said that people who belonged to him were to love their enemies.

Where to find it: *Matthew 5: 43-46; Romans 12: 14-21*

ENGEDI *(en-GHEE-dye)* is an oasis west of the Dead Sea where there is a natural spring of water. Its rich soil produces flowers and vineyards. David hid from Saul at Engedi.

Where to find it: *1 Samuel 24: 1*

ENGRAVING *(en-GRAVE-ing)* is the work of carving designs or words on gold, silver, brass, stones, or wood. Signet rings, breastplates, and tablets were often engraved. Two craftsmen, Bezalel and Oholiab, engraved the furnishings for the Tabernacle and taught others their skills.

Where to find it: *Exodus 28: 9-21; 31: 1-6; 35: 30-35*

ENOCH *(EE-nuk)* was one of the two persons in the Bible who never died. Instead, the Bible says, "God took him." (The other person who did not die was Elijah the prophet, who was taken to heaven in a whirlwind and chariot.)

Enoch was born seven generations after Adam. When he was 65 years old, his son Methusaleh was born. Methusaleh lived to be the oldest man in the Bible.

The Bible says that Enoch "walked with God" and that his faith pleased God. Enoch lived to be 365 years old, and then God took him to heaven.

Where to find it: *Genesis 5: 18-24; Hebrews 11: 5*

ENROLLMENT *(en-ROLL-ment)* means making a list of all the people in a country. The list had information about each person's family, position, and tribe.

In Bible times, enrollments were made to keep official records straight. The records were used to call soldiers for an army and to check taxes and tax records.

The Romans ordered an enrollment at the time of Jesus' birth. That is why Mary and Joseph had to make the trip from Nazareth to Bethlehem, where Jesus was born.

Where to find it: *1 Chronicles 7: 7-9; Luke 2: 2*

ENVY means jealousy that usually is based on rivalry and unkind feelings. The Bible says envy is a sin. In the New Testament the chief priests wanted to destroy Jesus because they envied him. They saw that he was more popular with many people than they were. The New Testament tells Christians not to envy each other.

Where to find it: *Matthew 27: 17-18; Mark 15: 6-10; Galatians 5: 19-26; 1 Peter 2: 1*

EPAPHRAS *(EP-uh-fruss)* helped the Christians at Colosse, Laodicea, and Hierapolis. Paul called Epaphras his "beloved fellow servant." Epaphras visited Paul in prison and encouraged him with a report of the Colossians' love. Epaphras prayed earnestly for his Christian friends.

Where to find it: *Colossians 1: 7-8; 4: 12-13*

EPAPHRODITUS *(ee-PAF-ro-DIE-tus)* was a messenger between the church at Philippi and the apostle Paul. The church at Philippi sent Epaphroditus with gifts for Paul, who was in prison in Rome. Paul appreciated the gifts and was cheered up by Epaphroditus.

Epaphroditus got sick and almost died while he was with Paul. When he got well, Paul sent him back to the church with the letter to the Philippians that is now a part of our New Testament.

EPHAH

Paul thanked the believers in Philippi for the gifts they had sent and told them to welcome Epaphroditus back with honor because he had risked his life while serving Christ. Paul called him "my brother and fellow worker and fellow soldier."

Where to find it: *Philippians 2: 25-30; 4: 18*

EPHAH (see *Measure*)

EPHESIANS *(ee-FEE-shunz)* is a New Testament letter that Paul wrote, probably when he was a prisoner in Rome around A.D. 59-61. Biblical scholars believe the letter was sent to more churches than just the one at Ephesus. It probably went to many small churches in the province of Asia, an area in what is now known as Turkey.

Paul's friend Tychicus took the letter and personal news about Paul to the churches. Tychicus delivered the letters we call Colossians and Philemon at the same time.

The letter to the Ephesians has two sections. In the first part, Paul talks about God's plan to bring all creation together in Christ. Paul tells how God chose his people, forgave their sins, and gave them the Holy Spirit. Paul also points out how Christ and his Church are a part of each other.

In the second part, Paul urges Christians to show that they love each other in their daily lives. In this way, the Church would help bring about God's plan of unity.

Paul uses many pictures to show how the Church is related to Christ. All Christians are like a body and Jesus is the head. Or Christians together are like a building and Jesus is the important cornerstone. Or again, Christians are like a wife and Jesus is the husband.

Where to find it

Christ and the Church   *Ephesians 1: 3–3: 21*
The new life in Christ   *Ephesians 4: 1–6: 20*

When the Christians at Ephesus understood God's truth, they burned their occult books and scrolls.

EPHESUS *(EF-uh-sus)* was the capital city of the Roman province called Asia (now a part of Turkey). It was an important, old, beautiful city during the time of the New Testament.

In Ephesus was an enormous white temple dedicated to the goddess Diana (whose Greek name was Artemis). It was known as one of the seven wonders of the ancient world. In the center of the temple was a sacred stone, perhaps a meteorite, that had fallen from the sky. People said it looked like the goddess. Diana was the goddess of fertility. The myths said she was the mother who nursed the gods, people, animals, and plants. Her images were ugly statues of a creature with many breasts. Worship in her temple included immoral sexual acts. Many merchants in Ephesus made their living by selling silver statues of the ugly goddess.

Paul stayed in Ephesus for nearly three years on his second missionary journey and helped many people become Christians. The merchants were afraid people would stop buying the idols they made, and so they started a riot. In spite of this, a strong church was established at Ephesus.

Where to find it: *Acts 18: 19, 24–19: 40*

EPHOD *(EE-fod)* was sacred clothing worn by the Jewish high priest. It was beautifully made

110

with many colors of materials, woven gold, and precious stones. Others who served in the Temple wore simple linen ephods.

Gideon and Micah turned the beautiful ephods into idols.

Where to find it

Beautifully made   *Exodus 28: 5-35*
Some are simple   *1 Samuel 2: 18; 2 Samuel 6: 14*
Gideon and Micah misuse them   *Judges 8: 27; 17: 5*

EPHRAIM *(EE-free-um)* was the younger son of Joseph. His mother, Asenath, was an Egyptian. When Ephraim's grandfather, Jacob, was old, he adopted both boys as his own sons. Jacob blessed them, but gave Ephraim the firstborn's rights, even though Joseph disapproved. Ephraim's descendants became one of the 12 tribes of Israel.

After the country was divided into the Northern Kingdom and the Southern Kingdom, the northern part was sometimes called Ephraim because it was the strongest tribe. (The southern part was known as Judah because it was the strongest southern tribe.)

Where to find it

Birth of Ephraim   *Genesis 41: 50-52*
Blessing of Ephraim   *Genesis 48: 8-20*
Northern Kingdom (Israel) called Ephraim   *Isaiah 7: 2, 5, 9; Hosea 9: 3-16*

EPICUREANS *(eh-pih-cure-REE-unz)* believed in the teachings of Epicurus, a Greek philosopher who lived in 341-270 B.C. He taught that a person's highest goal in life was to have pleasure, but without hurting anyone else. Christians know, however, that seeking pleasure can blot out their interest in God or other people. Paul spoke to some Epicureans in Athens.

Where to find it: *Acts 17: 16-34*

EPILEPSY (see *Diseases*)

EPISTLE *(ee-PIS-ul)* is a letter. Examples of epistles in the Old Testament include: David's letter to Joab in 2 Samuel 11: 14-15; Queen Jezebel's letter in 1 Kings 21: 8-9; and Sennacherib's letter to Hezekiah in 2 Kings 19: 14.

However, the word *epistle* usually refers to the 21 letters in the New Testament. These epistles were written by Peter, Paul, James, John, Jude, and the author of Hebrews. Paul wrote 13 letters.

Some letters were written to one church, others to several churches, still others to individuals or to all Christians. Many of the letters were written to help deal with specific problems, encourage the Christians, teach them, or correct false ideas.

An epistle usually began with the name or title of the author and the name of the people who were going to get the letter. Words of greeting came next, then the main message. The letter usually closed with the author's name.

The apostles probably wrote other letters that were lost or destroyed. 1 Corinthians 5: 9 refers to a letter written to Corinth before 1 Corinthians. In Colossians 4: 16, Paul mentioned an epistle written to the Laodicean church. Neither of these is in our New Testament.

ESAU *(EE-saw)* was the firstborn son of Isaac and Rebekah. His brother, Jacob, was his twin. Before their birth, God told Rebekah that the elder would serve the younger. This was the opposite of the custom of that time—usually the older person had more authority. The elder son always received a birthright, which was a special blessing and double inheritance from his father.

Esau loved hunting in the fields, but he seemed to care nothing for God or his blessings. Once when he was hungry, he sold his birthright to Jacob for a bowl of bean soup.

Esau had been hunting all day and was starving when Jacob talked him into trading his birthright for some soup.

When he was 40 years old, Esau married two Hittite women. These women made life bitter for Isaac and Rebekah.

When the time came for Isaac to bless his sons, Jacob tricked his father into giving him the blessing that belonged to the oldest son. Esau was angry and begged his father to bless him too. But Isaac's blessing had already said Esau would serve his brother. Esau planned to murder Jacob for this, but Jacob escaped.

Years later, when Esau was living at Mount Seir, he heard that Jacob was returning. Jacob sent a large gift of cattle and sheep to Esau because he was afraid. Esau took 400 men with him when he went to meet Jacob. But when he saw him, Esau ran to his brother and kissed him.

Hebrews 12:16-17 warns against being careless about God as Esau was.

Paul used the story of Esau and Jacob to show how God carries out his plans.

Where to find it

Esau's birth   *Genesis 25:21-25*
Esau sells his birthright   *Genesis 25:27-34*
Esau's two wives   *Genesis 26:34-35*
Esau's blessing   *Genesis 27:1-45*
Esau meets Jacob   *Genesis 33:1-9*
Esau as an example   *Romans 9:10-13*

ESCHATOLOGY *(ES-kuh-TAHL-uh-jee)* refers to teachings about what will happen in the future—especially the Second Coming of Christ, the judgment of God, and the future of the universe. These events are part of what the Bible sometimes calls the last days or the end of time.

ESSENES *(es-EENZ)* was the name of a group of Jews who lived in Palestine during the life of Christ. Most of them lived together in settlements away from the large cities. They shared all they owned with each other and followed the Jewish Law very strictly. They studied the Old Testament carefully.

In 1947 some Arabs discovered many old scrolls in the remains of a settlement near the Dead Sea. These became known as the Dead Sea Scrolls. Bible scholars have learned a lot about the Scripture and how people lived in

Jesus' time by reading these scrolls. The settlement where the scrolls were found was probably where a group of Essenes had lived.

Many of the Essenes died in the wars against the Romans from A.D. 66 to 73. The Essenes are not mentioned in the Bible.

ESTHER *(ES-ter)* was a Jewish orphan girl who became the queen of Persia about 475 B.C. Her story is told in the Old Testament Book of Esther.

Ahasuerus, who was then king of Persia, became very angry with his queen, Vashti, because she would not appear with him at a drunken feast. He divorced her and looked for a beautiful new queen. He chose young Esther out of many candidates.

Esther had been brought up by her cousin Mordecai, who told her not to tell anyone that she was Jewish. Mordecai kept in touch with Esther after she became queen. One day Mordecai heard of a plot against the king's life. He told Esther, and she told the king, so she saved his life.

Ahasuerus's chief assistant was Haman, who was very proud. He wanted everyone to bow before him. When Mordecai refused, Haman became very angry and looked for a way to get revenge. He got the king to sign a decree that all the Jews were to be killed. The king signed, not knowing that Esther was Jewish. But Haman was so angry at Mordecai that he couldn't wait for the general killing. He had a gallows built just to hang Mordecai.

Mordecai sent word to Esther about the new law that Jews were to be killed. At the risk of her life, Esther told the king that she was among those who would die because of his new law. He was so angry at Haman that he ordered him hanged on the gallows that had been built for Mordecai. He then made Mordecai his chief assistant in place of Haman. He could not change the law he had made, but he gave permission for the Jews to protect themselves.

Jews today still celebrate the Feast of Purim to remember how God delivered Esther and the Jews at this time. (See *Feast of Purim.*)

ETERNAL *(ee-TUR-nul)* **LIFE** means more than life that does not end. It means life under God's saving rule. It comes from God through Jesus Christ. It begins when we accept Jesus Christ as Savior and seek to do the things that please him instead of the things that please ourselves. The eternal life of the Christian keeps on growing through all of life on earth and into future life with God in his eternal kingdom. We share in the eternal life of Jesus Christ, God's Son, who died and rose again for us.

Where to find it: *John 3: 36; 10: 28; 17: 2-3*

ETERNITY *(ee-TUR-ni-tee)* means all that is past and all that is yet to come. It means time that didn't have a beginning and will not end. Psalm 90 is a beautiful poem showing God is eternal—he has neither beginning nor end.

ETHIOPIA *(ee-thee-OH-pee-uh)* is a country whose history stretches back to before Moses' time. It was south of Egypt along the Red Sea. In Old Testament times it included much of today's Sudan as well as modern Ethiopia. The Hebrews called Ethiopia "Cush" and its peoples "Cushites." Cush was the grandson of Noah, and his descendants formed Ethiopia. Moses married an Ethiopian woman.

In the days of King Hezekiah, the Ethiopian king, Tirhakah, attempted to conquer Judah, but failed. In New Testament times, Ethiopia was ruled by Queen Candace.

Where to find it

Cush, grandson of Noah   *Genesis 10: 6-10*
Moses marries Ethiopian   *Numbers 12: 1*
Ethiopia attempts to conquer Judah   *2 Kings 19: 9*
Queen Candace   *Acts 8: 27*

The tomb of Queen Esther as it appears today.

ETHIOPIAN EUNUCH *(ee-thee-OH-pee-un YOU-nuk)* was a treasurer for Candace, queen of Ethiopia. He was a Gentile who had become interested in the Jewish religion. One time, after he had gone to Jerusalem to worship, he was riding back to Ethiopia in his chariot, reading aloud in Isaiah 53. Philip, who was sent by the Holy Spirit, came alongside the chariot and asked if he understood what he was reading. Philip explained that Isaiah 53: 7-8 was a

prophecy about Jesus the Messiah. The eunuch believed in Christ, was baptized in water near the road, and went home rejoicing.

Where to find it: *Acts 8: 26-40*

EUCHARIST *(YOU-kuh-rist)* means "thanksgiving." This word has been used by the Christian church for the rite of the Lord's Supper (see *Lord's Supper*).

EUNICE *(YOU-niss)* was the mother of Timothy. She and her mother, Lois, taught Timothy the Old Testament Scriptures. They lived in Lystra, where they were probably converted through Paul. Eunice was Jewish, but her husband was Gentile.

Where to find it

Eunice's mother and son   *2 Timothy 1: 5*
Raised Timothy on Scriptures   *2 Timothy 3: 15*
Lived in Lystra   *Acts 16: 1*

EUNUCHS *(YOU-nuks)* were men who could not have sexual relations because their sexual organs were damaged or defective. These men were often put in charge of a king's

harem, as in Esther 2: 14. Sometimes the title *eunuch* meant a royal officer. These officers were not necessarily physically handicapped.

In Deuteronomy 23: 1 the Law of Moses says that a physically handicapped eunuch could not enter the religious congregation. Isaiah 56: 3-5 promises that the eunuch who loves and honors God will receive a blessing better than sons and daughters.

Jesus spoke of men making themselves eunuchs in Matthew 19: 12. These men remained unmarried so they could give more time and energy to God's work. It did not mean their sexual organs were damaged or defective.

EUODIA and **SYNTYCHE** *(you-OH-dee-uh and SIN-ti-key)* were two Christian women who worked hard with Paul in spreading the gospel. Euodia and Syntyche must have had some disagreement, because Paul urged them to agree in the Lord.

Where to find it: *Philippians 4: 2-3*

EUPHRATES *(you-FRAY-teez)* **RIVER** is an important river that runs 1,780 miles from Turkey through Syria and Iraq to the Persian Gulf. The Garden of Eden was somewhere near the Euphrates and Tigris rivers.

It was the largest river known to the Hebrews and is often mentioned in the Old Testament simply as "the river" or "the great river."

Where to find it: *Genesis 2: 10-12; Deuteronomy 1: 7; Isaiah 8: 7*

EUTYCHUS *(YOU-tih-kus)* was a young man who fell asleep during a sermon of Paul's. He was leaning against the frame of an open window, and when he went to sleep, he fell out the window and died. Paul went downstairs, threw his arms around him, and brought him back to life. The name *Eutychus* means "lucky" or "fortunate."

Where to find it: *Acts 20: 7-12*

EVANGELIST *(ee-VAN-juh-list)* is a person who announces the good news about Jesus, often to people who have never heard or understood it before. An evangelist may go from city to city, spreading God's message. Ephesians 4: 11 says that an evangelist's work is a gift from the Holy Spirit. Acts 21:8 and 2 Timothy 4:5 show that Philip and Timothy were evangelists.

EVE was the first woman. Her name means "life," and her husband, Adam, called her Eve because she was the mother of all people.

God made Eve from one of Adam's ribs. She was to be his closest companion. When Adam first saw her, he said with wonder, "This at last is bone of my bones and flesh of my flesh." The Bible says that the relationship between a husband and wife is meant to be even closer than the relationship between parents and children.

Adam and Eve lived in the Garden of Eden. They could walk and talk with God face to face. But Satan, appearing as a serpent, talked Eve into thinking God was keeping something good from them. She ate the one fruit God had told them never to eat, and she gave some to Adam. Their disobedience to God was the Fall of mankind. From that day on, their relationship with God, with each other, and with nature were all spoiled by sin.

Yet God promised that one day someone would be born from a woman who would have victory over Satan. He would bridge the gap between God and people. Christians know this person is Jesus Christ.

Eve was the mother of Cain, Abel, Seth, and many other children.

In 2 Corinthians 11:3, Paul warned Christians about being deceived by Satan, as Eve was.

Where to find it: *Genesis 2:15–4:2; 4:25–5:4*

EVENING SACRIFICE (see *Offerings*)

EVERLASTING LIFE (see *Eternal Life*)

EVIL is anything that is against the will of God. Evil causes moral or physical damage to ourselves or to other people. It also hurts our relationships with other people and with God. Evil damages everything God created.

Evil began in the world when Adam and Eve disobeyed God. Sometimes in the Bible, evil is called "the works of the flesh." These include bad thoughts, immoral actions, hatred, fighting, loving something more than God, trying to have supernatural power or knowl-

edge, wanting everything, complaining, dividing up into little groups, and getting drunk or taking drugs.

God did not create evil, but he permits it to exist in a world that is rebelling against God and going its own way. He created people so that they could choose for themselves whether to do evil or good. One day God will create a new heaven and a new earth, and evil will not exist.

Where to find it: *Romans 1:18-32; Galatians 5:19-21; Revelation 21:1-5*

EVIL ONE (see *Satan*)

EVIL SPIRIT (see *Demon*)

EXCELLENT means "the best" or "worthy of praise." The words *most excellent* were often used when speaking or writing to a high official. Acts 23:26 (KJV) quotes Paul's letter "unto the most excellent governor Felix."

In Romans 2:18 and Philippians 1:10, Paul urges his readers to "approve what is excellent," or choose the things that really matter.

Hebrews 1:4 speaks of Jesus as having obtained a more excellent name or reputation than the angels.

EXCOMMUNICATION *(ex-kum-MUNE-ih-KAY-shun)* is one way a religious group can punish one of its members. The group (or church) says the guilty member can no longer belong.

Christian believers were excommunicated, or banned, from Jewish synagogues just as Jesus said they would be in Luke 6:22: "Blessed are you when men hate you . . . exclude you . . . cast out your name as evil, on account of the Son of man!"

Jesus told his disciples how to treat a Christian brother or sister who rejected the truth or committed sin and wouldn't repent. Christian punishment is meant for the good of the sinner, so he or she will return to Christ and the church. If the sinner repents, the church should forgive freely, comfort, and love their former church member.

Where to find it

Jesus' teaching *Matthew 18:15-18*
Punishment is for the Christian's good *1 Corinthians 5:5*

The Jews never thought they would be forced to leave their country–but they were.

Church needs to forgive those who repent *2 Corinthians 2: 6-11*

EXHORTATION *(EX-or-TAY-shun)* means serious urging, encouragement, or comfort.

Where to find it: *Acts 13: 15; Romans 12: 8; Hebrews 13: 22*

EXILE means someone makes people leave their own country and live somewhere else. A country that had defeated another country in war would often make the leaders and most of the young people who could become leaders move to the country of the conqueror. The poor, the old, and those who were sick could stay in their own land, because they would not be able to stir up a revolution against the conqueror. Then the victorious nation would send some of its own loyal people to settle in the defeated land.

This is what happened to both the Northern Kingdom (Israel) and the Southern Kingdom (Judah). The Northern Kingdom was defeated by Assyria in 722 B.C. Many of its people were forced to move to Assyria. Only a few ever came back. The Southern Kingdom (Judah) was defeated by Babylon. Its leaders were exiled to Babylon. Their capital city and the beautiful Temple were finally destroyed by the army of Nebuchadnezzar in 586 B.C.

The term *The Exile* usually refers to the 70-year period when many of the people of Judah were forced to live in Babylon.

The people were not prisoners. They were free to build homes, start businesses, or work at their trade. But they could not go back to their own land. And that made them very sad, because God had told the Hebrew people that Palestine was the Promised Land that he had given them. The Book of Lamentations is a group of five poems Jeremiah wrote to show how he felt about the terrible destruction that had come to the land and why God had permitted this to happen.

While in Babylon, the Jews gathered in small groups to pray and study the Law of Moses. Many scholars believe these small groups were the beginning of Jewish synagogues.

After King Nebuchadnezzar of Babylon died, his country was conquered by the Persians in 539 B.C. The king of the Persians, Cyrus, allowed Jewish people to go back to their own land if they wanted to. Many of them did, and they rebuilt the Temple and the city of Jerusalem. The books of Ezra and Nehemiah tell about the rebuilding.

EXODUS, BOOK OF, is an Old Testament book written by Moses. It tells about the Hebrews going out of Egypt toward their Promised Land.

The first 12 chapters of Exodus tell how the Hebrews had to live as slaves. Many years after Joseph died, the Egyptian rulers became afraid of the Hebrews because there were so many of them in Egypt. They made all the Hebrews slaves. Later, God chose Moses to lead his people out of Egypt (see *Moses*). God had to send ten plagues on Pharaoh and the Egyptians before they were willing to let the Hebrews leave Egypt.

A large number of people took their flocks and household equipment and left Egypt with Moses and Aaron. Chapters 13 to 19 tell how God worked many miracles to keep them alive as they traveled across the wilderness. God destroyed Pharaoh's army in the sea; God fed the Israelites with manna and quail as they traveled southeast from Egypt to Mount Sinai. The rest of the Bible often talks about this deliverance out of Egypt.

Chapters 19 to 40 tell how God gave the Ten Commandments and other instructions to Moses on Mount Sinai. These instructions helped the Israelites live in the wilderness for 40 years. Even more important, God's words helped them realize what it meant to be his people.

Exodus includes God's instructions for building the Tabernacle and his instructions to the priests who would help the people worship God. God told Moses to tell the people why there has to be sacrifice for sin and why they should obey all his commands.

This book tells how God worked through his servant Moses to change a group of fearful, depressed slaves into a great, powerful nation.

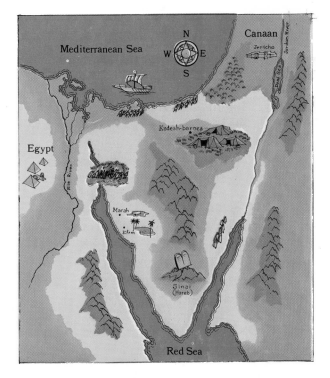

EXODUS ROUTE is unclear because although many places where the Israelites went are named, most of these places are unknown.

Exodus 12:37 says the Israelites left from Rameses in Egypt and went to Succoth. Archaeologists believe that Succoth was about 32 miles southwest of Rameses. Exodus 13:17 says, "God did not lead them by way of the land of the Philistines, although that was near," because the people would be so frightened they would turn around and go back to Egypt. The land of the Philistines was along the coast of the Mediterranean Sea and would have been the closest route to Canaan.

Exodus 13:20 says, "And they moved on from Succoth, and encamped at Etham, on the edge of the wilderness." The location of Etham is not certain.

Most scholars believe that the sea through which God miraculously brought the Israelites was the Reed Sea rather than the Red Sea. The Hebrew word actually means "reed." All we know about the location of the Reed Sea is that it was a boundary between Egypt and the Sinai wilderness. When the Suez Canal was built in the 1860s, the lakes in the area were changed, so the exact location can never be known.

After they crossed the sea, the Hebrews went into the wilderness of Shur and came to a place called Marah. Many scholars think this was an oasis in the Sinai desert about halfway down the coast. Then they camped at Mount Sinai, in the southern part of the peninsula, for about a year. God gave Moses the Ten Commandments and the rest of the Law on Mount Sinai. The places listed between Mount Sinai and Kadesh-barnea (where the Israelites wandered for nearly 40 years) are not known, although we do know where Kadesh-barnea was.

When the Israelites were ready to begin their war against Canaan, Moses led them by a long route to Ezion-Geber and then north toward the Dead Sea. Maps of the route are only approximate, since most of the places cannot be identified.

EXPIATION (EX-pee-AY-shun) means to cover over or to remove sin or sins. The New Testament teaches that Christ is the expiation for our sins; he covers over or removes them (see *Atonement*).

Where to find it: *Romans 3: 25; Hebrews 2: 17; 1 John 2: 2; 4: 10 (all from RSV)*

EYE was highly valued in Bible times as it is in our day. Exodus 21: 26 says a slave had to be set free if his owner blinded him. 2 Kings 25: 7 tells how prisoners were blinded by cruel heathen nations.

Eye is also a word picture of spiritual understanding. Psalm 19: 8 says the Word of God enlightens the eye.

EZEKIEL (ee-ZEE-kee-ul) was a Jewish prophet who lived in Babylon when many of the people of Judah were in exile there. He wrote one of the important prophetic books of the Old Testament. He foretold that the Jews would return to Jerusalem and rebuild the Temple. His prophecies emphasized that people are free to choose their own way and that they are responsible to God for what they choose.

Ezekiel was a priest as well as a prophet. He was forced to move from Jerusalem to Babylon in 597 B.C. The army of King Nebuchadnezzar captured the city and took many of the furnishings of the Temple. Nebuchadnezzar forced thousands of priests, scribes, and skilled workers to move to Babylon, about 900

miles away. This was the usual way conquerors in ancient times treated defeated countries (see *Exile*). In 586 B.C., when the city of Jerusalem was destroyed, more people were forced to move to Babylon.

Ezekiel built a house for himself and his wife in Babylon. He also continued to be a spiritual leader. He taught the people how to practice their Jewish religion even though they had no Temple in which to worship. He encouraged them to gather together to pray and study the Scriptures. Many scholars believe this was how Jewish synagogues became the place of worship instead of the Temple. Jews today still worship in synagogues.

When Ezekiel had been living in Babylon five years, God called him to be a prophet. He was walking in the country when a violent thunderstorm came. He had a vision of four strange living creatures, wheels of a heavenly chariot, and a vision of God on a throne. In that vision God commanded him to give a message to his people. It was the first of many visions that Ezekiel received. They are recorded in the Old Testament Book of Ezekiel.

Ezekiel was often told to help people remember his prophecies by acting out the message. Before Jerusalem was finally destroyed in 586 B.C., he foretold its fate by making a brick model of Jerusalem with armed soldiers around it. He lay down beside it and did not eat or drink much so that he could show the misery and hard times that were coming to Jerusalem.

He taught the people that God was with them in Babylonia just as much as he had been with them in Judah. Ezekiel said they must obey God wherever they were.

After the final destruction of Jerusalem, Ezekiel was able to encourage his people by prophesying that Jerusalem and the Temple would be restored. These prophecies began to be fulfilled about 50 years later, in 538 B.C., during the time of Ezra and Nehemiah. Ezekiel had no more prophetic visions for about 13 years. Later in his life, God showed him in visions that Israel and Judah would again be united and governed by a Messiah who would be a descendant of King David.

Ezekiel died in Babylonia without ever returning to his own land or seeing Jerusalem restored. He gave encouragement and

*When Ezra read
God's Law to the people,
it was news to many of them.*

spiritual help to his people in exile. He helped them keep on believing in God and looking forward to the day when they could return to their own land.

Where to find it

A priest in Babylonia   *Ezekiel 1:1-3*
First vision and call   *Ezekiel 1: 4–3: 15*
Dramatizes siege of Jerusalem   *Ezekiel 4*
Prophesies a restored kingdom   *Ezekiel 37: 24-28*
Emphasizes responsibility   *Ezekiel 18: 30-32*

EZRA *(EZ-ruh)* was a priest, scribe, and scholar who helped his people start worshiping God again. He probably wrote the Old Testament book called Ezra and might have also written Nehemiah and 1 and 2 Chronicles.

Ezra himself had been in exile in Babylonia. Many Jews like him had been forced to move to Babylonia after Nebuchadnezzar conquered Judah in 586 B.C. However, Babylonia was conquered by Persia in 539 B.C. The new Persian rulers told the Jews they were free to return to their own land. Many people did not want to go back. They had homes and businesses in their new land, and they were free to practice their own religion.

They studied the Old Testament in small groups in their own villages. The scribes among the exiles were men like Ezra who knew how to read and write Hebrew. They were kept busy making copies by hand of the Old Testament so these groups could use them.

But Ezra was also an adviser to the king of Persia about the Jews and their religion. He asked the king for permission to return to Judah so he could teach the Law of God there. The king approved and also gave him authority to appoint judges to enforce the Jewish laws.

Ezra took with him about 5,000 other Jews who decided to go back to their homeland. He found that many of the people who lived in Judah had wandered away from God and were not keeping God's commands. He wept in sorrow.

Ezra began offering sacrifices to the Lord at the Temple. He gathered the people of the land together and read the Law of Moses to them. The people listened. When they heard God's Word and realized how they were sinning against God, they cried.

Ezra also taught the people to celebrate the festivals of the Old Testament. On the eighth day of the Feast of Booths, Ezra led the people in a prayer of confession of sin. The people all agreed to renew their Covenant with God to keep his laws.

Ezra found that many of the men in Judah had married women who were not Jewish and who practiced pagan religions. The people agreed to obey the Law of Moses and no longer live with their foreign wives.

Ezra tried to arrange for each group of ten families to have their own copy of the Old Testament teachings to study. As they read God's Word for themselves, their faith was strengthened, and the Jewish people never again worshiped idols like the people in surrounding countries (see also *Exile* and *Nehemiah*).

Where to find it

King permits exiles to go to Judah   *Ezra 1*
Ezra goes to Judah   *Ezra 7–8*
Ezra confesses sins of the people   *Ezra 9: 7-15*
People put away foreign wives   *Ezra 10: 9-17*

FABLE is a story in which animals, plants, and objects talk and act as if they are people. Fables are sometimes funny, but they also teach a serious lesson. The Old Testament contains two well-known fables: Jotham's story about the "King Tree," and Jehoash's fable about the thorn bush.

In the New Testament the words *fable* or *myth* refer to stories that are not true. Christians were warned not to pay attention to these fables. The Bible states clearly that the apostles' reports of Jesus' life were not fables or myths.

Where to find it

Jotham's story *Judges 9: 7-15*
Jehoash's fable *2 Kings 14: 9*
Don't pay attention to untrue stories *1 Timothy 4: 7*
Jesus' life not a fable *2 Peter 1: 16*

FACE OF THE WATERS means the surface or top of the lakes or oceans. This expression is

Feasts in ancient times were major events that sometimes went on for hours.

121

found in Genesis 1: 2 where it says that "the Spirit of God was moving over the face of the waters."

FACE OF GOD means the presence of God. The name of God was so holy to the Jewish people that they sometimes used expressions like this instead of God's name. We find "the face of God" first in Genesis when Cain said, ". . . from thy face I shall be hidden" after he killed Abel. Jesus said that angels ". . . behold the face of my Father who is in heaven."

Where to find it: *Genesis 4:14; Psalm 27:8; Matthew 18:10; 2 Thessalonians 1:9*

FAITH has two meanings in the Bible: one meaning is trusting or believing; in other cases, when the Bible speaks of *"the* faith," it means the gospel of Christ—the message of Christianity.

1. Faith is the act of trusting or believing. Often a child has faith in his parents because he knows they love him and care for him. The Bible says people should place their trust—their faith—in God because he loves them very much.

In the Old Testament, the word *faith* does not appear often. But the Old Testament has many examples of faith. Abraham is the most famous. Genesis 15: 6 says that Abraham "believed the Lord; and he reckoned [counted] it to him as righteousness."

Abraham obeyed God because he had faith. Abraham had a close relationship with God because of his faith.

Hebrews 11 in the New Testament lists many other Old Testament examples of faith: Abel, Enoch, Noah, Joseph, Moses, and others. All of these people believed God. They had faith that God would care for them in every situation. They had experienced God's care. In the New Testament the words *faith* and *believe* (a word that means almost the same thing) are found more than 500 times.

Jesus said that faith is powerful and valuable. Only through faith in Jesus can we know God.

The writings of Paul in the New Testament explain what faith is and why we need it. Paul said God had fulfilled his promises by sending Jesus to die for our sins. "You have been saved through faith," Paul wrote to the Ephe-

sians. We cannot earn our relationship with God. It comes only through trusting who Jesus is and what he did. In Romans 4 Paul says that Abraham is "the father of us all [who believe]" because Abraham had faith in God. Like Abraham, we can trust God because he has shown his love and power to many people over many centuries.

But faith is not just believing certain facts about God. Paul also said that faith is obeying God's commands.

The Letter of James in the New Testament explains that faith is seen in what we do. When we trust God, we show our faith by obeying God. True faith is seen in how we act. If a person has faith in God but doesn't help others, his faith is dead, said James.

Hebrews 11: 6 says that without faith it is impossible to please God. And in Galatians 2: 20 Paul writes that Christians live by faith.

2. *The faith* sometimes means the whole message of the Christian gospel—the truth of Christ's coming to live and die for our sins so we can have a new relationship with God.

Where to find it

Old Testament faith *Psalm 119: 66; Jeremiah 17: 7*
New Testament faith *Ephesians 2: 8-10; Hebrews 11*
The faith *Colossians 1: 23; 2 Timothy 4: 7*

FALL refers to Adam and Eve's first sin in the Garden of Eden. God had told Adam and Eve—the first people—that they could eat from any tree in the garden except from "the tree of the knowledge of good and evil." But the serpent (Satan) tempted Eve, and she ate fruit from that tree. She gave some fruit to Adam and he also ate. Their disobedience caused the Fall.

The Fall describes what happened to Adam and Eve when they sinned. They "fell" out of their good relationship with God. Before they disobeyed God, Adam and Eve had been very close friends with God. After they sinned they felt guilty and hid from God. Their relationship with him was spoiled by sin. They even had to leave the Garden of Eden.

The Bible teaches that just as Adam and Eve "fell," so all people have "fallen." "All have sinned and fall short of the glory of God," says Romans 3: 23. Sin came into the world when Adam and Eve sinned, and ever since then sin has affected all people.

The Bible teaches that the remedy for our spoiled relationship with God is in Jesus Christ. He died for our sins so we can have a new relationship with God.

Where to find it: *Genesis 3; Romans 5*

FALLOW GROUND is farmland that is left unplanted during the growing season. The Jewish farmers let some of their land "lie fallow" each year so the soil would be built up. Jewish law required that farmland should be rested every seventh year, but that law was often ignored.

Where to find it: *Leviticus 26: 34-35; Jeremiah 4: 3; Hosea 10: 12*

FALSE APOSTLES *(falss uh-PAH-suls)* were a group of people mentioned in 2 Corinthians 11:13 who came to the church in Corinth claiming they were "ministers of Christ." But their real purpose was to turn the Corinthians against Paul. Paul said these false apostles "preach another Jesus . . . a different gospel" than the true one. It is not exactly clear who these people were or where they came from, but it is clear that they were hurting the young church.

FALSE CHRISTS are people who Jesus said would appear before he comes again. Jesus warned his disciples about these false Christs.

He said that by using miracles and clever stories they would attempt to lead Christians away from the truth. Jesus warned his followers not to believe these false Christs.

Where to find it: *Matthew 24: 3-5, 24*

FALSE TEACHERS were people who, in New Testament times, went from church to church saying they were followers of Christ but teaching things that were wrong.

They were often paid for their teaching, so they wanted to make big names for themselves. They used clever arguments to lead others away from God.

They taught that Christians did not need to live right but could do as they pleased. The apostle Peter said such teachings brought the whole Church into disgrace.

Where to find it: *2 Peter 2:13*

FAMILIAR SPIRITS, in the King James Version, refer to the spirits of dead people. During Old Testament times, as in our day, there were people called mediums who said they would talk with people who had died. The mediums said that in this way they could predict the future. The mediums said they could hear the familiar spirits by listening to whispers coming from the ground.

God said his people should not talk with mediums, but some people (including King Saul) disobeyed that command. Those who talked with familiar spirits could be sentenced to death.

Where to find it

Laws against mediums   *Leviticus 19: 31; 20: 6, 27*
King Saul and the familiar spirits   *1 Samuel 28: 7-25*
Warnings against mediums   *Isaiah 8: 19; 19: 3*

FAMILY, today, usually means a father, mother, and children. But in the Bible, *family* had broader meanings.

In the early Old Testament, a family included not only father, mother, and children, but also grandparents, uncles, aunts, cousins, servants, friends, and visiting strangers. Jacob's family included at least 66 people.

Hebrew families were the beginning of the Israelite nation. God promised Abraham that his descendants would fill the earth. As the family of Isaac became the 12 tribes of Israel, the people saw their whole nation as a family. Genealogies became important family records, and they were preserved carefully.

There were many reasons for the large Hebrew families in the days when they lived as shepherds. A large group was safer than a smaller group; they could protect each other against invaders. It was also easier for large families to take care of each other, since the governments did not help poor people or sick people. Each family group was like a small village.

Another reason Old Testament families were large was the custom of fathers to have more than one wife. This is called polygamy (puh-LIG-uh-mee). The Hebrews probably copied this custom from other countries around them. Having many children was very important to the Hebrew people, and extra wives meant more children. The Hebrew people thought having a large family meant God was pleased with them. A woman who had no children was thought to be cursed.

Since children in the Hebrew family were so important, there was much joy at the birth of a baby—especially of a son, since sons were necessary to inherit land. Firstborn sons had special family privileges—they got a double portion of the inheritance.

Like the pagan people around them, many Hebrews considered wives to be like property—something men owned. Men could divorce their wives, but wives could not divorce their husbands. The Old Testament commandments, however, teach that equal honor was to be given to fathers and mothers. Children are told to obey their parents and listen to the teachings of both father and mother.

Marriage customs were different in Bible times from our day. Almost all marriages were arranged by parents. The man would pay a price, either in money or work, for his bride. This did not mean, however, that the husbands and wives did not love each other. There are many beautiful pictures in the Old Testament of love and respect in marriage. The Song of Solomon is a series of beautiful love poems.

In the New Testament times, families were smaller. By then most men had only one wife, and families in cities lived in small houses.

The New Testament gives clear teachings about family relationships. In Ephesians 5 Paul tells Christians that family members should treat each other with love and respect. He says in a letter to Timothy that families should also take care of each other.

Jesus had a family with brothers and sisters. He apparently stayed with them until his baptism. One of the last things he did before he died was to make sure someone would take care of his mother.

The New Testament uses family relationships to describe our relationship with God and with other Christians. God is our Father, and we are members of his family. Christians sometimes call themselves brothers and sisters.

The first churches were formed in the New Testament when families of Christians met together in houses to study God's Word, pray, and worship.

Where to find it

The first family   Genesis 2:18-24
Respect for parents   Exodus 20:12; 21:15, 17; Proverbs 1:8; 6:20-21; 20:20; Ephesians 6:1-3; Colossians 3:20
Jesus' family   Matthew 13:55-56; Mark 6:3
Christians are God's family   Ephesians 2:19

FAMINE means there is not enough food in a country to keep people alive. Famines can be caused by war, lack of rain, bad storms, or by attacking insects (such as locusts) that eat crops. The Bible tells about many famines, including the one in Genesis 41 that brought Joseph's brothers to Egypt to look for food.

In Matthew 24:7, Jesus said that famines will be a sign that his Second Coming is near.

Where to find it: Genesis 12:10; Isaiah 14:30; Acts 11:28

FARMING (see Agriculture)

FARTHING (see Money)

FASTING means going without food or water for a period of time. The Bible mentions several reasons for fasting. Some people fast during times of grief or repentance. Others fast to gain God's answer to prayer or to draw closer to God. Isaiah warned the Israelites that fasting was useless unless their attitudes and actions were right.

Fasting was also practiced in the New Testament. Some religious Jews, including

Pharisees, fasted every Monday and Thursday. Jesus fasted when he was in the wilderness for 40 days after his baptism. He also warned his followers that fasting should be private rather than to show off how religious they were. Christians in the early church often fasted when faced with a big decision or special need.

Where to find it

Moses fasts for 40 days   *Exodus 34: 28*
Jesus fasts in the wilderness   *Matthew 4: 2*
Jesus' teachings on fasting   *Matthew 6: 16-18*
Fasting in the early church   *Acts 13: 2-3*

FATHER has different meanings in the Bible. The most common meaning is the male parent. Fathers in the Bible were important and respected leaders in their families.

Father is also used in the Bible to refer to ancestors. The fathers of Israel were men like Abraham, Isaac, Jacob, and David. When David died, 1 Kings 2: 10 says that " . . . he slept with his fathers."

Sometimes people used *father* as a title of respect for older men outside their own family. In 1 Samuel 24: 11 David called Saul "my father" even though he wasn't his son. In the early Christian church, some of the older, respected leaders were called fathers.

Father can also refer to a person who is the first one to do something. Jubal was the "father of musicians" (Genesis 4: 21). Abraham is said in Romans 4: 11 to be "the father of all who believe." And Satan, says John 8: 44, "is the father of lies."

In a very special sense the Bible uses *father* to describe God. "Have we not all one father?" asks Malachi 2: 10. "Has not one God created us?"

In the New Testament, God is the Father of Jesus Christ. All who believe in Jesus become "children of God." We follow Jesus' example and pray to God as "our Father who art in heaven" (Matthew 6: 9).

FATHERLESS describes boys or girls whose parents had died. They were also called orphans. The Israelites took special care of these children, giving them gifts of money and food. Both the prophets in the Old Testament, and James in the New Testament, said that God wants us to take care of the fatherless.

Where to find it: *Deuteronomy 14: 29; 24: 19-21; Jeremiah 22: 3; James 1: 27*

FATHER'S HOUSE is another name for *family* in the Old Testament. It included not only parents, brothers and sisters, but also close relatives, servants, and the belongings the family owned.

In the New Testament, Jesus called the Temple "my Father's house." He also called God's home "my Father's house" when he promised the disciples he was going to prepare a place for them.

Where to find it: *Genesis 46: 31; John 2: 16; 14: 2*

FATHOM (see *Measures*)

FATLING (FAT-ling) was a clean animal (such as a calf or lamb) that was well fed so it could be used as an offering to God.

Where to find it: *2 Samuel 6: 13; Psalm 66: 15*

FEAR usually means to be afraid of something. For instance, the disciples were fearful when they saw Jesus walking on the water. In the phrase *the fear of the Lord,* fear means a sense of respect and honor toward God. Proverbs 1: 7 says, "The fear of the Lord is the beginning of knowledge."

Where to find it: *Psalm 24: 11; Proverbs 9: 10; Matthew 14: 26*

FEASTS were holidays when the Jewish people celebrated God's goodness to them. Some feasts were like huge parties; the people ate, drank, sang, had parades, danced, and praised God. There were three main feasts each year: the Feast of Passover, the Feast of Weeks, and the Feast of Tabernacles. During these three feasts (called "pilgrim feasts") all Jewish men 13 years and older traveled to Jerusalem for the celebration if possible.

The Feast of Passover was the most important feast for the Hebrew people. It was held during the middle of April to celebrate God's rescue of the Hebrews out of slavery in Egypt. The name *Passover* comes from the way the death angel in Exodus 12 "passed over" the Hebrew homes on that terrible night in Egypt when all of the firstborn sons were killed. That plague—the tenth and final one God sent on the Egyptians—convinced Pharaoh to let the Israelites go.

God's death angel passed over homes with lamb's blood on the door frame.

The Passover has been celebrated by the Jews for thousands of years. It is a very holy day. It begins at sundown on the fourteenth day of the Jewish month Nisan and lasts for 24 hours. During Bible times, special meals were prepared using unleavened bread (to remind them of the bitter slavery they had endured in Egypt). Wine was served, and a lamb was cooked. The story of Israel's deliverance was told, songs of thanksgiving were sung, and prayers of praise were spoken to God.

In New Testament times, the Feast of the Unleavened Bread, which lasts seven days, was celebrated with Passover, making it an eight-day feast.

Thousands of Passovers have been observed. Some are very special to Jews, such as the original one in Egypt, the first one in the wilderness, and the first one in the Promised Land. However, during many long periods when the Israelites forgot about serving God, they did not hold Passover feasts.

Passover also has a special meaning for Christians. Jesus' last supper with his disciples was the Passover meal. At that time Jesus washed his disciples' feet and told them to "eat my body and drink my blood." That part of the meal became the Christian communion, or Lord's Supper. "Christ is our Passover [lamb] who is sacrificed for us," Paul wrote to the Corinthians.

Today many Jewish people still faithfully celebrate the Passover with special meals in their homes. It is a time when Jews remember that God took them out of slavery in Egypt to give them freedom in the Promised Land.

Where to find it: *Exodus 12; John 13; 1 Corinthians 5:7*

The Feast of Weeks or **Pentecost** was also called the Feast of the Harvest, because it was a one-day celebration at the end of the wheat harvest. The feast was held 50 days after Passover. The Jewish people sang and danced and gave sacrifices to thank God for watching over their crops. Later they also used this occasion to thank God for giving them his Law.

The Feast of Weeks or Pentecost received a new meaning for Christians when the Holy Spirit came to the Church on that day. Many churches celebrate Pentecost to thank God for sending his Holy Spirit.

Where to find it: *Exodus 23:16; 34:22; Numbers 28:26-31; Acts 2*

The Feast of Tabernacles or **Booths** was an important eight-day celebration in autumn. It began five days after the Day of Atonement. The Feast of Booths was the third and final "pilgrim feast" for which Hebrew men traveled to Jerusalem.

The Hebrews built outdoor "booths" once a year.

126

Because this feast was held at the end of the final harvest of olives and fruits, and because it was near the beginning of the Jewish year, the people celebrated it like Thanksgiving and New Year's Day rolled into one. They thanked God for giving them good crops, and they asked him to watch over them in the year ahead.

During the Feast of Booths the people camped out in little shelters (called "booths"). They did this to remember how their ancestors had lived while they wandered in the desert for 40 years.

Jesus secretly traveled to Jerusalem one year to go to the Feast of Booths. This feast has always been a very happy occasion for Hebrew people.

Where to find it: *Exodus 23: 16; Leviticus 23: 33-36; Numbers 29: 12-32; John 7*

Besides these three main feasts, the Jewish people also have other feasts during the year.

The Feast of Dedication or **Lights** is a happy, exciting holiday that lasts for eight days in December. It is also called Hanukkah (or Chanukah), which is the Hebrew word for "dedication." This celebration is to remember how Judas Maccabeus rescued, cleansed, and rededicated the Temple in Jerusalem in 165 B.C. (see *Maccabees, Revolt of*).

During the Feast of Dedication the Israelites marched to the synagogues carrying lighted torches. Singing and dancing filled the air with music. At the synagogues the children were told about the brave deeds of Judas Maccabeus.

Jesus was in Jerusalem for one Feast of Dedication, according to John 10: 22.

Jews today still celebrate this feast.

The Feast of the New Moon was a one-day festival held in October to celebrate the first day of the Hebrew New Year. (It was on the first new moon of the Hebrew month Tishri.) On this day silver trumpets were blown all during the day. All work was stopped, special sacrifices were offered to God, and families gathered together for a special meal. It also became a Jewish custom to have a public reading of God's Law on the Feast of the New Moon. The people celebrated after the Law was read, remembering that God has always kept his promises to his people.

Where to find it: *Numbers 28: 11-15; 2 Kings 4: 23; Amos 8: 5*

The Feast of Purim *(POOR-im)* celebrates the victory of Queen Esther and Mordecai over Haman, the wicked Persian who wanted to kill all the Jews. This two-day festival is held in the middle of March. It begins with all the people gathering in the synagogue to hear a reading of the Book of Esther. (Whenever Haman's name is mentioned, the people boo and hiss!) Afterwards large parties are held with much singing, dancing, eating, and excitement. Prayers of thanksgiving are also given to God for rescuing the Jewish people.

Where to find it: *Esther 9: 1-10; 20-32*

FEET (see *Foot*)

FELIX *(FEE-licks)* was the governor of Judea during Paul's missionary travels. His full name was Antonius Felix. He was a friend of the Roman emperors Claudius and Nero. He was known as a cruel and treacherous tyrant who had "the power of a king with the mind of a slave." He seduced Drusilla, the wife of the king of Emessa, and later married her.

When Felix and Drusilla were in Caesarea, Paul was brought before them after being arrested in Jerusalem. Paul pleaded for freedom, but Felix kept him in prison, hoping that Paul would give him some money. Paul didn't, and he was still in prison when Felix was replaced as governor in A.D. 59.

Where to find it: *Acts 23: 24–25: 14*

FENCE was a solid stone wall that ran around a field or town to protect the people from invasion. In Jeremiah 15: 20 God said he would make Israel like a stone fence so other countries could not conquer her.

FESTAL GARMENTS or **ROBES** were special clothes worn on holidays or days of celebration. Samson had to give festal garments to the thirty Philistine young men who got the answer to his riddle.

Where to find it: *Judges 14: 10-19*

FESTIVALS (see *Feasts*)

FESTUS *(FESS-tuss)* became the governor of Judea after Felix. After hearing Paul's defense,

Festus wanted to send Paul back to Jerusalem for trial. Paul preferred to go to Rome to be judged by the emperor, so Festus allowed him to go. Festus died in Judea in A.D. 62.

Where to find it: *Acts 24: 27–26: 32*

FETTER *(FET-er)*, a strong iron chain (like handcuffs), was used to tie up people. The Philistines used fetters on Samson to keep him prisoner after Delilah cut off his hair. Fetters were also used to try to control the man with the unclean spirit at Gadara.

Where to find it: *Judges 16: 21; Psalm 105: 18; Mark 5: 4*

FEVER (see *Diseases*)

FIERY SERPENTS *(FIRE-ee SUR-pents)* were snakes with a burning bite sent by God to punish the Hebrews. While they were in the wilderness, they kept complaining to Moses about not having enough water and the kind of food they wanted. Finally God was angered, and he sent the poisonous snakes. Many people died of the snakebites.

When the people were sorry for what they had done, God told Moses to make a serpent out of bronze and hang it on a pole. If persons who had been bitten looked at the bronze serpent, they would not die.

When Jesus came, he said he would be lifted up on a cross to die, and that whoever believed on him would live—something like people were saved by looking at the bronze serpent.

Where to find it

Bronze serpents   *Numbers 21: 4-9*
Jesus lifted up   *John 3: 14*

FIG TREE (see *Plants*)

FILLET *(FILL-et)* was a gold or silver rod at the top of the pillars in the Temple in Jerusalem. Metal hooks were attached to the fillets to hold up large curtains.

Where to find it: *Exodus 27: 10-11; 38: 10-19*

FINGER OF GOD is a word picture that means the power of God. The finger (or hand) was seen in Bible times as the part of the body that does the work. This is why the Bible says the finger of God brought the plagues on Egypt and wrote the Law on stone tablets for Moses. The stars, moon, and heavens are the creations of the finger of God. Jesus said he cast demons out of people by the finger of God.

Where to find it

Brings plague   *Exodus 8: 19*
Writes Law   *Exodus 31: 18*
Creates heavens   *Psalm 8: 3*
Casts out demon   *Luke 11: 20*

FIRE was probably discovered by people soon after God created them. The Israelites used fire for cooking their meals and refining their metals. The warriors of Israel also used fire to destroy captured enemy cities.

The Hebrews often saw fire as a special and mysterious sign from God. God spoke to Moses in a burning bush. At night, the Israelites were led to the Promised Land by a pillar of fire. "The appearance of the glory of the Lord was like a devouring fire on the top of the mountain," Moses wrote.

Both the Old and the New Testaments use *fire* as a word picture for God's punishment of sinners. Moses warned his people to remember their relationship with God, because "the Lord thy God is a consuming fire." Jesus referred to the "everlasting fire" that sinners will face if they do not repent. John told of a "lake burning with brimstone" into which the beast and the false prophet will be thrown. Peter wrote that the world will someday be destroyed by fire. These are all word pictures of suffering and separation from God.

Where to find it

God speaks to Moses   *Exodus 3:1-6*
Pillar of fire   *Exodus 13:21*
Glory of the Lord   *Exodus 24:17*
God a consuming fire   *Deuteronomy 4:24; Hebrews 12:29*
Everlasting fire   *Matthew 18:8*
World destroyed   *2 Peter 3:7-12*
Lake burning with brimstone   *Revelation 19:20*

FIRKIN (see *Measure*)

FIRST FRUITS

FIRST FRUITS were the first (and best) part of the crops. The Hebrew people presented the first fruits of the harvest to God. They did this to show they knew that all crops belonged to God and to show they believed God would give them more harvests.

When Christ arose from the dead, he was the "first fruits of those who had fallen asleep." Christ's resurrection is the promise of future resurrection for all believers.

The New Testament says that the Holy Spirit is given to Christians as a first fruit, a promise that even better things are coming.

Where to find it

First part of the crop   *Exodus 23:16; 34:22; Deuteronomy 18:4*
Holy Spirit is a first fruit   *Romans 8:23*
Jesus the first fruit   *1 Corinthians 15:20*

FIRSTBORN

FIRSTBORN was the oldest child in a family. A firstborn son had special privileges in a Hebrew family. He became the leader of the family after the father died, and he received twice as much inheritance as his brothers. This is the birthright that Esau sold to Jacob.

Israel was called the Lord's firstborn among the other nations, meaning the Israelites had a special relationship with God.

Where to find it

Esau and Jacob   *Genesis 25:21–34*
Firstborn has birthright   *Genesis 43:33*
Israel God's firstborn   *Exodus 4:22*

FIRSTLING

FIRSTLING (*FIRST-ling*) was the first lamb or calf born to a mother. The firstlings were brought as sacrifices to God. Abel gave God the firstlings of his flock, and God was pleased with this sacrifice.

Where to find it: *Genesis 4:4; Exodus 13:2; Leviticus 27:26*

FISH

FISH of many kinds were found in Palestine during Bible times. Fish were an important food for the Jewish people. Hooks, nets, and spears were used to catch fish.

Fish are mentioned in many parts of the Bible. One of the plagues against Egypt was the killing of all fish in the Nile River. Jonah was swallowed by a great fish. And at least seven of Jesus' disciples were fishermen. After he was resurrected, Jesus appeared to his disciples while they were fishing.

The fish is also used as a symbol. When it

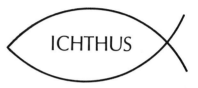

was illegal to worship Jesus, Christians in the Roman Empire used secret codes to announce meeting places. One of those secret codes was the Greek word for *fish: ICHTHUS.* The letters of that word in Greek were also the first letters of the words "Jesus, Messiah, God, Son, Savior."

Where to find it

Fish in Nile killed   *Exodus 7:20-21*
Jonah swallowed   *Jonah 1–2*
Disciples were fishermen   *Matthew 4:18-22; Luke 21:1-3*
Jesus appears to disciples   *Luke 21:1-8*

FLESH

FLESH has many meanings in the Bible. It often refers to the soft muscle and skin of a person or animal.

The Old Testament Law told the Jews which animal flesh they could eat ("clean" animals) and which they couldn't ("unclean"). The flesh of "clean" animals was also used as a sacrifice to God.

Sometimes *flesh* means living things—people and animals. God told Noah he was going to send a flood on earth to "destroy all flesh." John wrote that the "Word was made flesh," meaning that Jesus, who was the Word, became a man when he came to earth.

Flesh is also used to describe a person's relatives: his "own flesh."

Sometimes *flesh* is used to mean that people are weak—physically and morally.

Psalm 78:39 says God is patient toward people because he knows "they were but flesh, a wind that passes and comes not again." To say people are flesh means they are weak and will someday die.

Jesus used *flesh* to mean the opposite of spirit when he appeared to his disciples after the resurrection. At first they thought Jesus was a spirit or ghost. But Jesus showed them his hands and feet and told them to touch him to prove that he had a real body.

Paul often used *flesh* to describe the evil power of sin in a person's life. We can only have victory over the flesh, or sin, through Jesus.

Where to find it

All living things   *Genesis 6:13*
Relatives   *Genesis 29:14; 37:27*
"Clean" and "unclean" animals   *Leviticus 11*
People are weak   *Psalm 78:39*
Means a person   *John 1:14*
Opposite of *spirit*   *Luke 24:36-43*
Power of sin   *Romans 8*
Eating flesh   *Romans 14*

FLOGGING (see *Scourging*)

FLOOD refers to the time when God sent water to destroy wicked people. Only Noah and his family and the animals that were with them on the boat (or ark) were saved from the Flood.

When God saw how wicked people had become, he was sorry he had made them. He decided to destroy them all in a flood. But Noah was a good man who trusted God, so God warned Noah about the coming destruction. God told Noah how to build a huge boat. Noah spent many years building the boat. When it was finished, Noah and his family and pairs of every kind of bird and animal entered the ark.

Then the water came. It rained for almost six weeks without stopping! Water also rushed up from below the ground. Soon everything was under water. It stayed that way for more than a year. The people and animals outside the ark drowned.

Noah's ark finally landed on the mountains of Ararat. (There are mountains in Turkey today with this name.) Noah sent out birds to see if the land was drying up, and when a dove came back with a freshly picked olive leaf, Noah knew the Flood was over.

Noah, his family, and the animals spent more than a year on the ark.

Noah thanked God by building an altar and offering sacrifices. God made a covenant—an agreement—with Noah that he would never again send a flood to destroy the earth. The sign of the covenant was the rainbow. It still reminds us of God's promise.

The Flood is an important Bible event. Stories about a huge flood are also found in other ancient writings.

Where to find it

God tells Noah to build the ark   *Genesis 6:11-22*
The Flood comes   *Genesis 7:1–8:12*
God makes a covenant with Noah   *Genesis 9:8-17*
Flood mentioned in New Testament   *Matthew 24:37-39; Hebrews 11:7; 1 Peter 3:20; 2 Peter 2:5; 3:3-7*

FLOUR was crushed grain something like we use today, except that flour in Bible times was brown. The Israelites used flour in baking, even though it was very expensive. Sarah used flour to make cakes for three special visitors in Genesis 18:6.

FLUTE (see *Musical Instruments*)

FOLLY (*FAH-lee*) is a foolish or wicked act. The Bible calls folly the opposite of wisdom. The wise person believes in God and trusts him, but the fool ignores God and lives in disobedience and sin. "The fool says in his heart," wrote the psalmist, " 'There is no God.' " Even smart people can be fools if they ignore God. Paul warned the Ephesians to live "not as fools, but as wise."

To be called a fool was a very serious insult in the Bible. Jesus said that anyone who called another person a fool was in danger of the fire of hell.

Where to find it: *Psalm 14:1; Proverbs 18:7; Matthew 5:22; Romans 1:22; Ephesians 5:15*

FOOD in Bible times did not have much variety. Only rich people ate meat regularly. Poor people served meat when they had important guests, or at special celebrations, or when they made a sacrifice to God. Then a certain portion was given as a sacrifice, another portion to the priest, and the rest was eaten by the family. Since there was no refrigeration, meat had to be eaten within a few hours after the animal was killed, or else it would spoil.

People did not usually drink milk, but made it into cheese and yogurt. Cows and goats were raised for their milk rather than meat. Sheep were raised primarily for their wool rather than to be eaten.

The most common food in the Bible was bread. It was the main part of every meal. Poor people usually had bread made from barley. People with more money ate bread made of wheat.

Vegetables were not common, except for onions, cucumbers, leeks, garlic, beans, and lentils. Beans and lentils were used in soups and sometimes mixed with flour to make bread.

Grapes were the most common fruit, and they were usually made into wine. Olives were made into oil. The only fruits that were normally eaten raw were figs, pomegranates, and perhaps apples.

The Hebrews knew that all food was a gift of God, because unless God sent rain, there would be nothing to eat.

Food was important not only for staying alive, but also as a sign of friendship. People who were not friends never ate together. People who ate together were expected to be loyal to each other. All kinds of agreements were completed or sealed by eating together.

FOOL (see *Folly*)

FOOT is the lowest part of a person's body,

and so it is often used in word pictures to teach us to be humble. Mary sat at Jesus' feet to show she was a learner. The sinful woman who kissed Jesus' feet and washed them with her tears was showing her humility. God told Moses to stand barefoot near the burning bush because he was standing on holy ground.

Feet are also what we use to get us from place to place. The Bible uses *feet* in word pictures about going in the direction God wants us to go, or standing on something we know won't fall apart, like God's Word.

Where to find it

Take off shoes *Exodus 3:5*
God keeps feet from falling *Psalms 18:36; 40:2*
Going in the right direction *Psalm 119:59, 101, 105; Luke 1:79*
Falling at Jesus' feet *Mark 5:22; 7:25; Luke 17:16*
Kissing and washing Jesus' feet *Luke 7:38*
Sitting at Jesus' feet *Luke 8:35; 10:39*

FOOT WASHING was a special way to greet guests after they traveled. People traveled mainly by walking on the hot, dusty roads of Palestine. After a long journey, their feet would be tired and dirty. Servants would use a bowl of cool water and fresh towels to bathe the feet of the travelers.

Jesus washed the feet of his 12 disciples at the Last Supper. He was teaching them that

we must be each other's servants. Some churches today have foot washing services to remember Jesus' example.

Where to find it: *Genesis 18:4; 1 Samuel 25:41; John 13:1-17; 1 Timothy 5:10*

FOOTMAN was a member of the army who traveled on foot. Other soldiers would ride in chariots or on horses. The footmen sometimes ran ahead of the chariots and acted as messengers. Men who were royal bodyguards and messengers of the court were also called footmen.

Where to find it: *1 Samuel 22: 17 (KJV); 2 Samuel 8: 4; 1 Chronicles 18: 4; Jeremiah 12: 5*

FORBEARANCE *(for-BEAR-uns)* is patience, the opposite of a short temper. God's patience with sinful people is a sign that he loves us and that he wants us to ask forgiveness for our sins. Paul said that forbearance or patience is a fruit of the Spirit.

Where to find it: *Romans 2: 4; Galatians 5: 22; 1 Peter 3: 9*

FOREKNOWLEDGE *(for-NOLL-edge)* means knowing ahead of time. In the New Testament, the words are usually used about God. He knows about all persons who will be born and what they will do. But God does not make them do evil. They choose this for themselves. The Bible says that God has control of the world even though sometimes it's hard for us to see what he's doing. It also points out that God does what he needs to so that his divine plans and purposes happen.

Some Christians believe *foreknowledge* means that God chooses who will become a part of his family and who will not. Other Christians believe that *foreknowledge* means God knows in advance which people will choose to serve and obey him.

Where to find it: *Acts 2: 23; Romans 8: 29; 11: 2; 1 Peter 1: 2*

FORERUNNER was a scout or messenger in the army who ran ahead of the chariots to clear the path and to announce that the troops (or the king) were coming. John the Baptist was a forerunner for Jesus; he prepared the way for him. Jesus is a forerunner for us; he has gone ahead of us into the presence of God to prepare the way for us.

Where to find it: *Malachi 3: 1; Matthew 3: 11; 11: 10; Hebrews 6: 20*

FORESKIN (see *Circumcision*)

FORGIVENESS refers to blotting out sin and guilt. After this happens, the person who did wrong can again be friends with the one to whom he did the wrong.

All people sin against God. If they are to be friends with God and enjoy his love and kindness, they must be forgiven by God.

When people do wrong things to each other, forgiveness cannot really come until the person who did wrong is willing to pay his debt or make up in any way he can for what he did. However, there is no way we can make up to God for our sins. Instead, Jesus came to pay our debt. He gave his life in our place so we could be friends with God. Our sins and guilt have been blotted out if we let Jesus take our place.

However, Jesus said that God does not forgive our sins unless we are willing to forgive one another.

Where to find it: *Matthew 18: 23-35; 6: 12; Colossians 1: 13-14*

FORNICATION *(FOR-nih-KAY-shun)* means sexual intercourse between people who are not married to each other. The Bible says fornication is sin. In the Bible, the words *fornication, adultery, immorality* and *harlotry* mean almost the same thing.

In the Old Testament, *fornication* or *harlotry* was sometimes a word picture of how Israel was disloyal to God and went after other gods.

Where to find it: *Ezekiel 16: 15-43; Matthew 15: 19; 1 Corinthians 5: 9-13; Hebrews 13: 4*

FORTIFY *(FOR-ti-fy)* meant to build walls and towers around a city to defend it from invaders. People in ancient cities built thick walls of stone, some as high as 25 feet. Towers and moats also helped protect cities.

When the Israelites reached the Promised Land, they found Canaanite cities that were heavily fortified. Jerusalem was so protected that the Israelites did not capture it until the time of David. The Hebrews also fortified their cities to protect themselves.

Where to find it: *Deuteronomy 1: 28; 28: 52; Joshua 6: 5; Isaiah 25: 12*

FORTRESS *(FOR-truss)* is a tower or fort that ancient people built of stone or brick to protect their cities. A fortress usually had a blockhouse in the middle, surrounded by smaller houses or tents. A wall circled the fortress. Some fortresses had moats around them. Most fortresses in the Bible are called strongholds.

There was a fortress at Lachish that guarded the southern road leading into Jerusalem. The fortress at Megiddo guarded the Plain of Jezreel. David captured a fortress called Millo and turned it into what was called "the City of David."

Fortress is also a word picture for how God protects his people.

Where to find it: *2 Samuel 5: 7-9; Psalm 91: 2*

FORTUNATUS (see *Achaicus*)

FORUM was the open place or market in the center of a town where people would gather. When Paul was making his last journey to Rome, he met Christian friends at the forum (or market) of Appius, 43 miles southeast of Rome.

Where to find it: *Acts 28: 15*

FOUNTAIN is a spring of water flowing out of an opening in a hillside. Because Palestine was such a dry land, fountains were very important. Towns and cities often grew up around fountains, springs, or wells.

Because water is so important for life, the words *fountain, spring,* and *well* are often used as word pictures of spiritual truths: Jesus said, "The water that I shall give him will become in him a spring of water welling up to eternal life."

Where to find it: *Deuteronomy 8: 7; Psalm 36: 9; John 4: 14; Revelation 21: 6*

FOWLER *(FOW-lur)* was a person who used nets and cages to catch wild birds. Because fowlers had to be sneaky to catch the quick birds, the word *fowler* came to mean someone who tries to trick or lure other people into doing evil things. Psalm 124: 6-7 tells us that God helps us escape the trap set by wicked fowlers.

FOX (see *Animals*)

FRANKINCENSE *(FRANK-in-sense)* was a sweet-smelling perfume made from the sap that comes from a terebinth tree. These trees grew in warm, dry places. The Israelites used frankincense in religious ceremonies, and it was one of the special gifts that the wise men gave to Jesus in Bethlehem.

Where to find it: *Exodus 30: 34; Isaiah 60: 6; Matthew 2: 11*

FRIENDSHIP was very important in the Bible.

David and Jonathan were such close friends that the Bible says their souls were "knit together." The Book of Ruth tells of the beautiful friendship between Ruth and her mother-in-law, Naomi. Jesus called Lazarus his friend.

One of the deepest and highest friendships in the Bible was between Abraham and God.

Jesus told the people who followed him, "You are my friends if you do what I command you."

"A friend loves at all times," says Proverbs 17: 17. The writer of Ecclesiastes says that it is good to have a friend, because if either of them fell, the one could lift up his friend.

Where to find it

David and Jonathan   *2 Chronicles 20: 7*
A friend loves   *Proverbs 17: 7*
It is good to have a friend   *Ecclesiastes 4: 9-12*
Abraham, God's friend   *Isaiah 41: 8; James 2: 23*
Lazarus   *John 11: 11*
We are Jesus' friends when we obey   *John 15: 14*

FRONTLETS *(FRONT-lets)* were tiny pouches of leather that Hebrew men wore on their foreheads during prayer. Frontlets were also called phylacteries *(fil-LAK-tur-eez)*. In the

Some Jews in Israel today still wear phylacteries.

pouch were pieces of parchment with the words of Exodus 13: 1-16, Deuteronomy 6: 4, and Deuteronomy 11: 13-21 on them. Jesus criticized some Jews for using the frontlets to show other people how religious they were. Traditional Jews still wear frontlets when they pray.

Where to find it: *Matthew 23: 5*

FRUIT in Bible times was mostly grapes, olives, figs, and pomegranates.

Fruit is often used as a word picture.

Children are called the "fruit of the womb."

Often *fruit* as a word picture refers to outcome or results of actions. The Bible speaks of the "fruit of righteousness" or the "fruit of lies."

Jesus said that people would be known by their fruits. If we let the Holy Spirit rule our lives, our fruit will be such things as love, joy, and peace.

Where to find it: *Isaiah 3: 10; Matthew 7: 16-20; Luke 1: 42; Galatians 5: 22-23*

FUEL for cooking and heating in the Bible came from many sources. In the parts of Palestine where trees were plentiful, wood was used for fuel. Where trees were scarce, people burned shrubs, dried grass, cow and camel manure, charcoal, and the chaff of wheat from the threshing floor. Jesus used charcoal when he cooked breakfast for the disciples after his resurrection.

Where to find it: *Psalm 120: 4; Isaiah 44: 14-17; Ezekiel 4: 15; John 21: 1-14*

FULFILL means to complete or to satisfy. It is used in the Bible about granting a request, performing a vow, or obeying a command. But its most important use is in showing how the events of Jesus' life fulfilled or completed prophecies in the Old Testament. The Gospel of Matthew often says Jesus said or did something so that an Old Testament quotation about Jesus "may be fulfilled."

Where to find it: *Psalm 20: 5; Matthew 1: 22; 2: 23; 8: 17; 12: 17-21; 13: 35; Romans 13: 10; Galatians 6: 2*

FULLER (see *Occupations*)

FULLER'S FIELD is the name of a place outside Jerusalem where fullers washed, bleached, and dried their cloth. There was a running stream in this field as well as a dry, flat place where they could dry their cloth. The exact location of the Fuller's Field is not known. We know it was outside the city because their soaps and bleaches smelled bad.

Where to find it: *2 Kings 18: 17; Isaiah 7: 3; 36: 2*

FULLNESS OF TIME means when everything is ready. In Galatians 4: 4 it says that when the fullness of time came, God sent his Son. In other words, Jesus was born at the exact time in history that God planned.

In Ephesians 1: 10 *fullness of time* is that future time when all of God's plans for the world will be completed.

FURLONG (see *Measure*)

FURNACES in Bible times were not used in houses. They were used for baking pottery and bricks; for melting silver, gold, copper, brass, and bronze; and for smelting iron and other ores. They were of many sizes and were usually made of stone and brick.

Solomon built huge smelting furnaces. Daniel's three friends, Shadrach, Meshach, and Abednego, were thrown into a furnace for not obeying Nebuchadnezzar; but God rescued them. Jesus compared the agony of hell with the "furnace of fire."

Where to find it: *Proverbs 17: 3; Daniel 3: 13-30; Matthew 13: 42*

Gideon's raid on the Midianites was one of the most unusual attacks in the history of warfare.

GABBATHA *(GAB-uh-thuh)* means "the Pavement." It was an outdoor area paved with thick slabs of stone where a governor sat on a platform and held public trials.

Pilate sat at such a place when Jesus was brought before him for trial. We don't know exactly where it was—perhaps near the Tower of Antonia (the fortress of Roman soldiers next to the Temple in Jerusalem).

Where to find it: *John 19:13*

GABRIEL *(GAY-bree-ul)* is an angel mentioned four times in the Bible. Each time, he came with an important message from God.

He appeared twice to Daniel to explain visions that Daniel had. He also appeared to Zechariah, the priest, in 6 B.C. to say that he and his wife would have a son who should be called John. The son became John the Baptist.

Gabriel's most important appearance was to Mary. He told her she would have a child who would be the Son of God; his name was to be Jesus.

Gabriel once called himself "Gabriel, who stands in the presence of God."

Where to find it

Appears to Daniel *Daniel 8:16-26; 9:21-27*
Appears to Zechariah *Luke 1:8-20*
Appears to Mary *Luke 1:26-38*

GAD was the name of two different men: the seventh son of Jacob, and one of David's prophets.

1. Jacob's son founded one of the 12 tribes of Israel. The tribe of Gad was made up mostly of shepherds. They asked Moses to let them stay on the east side of the Jordan River when most of the Israelites went into Canaan. Moses said they could if their men would promise to fight in the battles to conquer Canaan. They did as Moses said.

Where to find it

Son of Jacob *Genesis 30:9-11*
Ask permission to stay east of Jordan *Numbers 32:1-36*

2. The prophet Gad was a court prophet who helped David during most of his life. Usually court prophets only prophesied good things to their king. But Gad delivered God's message to David whether it was good news or bad.

Gad once gave David advice on how to escape when Saul was trying to kill him.

After David became king, he sinned against God by counting his fighting men. Then Gad brought God's message about his punishment. Gad also told David to build an altar to God, and God stopped the terrible disease that was killing thousands of people.

Gad was also a musician and a writer. He helped David arrange musical services for the Temple and wrote a history of David's reign in Israel.

Where to find it

Advises David on fleeing from Saul *1 Samuel 22:5*
Tells David about God's punishment *2 Samuel 24:11-17; 1 Chronicles 21:9-17*
Tells David to build an altar *2 Samuel 24:18*
Helps David with Temple music *2 Chronicles 29:25*
Writes a history of David *1 Chronicles 29:29*

GADARENES *(gad-uh-REENZ)* were the people who lived around the city of Gadara, which was southeast of the Sea of Galilee.

Along the seashore was an area of limestone cliffs. Many holes were dug out of these cliffs for tombs.

Once when Jesus landed in this area, he met two demon-possessed men who lived in these tombs. He healed them and said the demons who had lived in them could go and live in a herd of pigs nearby. The pigs promptly ran into the sea and were drowned. The owners were so angry they asked Jesus to leave the area.

Where to find it: *Matthew 8:28-34; Mark 5:1-20; Luke 8:26-39*

GAIUS *(GAY-us)* is the name of three or four people in the New Testament:

1. A man from Corinth whom Paul baptized. This is probably the man in whose house the church met (Romans 16:23; 1 Corinthians 1:14).

2. A man from Macedonia who went with Paul on his third missionary journey (Acts 19:29). Some people think that the Gaius who is mentioned in Acts 20:4 is the same man. However, this Gaius is from Derbe, in Asia Minor, not Macedonia (a part of Greece).

3. The man to whom the apostle John wrote 3 John. John praised him for his kindness to traveling preachers of the gospel (3 John 3-8).

GALATIA *(guh-LAY-shuh)* was a large province in Asia Minor (now Turkey). Paul visited Galatia on his missionary journeys and wrote one of his letters (Galatians) to the churches in that province.

GALATIANS *(guh-LAY-shuns)* is a letter the apostle Paul wrote to the churches in the province of Galatia in Asia Minor. Some of these churches were at Antioch of Pisidia, Iconium, Lystra, and Derbe. They had all been started by Paul during his first missionary journey.

The Christians there had been growing well in their knowledge of the Christian message when Paul left them.

But then some Jewish teachers came who claimed to be Christians. Their teachings were not like Paul's. They said that Gentile Christians must be circumcised and must keep all the rituals of the Old Testament if they were to be Christians.

The new Christians in Galatia were very confused, so Paul wrote this letter to try to help them. He reminded them that Abraham was made right with God through faith— before the Old Testament Law of Moses was ever announced. Gentile Christians, he said, are the true "sons of Abraham." He also said that believers are now part of Christ. There is no place for race prejudice, sex prejudice, or class prejudice, because all believers are "one" (equal) in Christ.

The Letter to the Galatians says that the Old Testament Law was given so people would know that they are sinners. But sins are forgiven through faith in Christ. Christians are free to follow Christ.

But Paul also told the Galatians that they were not free to sin or live in ways that did not please God. The Spirit of God does not lead people to sin, but to be gentle and loving. Galatians 5:22 says, "The fruit of the Spirit is love, joy, peace, patience, kindness, goodness, faithfulness, gentleness, self-control."

Where to find it

Paul tells how God made him an apostle *Galatians 1:11-12; 2:18*
Abraham was saved by faith *Galatians 3*
Christians must follow the Spirit of God *Galatians 5:16-26*

GALILEAN *(gal-uh-LEE-un)* was a person who lived in the province of Galilee—in northern Palestine where Jesus grew up. People in this area had a distinctive accent in their speech.

Where to find it: *Matthew 26:73; Mark 14:66-70*

GALILEE *(GAL-uh-lee)* was the northern province of Palestine in Jesus' day. Jesus grew up in Nazareth, a city of Galilee, and preached his first sermon in the synagogue there. Almost all his disciples were from Galilee.

The southern part of Galilee, where Jesus grew up, had more cities and people than the northern part. Southern Galilee had fertile valleys and a mild climate that were good for farming. The northern part was not as good for farming because it was more hilly. Olive trees, however, grew well there.

The people in Galilee were not as "pure-blood" Jewish as those in Judea, and for this reason the people of Judea looked down on those in Galilee. This is why the area is called "Galilee of the Gentiles" in Matthew 4:15.

However, between Galilee and Judea was another province called Samaria. The people in Samaria were even more racially mixed than those in Galilee—so both the people in Galilee and those in Judea looked down on the Samaritans!

GALILEE, SEA OF *(GAL-uh-lee)* is sometimes called the Sea of Gennesaret, the Sea of Tiberias, and the Sea of Chinnereth. It is a freshwater lake about 13 miles long and 8 miles wide in northern Palestine near where Jesus grew up.

During the time of Jesus, the Sea of Galilee had rich fishing industries. Four of Jesus' disciples were men who fished in the Sea of Galilee.

Many of Jesus' sermons and miracles took

The Sea of Galilee still has its fishing boats.

place along the shore. The sea was known for its sudden and violent storms. Jesus rescued his disciples in two such storms. Jesus sometimes taught large crowds from a boat anchored near the shore.

During Jesus' time there were nine large, thriving cities around the lake. Only Tiberias still exists, plus one tiny village, Magdala.

Where to find it

Jesus calls fishermen as disciples *Matthew 4:18-22; Luke 5:1-11*
Jesus calms the storm *Matthew 14:22-33; Mark 4:35-41; John 6:16-21*
Jesus teaches by the shore *Mark 4:1*

GALL *(gawl)* was a bitter and poisonous plant that might have been used as a painkiller for men being crucified. Matthew 27:34 says that Jesus was offered wine mixed with gall on the cross, but he refused to drink it.

GALLIO *(GAL-ee-oh)* was a Roman official known for his fairness. Some Jews in Corinth brought the apostle Paul before Gallio, saying that he persuaded people to worship "contrary to the law." But Gallio refused to listen to their charges, since they had to do with the Jewish religion, and Paul was freed.

Where to find it: *Acts 18:12-17*

GAMALIEL *(guh-MAY-lee-ul)* was a famous Jewish Pharisee and teacher who lived in Jerusalem. The apostle Paul was one of his students before Paul became a Christian.

When the church was just beginning in Jerusalem, the Pharisees and priests ordered the apostles not to preach about Christ. The apostles said they must obey God rather than men. The Pharisees and priests were so angry they wanted to kill them. The highly respected Gamaliel advised against it, saying that if this new teaching were just the idea of the apostles, it would die by itself. If it were of God, no one could stop it anyway. The council took his advice.

Where to find it: *Acts 5:27-40; 22:3*

GAMES were part of life in Bible times, even though only a few kinds are mentioned. Music and dancing were common, both as part of celebrations and as part of worship.

In Zechariah 8:5, the prophet speaks about the coming day when "the streets of the city shall be full of boys and girls playing in the streets." This shows that children playing in the streets had been part of everyday life in Jerusalem. The kind of play is not mentioned.

The Old Testament frequently refers to rid-

WHAT DID JESUS PLAY?

dles so we can guess that they were popular. Archaeologists have dug up many game boards from Old Testament times. Some were quite difficult. Chess is a very old game and may have been played in Palestine. Some old carvings from Egypt suggest that boys played tug-of-war and girls juggled balls.

In the New Testament, Jesus speaks of children playing make-believe weddings and funerals with music.

The New Testament also refers to the Greek footraces and other contests that were well known in that time. These included chariot races, throwing the discus and javelin, wrestling, boxing, and horse racing.

Where to find it

Music and dancing *Jeremiah 31: 4, 13-14; Luke 15: 25*

Riddles *Judges 14: 12-18; Proverbs 1: 5-6; Ezekiel 17: 2*

Jesus' mention of make-believe *Matthew 11: 16-19; Luke 7: 31-35*

Reference to Greek games *1 Corinthians 9: 24-27; 2 Timothy 2: 5*

GARDEN OF EDEN (see *Eden*)

GARDEN OF GETHSEMANE (see *Gethsemane*)

GARRISON *(GARE-uh-sun)* was a group of soldiers stationed somewhere to defend a place—usually an outpost away from the homeland. When Israel was at its strongest, King David had garrisons of soldiers in Damascus and in Edom. When Israel was weak, other countries had garrisons within its borders.

When the apostle Paul was in Damascus after his conversion, the king ordered a garrison of soldiers to arrest him. But they failed.

Where to find it

David's garrisons *2 Samuel 8: 6, 14*

Philistine garrisons in Israel *1 Samuel 10: 5; 13: 3*

Garrison at Damascus *2 Corinthians 11: 32 (KJV)*

GATE (see *City Gate*)

GAZA *(GAY-zuh)* was a Philistine city on the coast of the Mediterranean Sea. It still exists, but is now called Chazzah. It is the most important city on the Gaza Strip in the southwest corner of Israel.

Gaza is best known in the Bible as the city

Samson's last act was to collapse Gaza's temple.

where Samson died. He pulled down the pillars of the temple of Dagon and killed the crowd inside—including himself.

The city was not fully defeated by the Israelites until the time of Hezekiah, about 713 B.C.

Gaza is mentioned in the New Testament only once. Philip, the evangelist, was told to go to the road that ran from Jerusalem to Gaza. There he met an Ethiopian who wanted to know about Christ.

Where to find it

Samson pulls down Dagon's temple *Judges 16: 21-30*

Hezekiah conquers Gaza *2 Kings 18: 8*

Philip on road to Gaza *Acts 8: 26*

GAZELLE (see *Animals*)

GEDALIAH *(ged-uh-LIE-uh)* was the last ruler of Judah. He was appointed by Nebuchadnezzar to govern the people who were left after the leaders and many others had been taken captive to Babylonia. He protected the prophet Jeremiah, who had chosen to stay in Judah.

Gedaliah was warned that a group of men were planning to kill him, but he did not believe it. He was killed after ruling only two months.

Where to find it: *2 Kings 25: 22-25; Jeremiah 39: 14; 40: 1-16; 41: 1-3*

GEHAZI *(guh-HAY-zye)* was a servant of the prophet Elisha.

Once a Shunammite woman came to Elisha for help when her son died. Elisha told Gehazi to hurry to the child and place Elisha's staff across the body. Gehazi did this, but nothing happened. Later, God raised the child from the dead through Elisha.

Gehazi was also with Elisha when Naaman, the Syrian commander, was cured of leprosy. Naaman wanted to give Elisha a present, but Elisha refused.

After Naaman left, Gehazi ran after Naaman and said Elisha had changed his mind, so Gehazi got the gift. He was punished for his dishonesty by getting Naaman's leprosy.

Where to find it

Shunammite woman   *2 Kings 4: 1-37*
Dishonest with Naaman   *2 Kings 5: 1-27*

GEHENNA *(guh-HEN-uh)* was also called the Valley of Hinnom. In Old Testament times, it was a place where pagans and some ungodly kings of Israel sacrificed their own children to pagan gods. Because of the things that had happened there, *Gehenna* was used as the word for hell—the place of final punishment.

Where to find it: *Matthew 5: 22, 29-30; 10: 28; 18: 9; 23: 15, 23; Luke 12: 5; Mark 9: 43, 45, 47; James 3: 6*

GENEALOGIES *(JEN-ee-AHL-oh-jeez)* are lists of family members, usually just fathers and sons. People could use these lists to trace their ancestors, show tribal memberships, and to decide who should get inheritances.

Bible genealogies are rarely complete. Often a grandson or great-grandson is called "the son of." For this reason, sometimes genealogies do not agree, and scholars cannot use genealogies to figure out periods of time.

The genealogy of Jesus Christ is recorded in two places. In Matthew 1: 1-16, Jesus' ancestry is traced back (through Joseph) to Abraham. In Luke 3: 23-38, his ancestry is traced back to Adam.

Some scholars think that the Matthew list is really the one that traces Jesus' relationship to the Old Testament throne of David—to show that he was really born to be King of Israel. The list in Luke may have been a listing to show his actual family relationships to David through his mother, Mary. Mary is not listed in the Luke genealogy, but some scholars think that Joseph was the *son-in-law (rather than son)* of Heli, which means that Mary was the daughter of Heli.

The Matthew genealogy for Jesus includes five women—Tamar, Rahab, Ruth, Bathsheba, and Mary.

GENESIS *(JEN-uh-sis)* is the first book of the Bible. It is a book about beginnings. It tells how God created the world and people. It tells about the beginning of sin, the beginning of God's judgment on sin, and his mercy to sinners. It also tells about the beginning of the nation of Israel, from which the Redeemer of the world—Jesus Christ—would be born many years later.

Genesis 1 and 2 tell about the creation of the world. The words do not tell exactly *how* God created, but they state clearly that God did it and that he cared deeply about what he had made. He called everything he made "very good."

God had close fellowship with Adam and Eve, who were made "in the image of God." That fellowship was destroyed when Adam and Eve sinned. But God began his work of redemption with them. He did not destroy them, but he sent them away from the Garden of Eden. God said the seed of the woman (Jesus) would crush the head of the serpent (Satan). This was the first promise that Satan and sin would finally be conquered.

Genesis also tells about God sending the Flood because people became so sinful. But God was merciful again and saved Noah and his family and some of each kind of animal so life on earth could go on.

Genesis also tells about the beginning of the Hebrew people. They came from Abraham, "the man of faith," his son Isaac, and his grandson Jacob. Jacob's son Joseph helped all the people come to Egypt. He got food for them during the years when the farmers couldn't raise enough.

GENNESARET *(guh-NESS-uh-ret)* is a fertile stretch of land along the northwest shore of the Sea of Galilee. It is about a mile wide and three miles long. It is the only good agricultural land along the Sea of Galilee. There are many fig, olive, palm, and walnut trees there. Jesus healed many people in this area.

Where to find it: *Matthew 14: 34; Mark 6: 53*

GENNESARET, Lake of, is the same as the Sea of Galilee (see *Galilee, Sea of*).

GENTILES *(JEN-tiles)* means all people who are not Jewish by nationality or religion. In Bible times, Jews and Gentiles did not have much to do with each other. The Gentiles often persecuted the Jews for their religion, and the Jews hated the Gentiles and looked down on them.

Jesus did most of his teaching and miracle working among Jews. He rarely taught Gentiles, but he healed them when they came to him. He healed the servant of a Gentile soldier. He taught Greeks who came to see him.

After Jesus' death and resurrection, the Church began to include both Jews and Gentiles who believed in Christ. The apostle Paul said that the gospel of Christ has broken down the wall between the two groups.

The Church today is made up mostly of Gentiles. But the people of God in Old Testament times were mostly Jews. It was through the Jews that God brought salvation to all people.

Where to find it

Jesus teaches and heals Gentiles *Luke 7: 2-10; John 12: 20-36*
Gospel breaks down walls between Jews and Gentiles *Ephesians 2: 11-22*

GERIZIM *(guh-RYE-zim)* is a mountain in Samaria about thirty miles north of Jerusalem. On this mountain the Samaritans built a temple to worship God. Jesus and the Samaritan woman talked about this temple in John 4: 19-24.

GERASENES (see *Gadara, Gadarenes*)

GETHSEMANE *(geth-SEM-uh-nee)* was the garden where Jesus prayed just before he was arrested and then crucified. It was on the Mount of Olives, just outside Jerusalem.

The Garden of Gethsemane is beside the church along the road (right center).

Where to find it: *Matthew 26: 36-56; Mark 14: 32-50; Luke 22: 39-54*

GHOST is a word used often in the King James Version to mean "the breath of life." When the Bible says, "he gave up the ghost," it means "he died." When it says "Holy Ghost," it means the Holy Spirit.

Where to find it: *Genesis 25: 8; Job 11: 20; Matthew 27: 50; John 19: 30; Acts 5: 5*

GIANT in the Bible refers to actual human beings (not make-believe creatures) who are large, tall, and powerful. Tribes of these very large people lived in Canaan before the Israelites conquered it. Perhaps Goliath, who fought David, was one of these. He was more than nine feet tall. Very large people are often called *Rephaim* or *Nephilim* in the Old Testament. There is no reference to these people in the New Testament.

Og, the king of Bashan, slept in a bed 9 cubits long and 4 cubits wide (13½ feet by 6 feet). He was the last of the Rephaim.

Where to find it

Og sleeps in a long bed *Deuteronomy 3: 11*
Spies find large people in Canaan *Numbers 13: 32-33*
David fights Goliath *1 Samuel 17: 1-51*

GIBEAH *(GIB-ee-uh)* was a city a few miles north of Jerusalem. The Israelites destroyed the town because an awful murder took place there.

141

GIBEON

.Later it was rebuilt and was the birthplace of King Saul. He lived there during some of his battles with David.

Archaeologists have found that the town was destroyed and rebuilt several times. There is no city there now.

Where to find it: *Judges 19–20; 1 Samuel 10: 26; 22: 6; 26: 1*

GIBEON *(GIB-ee-un)* was a city in Canaan about 15 miles west of Jerusalem. When the Gibeonites heard that the Israelites had defeated Jericho and other cities, they tricked Joshua into making a treaty with them.

They said they had walked many days to come see Joshua. They showed him moldy bread and worn-out shoes as proof. So Joshua made a treaty not to destroy them. When Joshua discovered they lived in the area, he said they would have to become servants of the Israelites, but he would keep his word and see that they were not destroyed.

Later, other people attacked the Gibeonites because they had made peace with Joshua.

The Gibeonites called for help, and Joshua came with his army. God sent giant hailstones on the enemies and miraculously lengthened the day to give time to defeat them.

Saul once tried to kill the Gibeonites in spite of the treaty, but God sent punishment on his family as a result.

Where to find it

Treaty with Joshua   *Joshua 9: 3-27*
Joshua fights their enemies   *Joshua 10: 1-14*
Saul tries to kill Gibeonites   *2 Samuel 21: 1-14*

GIDEON *(GID-ee-un)* was one of Israel's great ruler-judges. During his time the Midianites made life miserable for the people of Israel, stealing their cattle and destroying all their crops.

One day as Gideon was working, God's angel appeared to him and told him that the Lord would help him defeat the Midianites. God told Gideon to tear down the altars to false gods and build an altar to the true God. Gideon did this, but the people in Ophrah, his

The Gibeonites tricked Joshua and his army by pretending to have come from a long distance.

142

Gideon and his servants tore down an altar to a false god one night.

city, were so angry they wanted to kill him.

Gideon was afraid to fight the Midianites. He asked God to let him know for sure that God would lead him. Gideon put a sheep fleece on the ground. In the morning the fleece was soaking wet, but the ground was dry. The next night, the fleece was dry but the ground was wet. Gideon was satisfied that God would be with him.

Gideon called for men to help him defeat the Midianites, and 22,000 responded. God said it was too many. By a series of tests, Gideon cut the number to 300.

Gideon gave each of the 300 men a trumpet and a jar with a torch inside. One hundred men went to each of three sides of the Midianites' army camp. They all broke their pitchers and blew trumpets at the same time. The Midianites were so frightened and confused they began killing each other. Gideon's men won a great victory.

Later, the Israelites wanted to make Gideon king, but he refused. He said God should rule over them. The Israelites had peace for 40 years. But after Gideon died, the Israelites again began to worship false gods.

Where to find it: *Judges 6: 1–8: 33*

GIFTS, SPIRITUAL (see *Spiritual Gifts*)

GILEAD (*GIL-ee-ad*) was the name of the land east of the Jordan River that belonged to Israel. It was about 30 miles wide and 120 miles long—extending from the Sea of Galilee to the Dead Sea. It was good grazing land with some forests. Three tribes of Israel settled in this region—Reuben, Gad, and part of Manasseh. Gilead is most famous for its balm—a healing ointment made from a small tree.

Where to find it: *Genesis 37: 25; Jeremiah 8: 22; 46: 11*

GIRDLE (*GUR-dul*) was a belt made of leather or cloth worn by men and women. Cloth girdles were often wide squares folded to form pockets in which things could be carried.

GILGAL (*GIL-gal*) was a place west of the Jordan River near Jericho. The Israelites camped there after they crossed the Jordan into the Promised Land. They held a Passover feast in Gilgal. After the Passover, no more manna appeared on the ground for them to eat, and they ate food that grew in their new land.

Hundreds of years later, Saul was proclaimed king in Gilgal. Saul later offended God by trying to serve as priest and offer sacrifices to God in Gilgal.

Where to find it

Israelites camp in Gilgal *Joshua 4: 19–5: 12*

Ruth first met Boaz by gleaning in his fields during harvest.

Saul is proclaimed king *1 Samuel 11:14-15*
Saul tries to be priest *1 Samuel 13:8-15*

GLAD TIDINGS *(TIE-dings)* means good news that brings joy. It is a phrase used in the King James Version. Other translations use "good news."

Where to find it: *Luke 1:19; 8:1; Acts 13:32; Romans 10:15*

GLEANING *(GLEEN-ing)* means going into the fields after the main picking or harvesting to find whatever has been missed. In the Old Testament Law, farmers were told they should let the poor come into their fields and glean the grain that was left.

Where to find it: *Leviticus 19:9; 23:22; Deuteronomy 24:19-21*

GLORY means splendor or honor that can be seen or sensed. In the Old Testament, the glory of the Lord was seen in the cloud above the Tabernacle. On Mount Sinai, Moses saw the glory of the Lord.

At the birth of Christ, the glory of the Lord shone around the shepherds on the hillside. Peter, James, and John saw the glory of Christ on the mountain with Jesus.

Christians are told to "glorify" God in our bodies—to show in our lives the splendor and honor of God.

Where to find it

Glory of God in the cloud above Tabernacle *Exodus 16:10*

Moses sees the glory of God *Exodus 24:16-17*
Shepherds see the glory of God *Luke 2:9-14*
Christ on the mountain *Luke 9:28-36*
Christians should glorify God *1 Corinthians 6:20*

GLOSSOLALIA (see *Tongues, Gift of*)

GLUTTON *(GLUT-un)* means a person who eats more than he should. The Bible says gluttony is wrong. When Jesus' enemies wanted to say something mean about him, they accused him of being a glutton, and of eating with people they believed were sinful.

Where to find it: *Proverbs 23:20-21; Matthew 11:19; Luke 7:34; Titus 1:12*

GNOSTICISM *(NAH-stuh-siz-um)* was a wrong Greek idea that hurt the Christian church in the first and second centuries.

Those who followed this belief thought they knew things that no one else knew. They believed that everything that could be touched was evil. So a person's body was evil and only the inner spirit was good.

This led to many other wrong ideas. Some people thought they could do as they pleased with their bodies (such as be immoral) because it had nothing to do with their good inner person. Others who were Gnostics thought they must punish their bodies by hurting themselves or not eating. Some insisted that Jesus Christ, since he was God, could not have had a real body because a body was evil.

Some scholars believe that the letter of 1 John in the New Testament was written to help Christians who were being confused by these wrong teachings.

GOAD was a long pointed stick or piece of metal used to push oxen to keep them moving. *Goad* is used as a word picture for a person's conscience in Acts 26:14 in the story of Paul's conversion. The voice from heaven said, "It hurts for you to kick against the goads."

GOATS (see *Animals*)

GOD lives, the Bible says. It never tries to prove God exists; it assumes that everyone knows he does.

The Bible shows us what God is like by letting us see what he does and how he responds to people and the things they do. But the most important way we know who God is and what he is like is to see who Jesus Christ is and what he is like. Jesus Christ was God in a human body. He said, "He who has seen me has seen the Father; I am in the Father and the Father [is] in me."

Many names are used for God in the Bible. These names show certain qualities about God. Psalm 23:1 says "The Lord is my shepherd," showing that he cares for his people. "The Lord, your healer" is a name God gave himself in Exodus 15:26.

The Bible tells us many other things about God. Among them are these:

1. *God loves us.* God loved the world so much that he gave his Son so that whoever believes in him (Christ) has everlasting life (John 3:16).

2. *God is everywhere.* He is not confined to one place. No matter where we go, God is there (Psalm 139:7-12).

3. *God knows everything.* He is truth itself (Job 28:20-28; Titus 1:2).

4. *God has always been and always will be.* He neither began (like a baby is born) nor will he end (he will not die) (Isaiah 44:6).

5. *God is holy.* Unlike people, he has never sinned, and could never sin (Leviticus 11:44).

6. *God is angry with sin* because it has spoiled the perfect world he created. It also hurt the friendship he could have had with people. Someday God will destroy Satan, the author of sin.

7. *God is Spirit.* He does not have a physical body as people have, although Christ had a physical body when he was on earth (John 4:24).

These are only some of the things we learn about God from the Bible. The Bible does not tell us everything about God. God is so big, so great, so wonderful that our minds can never understand or imagine it.

But we can understand enough to know that God wants us to believe him, to trust him, to love him, to obey him. We can start by learning about Christ, God's Son, who came to earth to be our Savior and to reveal God to us.

GOD-FEARING in the New Testament usually describes a Gentile person who was following the Jewish religion or had shown interest in it.

Where to find it: *Acts 10:2, 22; 13:16, 26*

GODHEAD is another word for God or the qualities of God. It appears in the King James Version in Acts 17:29; Romans 1:20; and Colossians 2:9. Most other versions use "God" or "deity" in these places.

GODLESS means wicked, evil, caring nothing about God or his laws.

GODLINESS, GODLY (*GOD-lee-ness, GOD-lee*) means having an attitude of respect and reverence toward God and obeying him.

Where to find it: *1 Timothy 2:2; 4:7-8; 6:3, 5-6, 11*

GOG and **MAGOG** (*MAY-gog*) are names of nations or groups of people who the Bible says will be enemies of God's people. Scholars differ as to who they are and when they will attack. But in the end, God will defeat them.

Where to find it: *Ezekiel 38–39; Revelation 20:8*

GOLD is mentioned hundreds of times in the Bible—from Genesis to Revelation.

Gold was valuable in early times for the same reason it is valuable now—it is beautiful, it is almost indestructible, and it is scarce.

In Bible times it was used for jewelry, for

Moses was so furious about the golden calf that he smashed the stone tablets God had given him.

money, and to decorate fine furniture, pottery, spoons, and other household things. But its main use was in decorating palaces and temples and the things used inside them.

The word *gold* is also sometimes a word picture to describe heaven.

Where to find it: *Genesis 2:11-12; Exodus 25:3, 11; Matthew 2:11; Revelation 21:15, 18, 21*

GOLDEN CALF was an image Aaron made while Moses was on the mountain receiving the Ten Commandments from God. The people had become impatient because Moses

had been gone so long. The statue was probably similar to the Egyptian bull-calf images that the people had known. Moses said Aaron's act was a terrible sin.

Much later, King Jeroboam made two golden calves. After the Hebrew people were divided into two countries, he did not want his people to go to the Temple in Jerusalem to worship because it was in Judah. So he made new places of worship in Dan and Bethel and created golden calves for the people to worship. This was sinful and is mentioned several times in the Old Testament as an example of Israel's going away from God.

Where to find it
Aaron   *Exodus 32: 1-35*
Jeroboam   *1 Kings 12: 25-33; Hosea 8: 5-6; 13: 2*

GOLDEN RULE is what we call Jesus' command, "As you wish that men would do to you, do so to them."

Where to find it: *Luke 6: 31; Matthew 7: 12*

GOLGOTHA *(GOL-gah-thuh)* is an Aramaic word that means "place of the skull." It is the name of the place where Jesus was crucified.

Where to find it: *Matthew 27: 33; Mark 15: 22; John 19: 17*

GOLIATH *(guh-LIE-uth)* was a huge Philistine soldier, more than nine feet tall. In a battle, Goliath challenged the Israelites to send one man to fight him instead of having the armies fight. When no one from the Israelite army dared to go, David, the young shepherd boy, volunteered. He believed God would save him from Goliath.

With his sling and a smooth stone, David hit Goliath in the forehead. Goliath fell to the ground. David then ran to him and killed him with Goliath's own sword.

David became more and more popular after this, and Saul began to get jealous of him.

Where to find it: *1 Samuel 17: 1-58*

GOMORRAH *(guh-MOR-uh)* was one of two cities destroyed by God for its wickedness. It was located along the shores of the Dead Sea. God sent "fire and brimstone from heaven," probably in the form of an earthquake and volcano explosion that destroyed the cities

and caused the Dead Sea to spread over the remains. Lot's family, except for his wife, escaped.

Where to find it: *Genesis 18: 20-21; 19: 24-29*

GOPHER WOOD *(GO-fur)* was the material from which Noah built the ark. Scholars do not know exactly what kind of wood it was.

Where to find it: *Genesis 6: 14*

GOSHEN *(GO-shun)* was the part of Egypt where the Israelites lived for the 400 years between the time of Joseph and the time Moses led them out. It was about 900 square miles, in the northeast section of the delta of the Nile River. (See *Nile River.*)

Where to find it: *Genesis 45: 10; 47: 6, 27*

GOSPEL *(GOS-pul)* means "good news." The good news is that God has provided a way for any person to become his child, part of his family. This way is through faith in Jesus Christ, who gave his life so believers could live forever in fellowship with God. The story of the life, death, and resurrection of Jesus Christ is given in the four Gospels—the first four books of the New Testament.

GOSPELS are the first four books of the New Testament—Matthew, Mark, Luke, John. Each one tells about the life, death, and resurrection of Jesus Christ.

Information about the life of Christ was spread by word of mouth for about 30 years after the resurrection and ascension of Jesus. But the young church needed a more permanent record of the things Jesus said and did. The four Gospel writers each collected information from their own experiences and from other sources and wrote their histories.

We are not sure which Gospel was written first. Many believe the Gospel of Mark was first. It is the shortest and it emphasizes the things Jesus did.

The Gospel of Matthew seems to have been written especially for Jewish Christians. It tells more about Jesus' teachings than Mark's Gospel.

The Gospel of Luke tells more about Jesus' last visit to Jerusalem than do Matthew or Mark. It also tells more about some of the important women in the life of Jesus. It tells about Mary, the mother of Jesus, and Elizabeth, the mother of John the Baptist.

Matthew, Mark, and Luke are called "synoptic" Gospels. *Synoptic (sin-OP-tik)* means "seen together." These three accounts tell many of the same things, sometimes in ways that are very much alike.

The Gospel of John is different from the Synoptics. Most writers think John wrote his Gospel last. He tells many things that the other writers did not tell—especially about the last week of Jesus' life.

GOVERNMENT in Old Testament times had several forms. After the Israelites escaped from slavery in Egypt, they were supposed to live under a theocracy. This means "rule of God." Moses received instructions from God, and the people were to carry out those instructions. Sadly, the people did not always obey what God said through Moses. During the forty years in the wilderness, Moses appointed people to help him judge or settle disputes.

After the Israelites settled in Canaan, they had "judges" as chief rulers. These judges were leaders in battle and rulers in peace. The Bible is not clear whether each judge was responsible for all the tribes or only a few. This period lasted for several hundred years.

Later the Israelites wanted a king, like the nations around them. From that time until Israel was conquered by its enemies, there were kings. Some were good; some were evil. In 722 B.C. the Northern Kingdom of Israel was conquered by Assyria and most of its people forced to move to Assyria. In 586 B.C. the Southern Kingdom of Judah was conquered by Babylonia.

When some of the Israelites came back to Palestine after their exile in Babylon, Persia was ruling Palestine. However, the people had local officials who were called princes. The Jewish priests also had strong powers. Later, when the Syrians gained control of Palestine, the high priest became the ruler with the most authority, even though he was always subject to Syria.

In New Testament times, Palestine was ruled by the Romans. The Roman government, however, gave a great deal of self-rule to its various areas. Palestine was divided into three parts—each part had a king appointed by Rome. In New Testament times, these local kings were part of the Herod family and were themselves Jewish.

The city of Jerusalem was ruled by the Sanhedrin—a council of 70 Jewish religious leaders. They had power over most local matters, but they could not put anyone to death. That is why Jesus had to be brought before Pilate, the Roman procurator of the area.

The Jewish people hated the Roman rule—they wanted a kingdom of their own as they had under David. Some Jewish people became terrorists, called Zealots. Simon the Zealot was one of Jesus' disciples. Other people withdrew from all contact with the Romans and lived in small colonies or communes far away from cities. Others, called Sadducees, worked right with the Romans.

In A.D. 68, about 38 years after the crucifixion of Christ, the Jews rebelled against the Romans. The Romans crushed the rebellion and destroyed the city of Jerusalem.

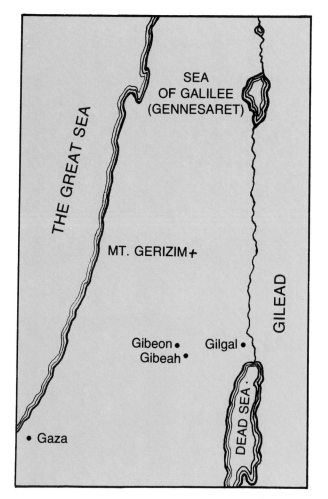

GOVERNOR *(GUV-uh-ner)* in the Bible means someone who is in charge of a country but who works for a higher ruler. Joseph was governor in Egypt, second only to Pharaoh. Pilate was a governor of Judea; he was appointed by the emperor of Rome. Governors could always be removed from office by whoever appointed them.

Where to find it: *Genesis 42: 6; Matthew 27: 2; Acts 23: 26*

GRACE usually refers to God's love showing itself in acts of kindness to us even though we don't deserve it. God's grace is especially seen in giving his Son, Jesus Christ, to be our Savior. When we respond to God's grace, we can become what God has always intended for us to be. We don't deserve God's grace, because we sin against God. That is why the Bible says, "By grace you have been saved through faith; and this is not your own doing, it is the gift of God" (Ephesians 2: 8).

GRAIN is seed from which bread is made. The main grains in the Bible were wheat and barley. Poor people usually ate barley. The King James Version usually uses "corn" for grain, but it is not the corn we have in America.

Where to find it: *Genesis 41: 57; Psalm 65: 13; John 12: 24*

GRASSHOPPER (see *Locust*)

GRATITUDE (see *Thanksgiving*)

GRAVE is a place of burial. Since most of Palestine is very rocky with only a small layer of topsoil, graves were usually holes in the limestone hills. Sometimes they were natural caves; other times they were holes dug into the hillsides. These places often became family graves. Abraham, Sarah, their son Isaac and his wife Rebekah, and their son Jacob and his wife Leah were all buried in the family cave at Machpelah.

If a person died a distance away from the family grave, he or she might be buried under the ground, as Rachel was buried beside an oak tree.

The grave of Jesus was cut into the side of a rocky hill. It was apparently the family grave of Joseph of Arimathea, but it had not been used at the time of the crucifixion.

Where to find it

Grave of Abraham's family *Genesis 23: 19-20; 49: 29; 50: 13*
Grave of Rachel *Genesis 35: 19-20*
Grave of Jesus *Matthew 27: 59-60*

GRAVECLOTHES were the strips of linen cloth that were wrapped around a body before burial. Hands and feet were tied with more pieces of linen, and another piece was placed

over the face. This is the way Lazarus appeared when Jesus raised him from the dead.

Where to find it: *John 11: 38-44*

GRAVEN IMAGE *(GRAY-vun IM-aj)* was an idol shaped of wood, metal, or stone. Such idols were worshiped by the Canaanites, Babylonians, and Chaldeans. God told the Israelites in the Second Commandment that they were not to make such things, but they often disobeyed him.

Where to find it: *Exodus 20: 4; Isaiah 45: 20*

GREAT SEA refers to the Mediterranean Sea—the largest body of water the Israelites knew. It is also called the Western Sea and the Sea of the Philistines, because the Philistines lived along its coast.

GREECE is the peninsula and surrounding islands in the Mediterranean Sea east of Italy. People have lived in Greece since about 4000 B.C. From about 400 to 300 B.C., it was the most advanced civilization of its time. Ancient Greek culture, ideas, and form of government still influence our world.

By 300 B.C. Greek language and culture had spread over all the countries around the Mediterranean Sea. Greek language and culture were most important during New Testament times, although the ruling power was then the Roman Empire. Jesus and the disciples spoke mainly Aramaic, the native language of Palestine, but the New Testament was written in Greek, and the Christian message spread around the then-known world in the Greek language.

During New Testament times, the area we now know as Greece was divided into two Roman provinces—Macedonia in the north, and Achaia in the south. The apostle Paul visited both parts on his missionary journeys.

People who lived in Greece or spoke the Greek language were called Grecians.

GREEK LANGUAGE is the language in which most of the New Testament was originally written. It was the language of business all through the Roman Empire in New Testament times.

It was originally the language of just Greece. But when Alexander the Great was conquering the world (about 336-323 B.C.), the Greek language spread to all the countries around the Mediterranean. Even after Greece became part of the Roman Empire in 146 B.C., Greek remained the most important language of its time.

The gospel of Christ was able to spread much more rapidly because so many people in different countries understood the Greek language.

GREEKS was a term used in New Testament times to mean people who were not Jews—it meant the same as "Gentiles." Paul uses it this way in Romans 1:16: "For I am not ashamed of the gospel; it is the power of God for salvation to every one who has faith, to the Jew first and also to the Greek."

GROVES in the Old Testament referred to the places of false worship. The King James Version uses the word *groves* where newer translations use *Asherah*, the name of a pagan goddess. The goddess's symbol of worship was the trunk of a tree. This is why God told Moses, "You shall not plant any tree as an Asherah beside the altar of the Lord."

God-fearing kings of Israel often cut down the pagan groves.

Where to find it: *Deuteronomy 16:21; Micah 5:14*

GUILE (*gile*) means dishonesty or trickery, pretending one thing while doing the opposite.

Where to find it: *John 1:47; 1 Peter 2:22; 3:10*

GUILT (see *Sin*)

GUILT OFFERING (see *Offerings*)

GULF (see *Chasm*)

HABAKKUK *(huh-BACK-uk)* was a little-known prophet who wrote an Old Testament book sometime between 605 and 586 B.C. In this book, he asked why the Jewish people had become so wicked. He told them to be sorry for their sins and to repent. If they didn't repent, he said, God would allow their enemies to the north, the Chaldeans, to destroy Judah. And then God would let the Chaldeans—who were even more wicked—be destroyed also.

But even after bad times come to God's people, Habakkuk said, they must remember God's faithfulness and trust him. In his book, Habakkuk asked questions and then quietly listened to God's answers.

The last chapter of Habakkuk is a lovely poem that was meant to be sung. The words "according to Shigionoth" in the first verse told the readers what tune to use when they sang it.

The poem expressed Habakkuk's faith in God's power and control of the world. He is sure that God will do what is right, and that he can always rejoice in God.

Where to find it

Habakkuk's prophecy and warning *Habakkuk 1–2*
Habakkuk's poem about God's power and goodness *Habakkuk 3*

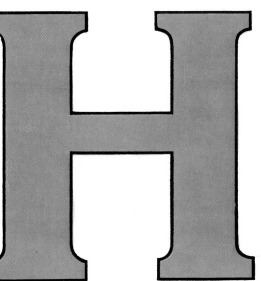

Hannah prayed to the Lord with such emotion that Eli the priest thought she was drunk. But she was simply pleading with the Lord for a son. God answered by giving her Samuel.

HADORAM (see *Adoniram*)

HADES (*HAY-dees*) is the Greek word for the place of the dead. In Greek, the original language of the New Testament, the word for the place of the dead is not the same as the word for hell—the place of eternal punishment. However, the King James Version translated both words as "hell." The Revised Standard Version and other newer translations show the difference.

In Jesus' story of the rich man and Lazarus, the rich man was in hades—the place of the dead. In Peter's sermon after Pentecost, he said that Christ had been raised from the dead and not left in hades.

Peter says that God did not spare the angels when they sinned but cast them into hell—the place of eternal punishment. This shows the difference between the two terms. At the end of time, both death and hades will be "thrown into the lake of fire"—hell.

Where to find it

Parable of Lazarus and the rich man   *Luke 16: 19-31*
Christ not left in hades   *Acts 2: 31*
Angels cast into hell   *2 Peter 2: 4*
Death and hades will be thrown in lake of fire   *Revelation 20: 13-14*

HAGAR (*HAY-gar*) was Sarah's Egyptian maid. She was also the mother of Abraham's son Ishmael. Sarah became jealous of Hagar and her son, even though it had been Sarah's idea for Hagar and Abraham to have the child. Sarah treated Hagar badly because Sarah wished she could have a son. Abraham did not stop Sarah from being mean to Hagar, and eventually Hagar took her son and ran away. But God promised Hagar that the descendants of her son Ishmael would become a large nation. When God heard Hagar crying in the wilderness, he said, "What troubles you, Hagar? Fear not. Arise, lift up the lad. I will make him a great nation."

God was with Ishmael, and he grew to be a strong man and a good hunter. His descendants became a part of the Arab people, who still live in the Middle East.

Where to find it: *Genesis 16; 21: 1-21*

HAGGAI (*HAG-ee-eye*) was a prophet who wrote an Old Testament book about 520 B.C. The Jews had returned from captivity in Babylon and had started to rebuild the Temple at Jerusalem. But they stopped work because lack of rain had ruined their crops, and poverty had discouraged them. Haggai encouraged the Jews to go back to the rebuilding. He said they should work hard to complete the Temple so the Jews could have a place to worship God.

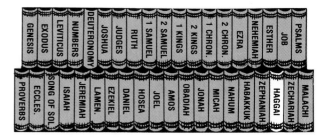

The prophet told the people that the Lord promised to fill the building with his glory when it was finished. Haggai reminded them of the glory given to the Lord by Solomon's Temple long ago. He wrote about the power of the Lord over the whole universe, using a word picture of the Lord shaking the world. Such a Lord deserves to be given glory, Haggai said.

Where to find it

God's promise to fill the Temple   *Haggai 2: 7*
Song about God's power   *Haggai 2: 21-23*

When Hagar and young Ishmael had to leave Abraham's home, they almost died of thirst.

HAIR, to some Jews in Old Testament times, was a picture of life itself because it keeps on growing. Some people, known as Nazarites, made vows never to cut their hair. Their long hair was presented to God as a picture of their lives being given to him. Samson's strength was in this dedication to God, so when his hair was cut, he lost his strength.

In both the Old Testament and the New Testament, hair was a mark of beauty. In Old Testament times long hair on men was greatly admired, but in New Testament times men's hair was shorter and long hair on women was considered beautiful.

Where to find it

Old Testament hair beauty *2 Samuel 14: 25-26*
New Testament hair beauty *1 Corinthians 11: 14-15*

HALLELUJAH *(HAL-uh-LOO-yuh)* means "you, praise the Lord" in Hebrew.

HALLOW *(HAL-oh)* means to dedicate for a holy purpose. When we are told to "hallow" the Sabbath Day, it means we are to treat it as a holy day and make it special for God's worship. When we say "Hallowed be thy name" to God, we are saying that we sense his holiness and pray that all other people may recognize it.

HAM is the name for three people or groups of people in the Bible:

1. Ham was the youngest son of Noah. He lived through the Flood on the ark with his family. Because Ham looked at Noah when Noah was naked and drunk, his father later cursed him and his son. However, Ham still became the father of many nations.

2. The group of descendants from the original man named Ham is also called by his name. In the Psalms the word refers especially to those descendants of Ham who became Egyptians.

3. Ham was a city east of the Jordan River in Abraham's time.

Where to find it

Ham, Noah's son *Genesis 9: 20–10: 20*
The city *Genesis 14: 5*
Ham's descendants *Psalms 78: 51; 105: 23; 106: 22*

HAMAN *(HAY-mun)* was a selfish man who tried to destroy the Jewish people during the days of Queen Esther. He was a prime minister of Persia about 480 B.C., but he wanted to be treated like a king. He wanted all the people to bow down to him when he passed by. Because Mordecai, a Jew, would bow only to God, Haman tried to trick the king into hanging Mordecai. But Queen Esther showed the king what Haman was up to, and Haman himself was hanged on the gallows he had built for Mordecai.

Where to find it: *Esther 7*

HAMMER is a hand tool, but in the Bible it is also a word picture for any crushing power.

An ancient hammer was made of stone. It was used for smoothing metal or for breaking rocks. It was also used as a mallet for driving tent pegs into the ground.

As a word picture, *hammer* describes the power of a nation, as in Jeremiah 50: 23, or the power of God's Word, as in Jeremiah 23: 29.

HAMSTRING is the tendon at the back of the knee in humans and in animals. When that tendon is cut, the animal or person is helpless. Jacob's sons Simeon and Levi were cursed because they cut the hamstrings of some oxen.

Where to find it: *Genesis 49: 6*

HAND is an actual part of the body and is also used as a word picture in the Bible.

Sometimes it is a word picture of God's care, as in John 10: 29. He keeps us in his hand. He wants us close to him where he can take care of us.

Sometimes it is a word picture of God's power, as in Hebrews 10: 31 or Isaiah 41: 20. God's hand is strong to do his will in nature and in the lives of people.

When the Bible says God's hand was upon a person, it often means God enabled that person to tell God's message.

To sit at the right hand of someone is a word picture for being in an honored position. Psalm 110: 1 tells us that Christ the Son sits at the right hand of God the Father.

HANDKERCHIEF was a piece of cloth used for several purposes—to wipe away sweat, to carry money, etc. Sometimes our Bibles say napkin or cloth for what we today would call handkerchief.

HANDMAID (see *Maid*)

HANDS, LAYING ON OF, is a ceremony in which persons placed their hands symbolically on something or someone. It is recorded in both the Old and New Testaments.

Sometimes the ceremony means someone or something is dedicated to God's service. In the Old Testament, the priests laid their hands on an animal that was going to be sacrificed.

Sometimes a blessing, such as healing, came with a laying on of hands in the Bible.

Today when people are set apart to be priests or pastors, they often are in a ceremony of the laying on of hands. This is a picture of passing on spiritual strength from one servant of God to another, of setting a person apart for God's service.

Where to find it

Laying on of hands for animal sacrifices   *Exodus 29:10*
Laying on of hands for God's service   *Deuteronomy 34:9*
Laying on of hands for healing   *Mark 5:23*
Laying on of hands to receive the Holy Spirit   *Acts 19:6*

HANNAH *(HAN-uh)* was a godly woman who dedicated her firstborn son Samuel to serve God. When Hannah had no children, she prayed for a long time that she would have a child. One feast day in the Tabernacle she

promised God that if he gave her a son she would bring him to serve in God's house. Later, when Hannah and her husband Elkanah had a baby boy, Hannah dedicated him to the Lord. She was so happy she sang a beautiful song of praise. After her son Samuel moved into the Tabernacle to serve the priest Eli there, the Lord gave Hannah three more sons and two daughters to love.

Where to find it: *1 Samuel 1–2*

HANUKKAH *(HAHN-uh-kuh)* is a Jewish festival of dedication in early December. It reminds the Jewish people of one of their brave heroes, Judas Maccabeus. In 165 B.C. he removed the signs of pagan worship that had been placed in the Temple by the Romans. Then he rededicated it for the worship of God. Jewish people each year light candles to remember God's miraculous help at that time.

HARAN *(HAY-run)* was a city in northern Mesopotamia. Here Abraham buried his father, Terah, after they had both left the city of Ur. In this city Abraham's brother, Nahor, decided to stay while Abraham set off for Canaan. Later Abraham sent his servant to find a wife for his son Isaac among his relatives there. Still later, Isaac's son Jacob fled to Haran and met his wives there.

Haran is also the name for several people in the Bible.

Where to find it

Abraham's family settles in Haran and later leaves for Palestine   *Genesis 11:31; 12:4*
Isaac's wife comes from Haran   *Genesis 24:4*
Jacob flees to Haran   *Genesis 29:4-5*

HARDEN THE HEART is a word picture for stubbornness and refusing to understand. People with hard hearts will not take God's love or listen to God's message.

The Bible says that sometimes people deliberately harden their hearts. Pharaoh did this when he would not let the Israelites leave Egypt, even though he knew he should. The Bible also says that God hardened Pharaoh's heart. This may have been part of the punishment for Pharaoh's hardening his own heart.

Jesus said people sometimes choose to close their ears and their hearts to God's message because they do not want to respond.

Jesus was sad when his disciples' hard hearts kept them from seeing the spiritual truth he was trying to teach them as he fed the 5,000.

God also said his people were not to harden their hearts against those who are in need, such as poor people.

Where to find it

Pharaoh hardens his heart   *Exodus 8:15*
God hardens Pharaoh's heart   *Exodus 14:4*
Don't harden hearts against poor   *Deuteronomy 15:7*
People don't want to know God   *Matthew 13:14-15*
The disciples' hearts are hard   *Mark 6:52*

HARLOT *(HAR-lut)* is a woman who has sexual relations with men other than her husband, often for money. Harlotry is a sin, but like other sins, it can be forgiven. And sometimes God used even harlots to fulfill his purposes. The best known story is about Rahab, a harlot who helped God's people find out how to enter the Promised Land.

The Bible also uses *harlot* as a word picture for people who turn away from God. Harlotry means idolatry, especially for the Israelites. God pictured Israel as his "bride," because he loved that nation as much and more than any husband loved his wife. When Israel rejected God and worshiped idols, God said Israel was like a harlot turning to other lovers.

Where to find it

Rahab   *Joshua 2:1-21*
God's people   *Hosea 1–3*

HARMONY OF THE GOSPELS is a term used for books that arrange the material in the Gospels—Matthew, Mark, Luke, John—to give a more complete story of Jesus' life on earth. Usually a harmony of the Gospels has four columns on each page, one for each Gospel. Where the material is the same in all the Gospels, the paragraphs are printed side by side in the columns. Where information is only in one Gospel, the other columns are blank.

None of the Gospel writers was trying to give a full account of Jesus' life. They didn't include every event. A harmony of the Gospels puts the events in order to show how the four accounts together give a more complete picture of the life of Christ.

HARP (see *Musical Instruments*)

HART (see *Animals*)

HATE is a word used in two different ways in the Bible. God hates evil, idolatry, unfairness, and religious pretending. Believers also should hate these things. Even though God hates these sins, he still loves the persons who do them, and Christians are to do the same. Christ said we are to love our enemies. John says that anyone who hates his brother is a murderer and is in darkness of sin.

Secondly, *hate* in the Bible is sometimes a word picture of turning away from something or someone. When God said he "hated" Esau, it meant that Esau and his descendants were not chosen by God as his special people.

Jesus used *hate* as an exaggerated word to show us that we should not love someone more than God. Jesus said in Luke 14:26, "If anyone comes to me and does not hate his own father and mother and wife and children and brothers and sisters, yes, and even his own life, he cannot be my disciple." However, he did not mean an active dislike. He meant, "Whoever does not put me first— before even his family or himself—cannot be my disciple."

Where to find it

God hates sin   *Deuteronomy 12:31; Proverbs 6:16-19*
God "hates" Esau   *Malachi 1:2-3*
We are to love enemies   *Matthew 5:44*
Hatred is murder and darkness   *1 John 3:15*

HEAD in the Bible usually means the top part of a person's body. However, it is sometimes used in other ways.

1. The top of some object, such as a mountain, tower, ladder, lampstand, or pillar.

2. The leader or chief of a group.

3. The first in line, or the beginning. It is used this way when speaking of the "head of a tribe," the "head of a river," or the "head of a line of march."

When the Bible uses *head* as a word picture, it is important to try to decide which of these meanings it has. In Colossians 1:18, Christ is called the "head" of the church. We know that Christ is the leader of the church, but in this verse *head* does not mean "leader." It says he is the "beginning, the first-born from the dead," showing that the meaning here is "first in line, or the beginning or source of the church."

Our modern understanding of the body says that the head or brain is the place of thinking and decision making. However, people in the Bible used the word *heart* for this.

HEALTH of mind and body was important to people in Bible times. Some of the laws God gave in the Old Testament about which foods to eat helped to prevent diseases. God's laws about the Sabbath Day helped the people get rest and time for thinking.

The people in the Old Testament were mostly farmers or wandering shepherds. Living outdoors and getting lots of exercise in their work kept many people healthy. However, when people did get sick, others often said it was punishment for sin. When Jesus came, he said that was not always true. When he healed a man who had been blind from birth, people asked if his blindness was due to his sin or his parents' sin. Jesus answered, "Neither." Jesus healed people whose minds or bodies were sick.

The Bible teaches that the Christian's body is the temple of the Holy Spirit and a member of Christ. Therefore it is to be well cared for with nourishing food and proper exercise.

Where to find it

Old Testament food laws *Leviticus 11*
Jesus' concern for health *John 3: 16; 10: 10*
Jesus heals the blind man *John 9: 1-41*
Bodies belong to God *1 Corinthians 6: 15, 19*
Exercise is good *1 Timothy 4: 8*

HEALING was an important part of Jesus' ministry. When he sent his disciples out to tell about salvation, he gave them a special gift— the ability to heal as he did.

After Jesus left this earth, the leaders of the early church received gifts of healing. "In the name of Jesus," sick people were restored to health by Jesus' followers.

Where to find it

Jesus' early healings *Luke 4: 33-39*
The disciples' gift of healing *Luke 9: 1*
Early church's gift of healing *Acts 3: 6, 16*

HEAP OF STONES is an expression for two things in the Bible.

1. A marker for an agreement between two people, such as Jacob and Laban, or a marker for a grave.

2. The remains of a city or house or pagan altar that had been destroyed.

Where to find it

Marker for agreement *Genesis 31: 46-54*
Marker for grave *Joshua 7: 26*
Remains of a house *Job 15: 28*

HEART in the Bible seldom means just the organ that pumps blood through a body. To people in Bible times, all the emotion or feelings of a person came from his heart. People talked about their hearts being glad, sad, fearful, full of hatred, full of love, or having secrets.

The heart was also considered the place of intelligence. The heart was the innermost part of a person, where all his thinking and deciding was done. So the heart was also the center of the will.

The heart, because it involved the emotions, mind, and will, was also the place of meeting with God. The Bible says God looks on the heart and knows its secrets. A person speaks to God from his heart and can keep God's Word there.

Sometimes *heart* also means a person's whole nature.

Where to find it

Hateful heart *Leviticus 19: 17*
Heart full of love *Deuteronomy 13: 3*
We keep God's Word in the heart *Deuteronomy 30: 14*
God looks on the heart *1 Samuel 16: 7*
Intelligence comes from heart *1 Chronicles 29: 18; Psalms 4: 4; 10: 6; Mark 2: 6*
Sad heart *Nehemiah 2: 2*
We speak to God from the heart *Psalm 27: 8*
God knows secrets of the heart *Psalm 44: 21*
Glad heart *Proverbs 27: 11*
Fearful heart *Isaiah 35: 4*
Heart means whole person *Jeremiah 17: 9*

HEAVE OFFERING (see *Offering*)

HEAVEN (*HEV-un*) in the Bible may mean either the part of the world that seems to arch over the earth, or it may mean the place where God lives.

1. Ancient peoples saw the universe as

being in two parts: the earth and the heavens. They saw the heavens as a kind of dome over the earth. From the heavens—sometimes called the firmament—came the rain and the sunlight needed for life. The beauty of the heavens reminded the people of God.

2. Heaven is also the place where God lives and where his children will live with him after the resurrection. Right now, Jesus is in heaven praying for his followers and helping to run the universe. We don't know where heaven is or what it looks like, but the word pictures in the Book of Revelation tell us it is a happy place where everyone enjoys God.

Where to find it

Beauty of heavens *Psalm 8*
God lives in heaven *Genesis 28:17*
Christians will join him there *Matthew 5:12*
Jesus is praying for us in heaven *Hebrews 9:24*

HEBREW *(HEE-bru)* is a name for the nation that descended from Abraham and Sarah. It is also the name for any member of that nation as well as the language they speak.

Another name for the Hebrew nation is the nation of Israel. God promised Abraham that his descendants would be a great nation. The Hebrews have remained a great people for over 4,000 years. Some of the Hebrews now live in the nation of Israel, but many others are scattered around the world. In our day, Hebrew people are often called Jews.

HEBREW LANGUAGE is the major language of the Old Testament. Most of the Old Testament books were written in Hebrew; only half of Daniel and a few parts of Ezra were in Aramaic, a kind of "cousin" language of Hebrew.

Hebrew was the language the Israelites spoke in Old Testament times. However, after the Northern Kingdom and the Southern Kingdom of Israel were carried into exile in 722 and 586 B.C., the Hebrew language slowly began to die. The people began to speak Aramaic like the nations around them did. By the time of Christ, Hebrew was a "dead" language—it was not spoken by anyone in normal conversation. It was used primarily by rabbis and teachers to study the Old Testament and to write about Judaism.

But in the new nation of Israel that began in

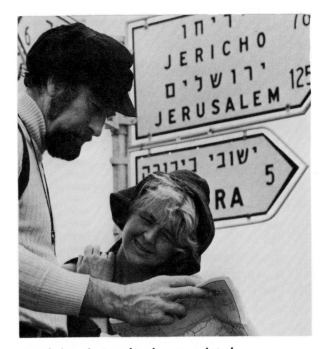

Road signs in Israel today are printed both in Hebrew and English.

1948, Hebrew is the official language, although it has changed some since Bible times.

Hebrew is read from right to left instead of left to right as we read English. Also, all the letters in Hebrew are consonants. Although some consonants can be used as vowels, there are no letters for vowels—*a, e, i, o, u*—only dashes and dots. These dashes and dots are placed between the consonant letters or above and below the line of print to tell what vowel sounds should be used.

HEBREWS, HISTORY OF (see *Israel*)

HEBREWS *(HEE-brooz)*, **LETTER TO,** is a New Testament book written to Christians, many of them Jewish, to remind them that Jesus' way to know God was better than the old way described in the Law. We do not know who wrote the Book of Hebrews. The book itself does not say, and no other New Testament books tell us for sure.

Whoever the author was, he was a very good writer who knew the Old Testament well. The letter shows that he also expected his readers to know the Old Testament well. His purpose was to show his readers that Christ was greater than angels, than Moses, than Old Testament priests and Law. Christ was the highest revelation of God.

His readers thought highly of angels as ministers of God. The author of Hebrews showed that Jesus is higher than the angels. The author showed that Jesus is greater than any high priest. The Jewish people felt they owed everything in their religion to Moses. But Jesus is far above even Moses.

The author wanted his readers to renew their commitment to Christ. He reminded them of people in the past whose faith remained true even when they were tested. Hard times were coming for the Christians who would read that letter, just as they may be for Christians at any time. The writer said that Christians are on a pilgrimage—a kind of camping trip—on their way to a heavenly city to which Christ has already gone. Through Christ we already have citizenship in this heavenly city. Christians will find eternal rest and joy at the end. So we shouldn't be weary or lose hope. We must keep on following Jesus.

Where to find it

Christ is greater than angels   *Hebrews 1: 4-14*
Christ is greater than Moses   *Hebrews 3: 1-6*
Christ is greater than high priests   *Hebrews 4: 14-16; 5: 1-10; 7: 1-26; 9: 11-28*
Faithfulness will be rewarded   *Hebrews 10: 19–12: 29*
Don't become indifferent   *Hebrews 10: 19-38*
Many saints have been tested   *Hebrews 11*

HEBRON (*HEE-brun*), one of the oldest cities in the world, is 19 miles southwest of Jerusalem.

The tomb of Abraham, Sarah, Isaac, Rebekah, Jacob, and Leah was a cave in a field near the ancient city. This place is now a part of the much larger modern city of Hebron.

Hebron was an early camping place for Abraham when he went to Canaan. There he built an altar to God. Later, when the Israelites came to Canaan, Caleb and his men conquered Hebron.

For the first seven and a half years of King David's rule, Hebron was the capital of Israel. After David conquered Jerusalem, he moved there. When Absalom rebelled against David, he made Hebron his headquarters.

Where to find it

Abraham camps at Hebron   *Genesis 13: 18*
Tomb of the patriarchs   *Genesis 23: 17-20*
Caleb conquers Hebron   *Joshua 14: 13-15; 15: 13-14*
David is king at Hebron   *2 Samuel 2: 1-11*
Absalom made king at Hebron   *2 Samuel 15: 7-11*

HEEL, LIFT UP, is to act unkindly, proudly, or selfishly toward a person—usually a person who had been your friend. It was like an animal kicking the owner who was feeding it. Sometimes "lifting up his heel against . . ." meant the person was being a traitor. John 13: 18 says Judas had that attitude toward Jesus, even though they had been close friends for three years.

HEIFER (see *Animals*)

HEIR (*air*) is a person who receives or has the right to receive someone's property or position after that person dies. In Bible times, the heir was always the son of the property owner. He was a very important person in a household. Everyone who has Jesus as Savior is an heir of God. Each one of us is important to him.

Where to find it: *Romans 8: 17; Galatians 4: 4-7*

HELL is both separation from God and the eternal place of those who choose to be separated from God. It is a place of punishment for those who have chosen to turn away from God. It is the place of the devil and his angels. The Bible has many word pictures to show how terrible it is to be forever separated from God.

Hell is not the same as hades or sheol—the place of the dead. However, the King James translation uses the word *hell* for hades and sheol as well as for actual hell. To tell which word is meant, check with the Revised Standard Version or one of the other newer translations.

Where to find it: *Matthew 5: 22, 29-30; 18: 9; 23: 15, 33; Mark 9: 47; James 3: 6; 2 Peter 2: 4*

HELLENISTS *(HELL-un-ists)* were Jews in New Testament times who spoke Greek as their native language instead of Aramaic, like the Jews in Palestine. Having groups that spoke different languages sometimes led to problems in the early church.

Where to find it: *Acts 6:1; 9:29*

HELMET is a covering to protect the head, often worn during battle. In the Bible it is also

A Roman helmet.

a word picture of salvation. The helmet of salvation is a protection against those who want to keep the believer from serving the Lord.

Where to find it: *Ephesians 6:17*

HELPERS are those people who lend a hand to another in a task. The gift of being a helper is one of the gifts of the Spirit (see *Spiritual Gifts*). In the New Testament deacons are often called helpers.

Where to find it: *1 Corinthians 12:28*

HELPMEET is a word that comes from the King James Version of Genesis 2:18, where it is actually two words, "I will make him an help meet for him." It means "suitable" or "equal to." For Adam, the first man, God made a woman suitable and equal to him, one who could work side by side with him. The Revised Standard Version says "a helper fit for him."

HERDSMAN (see *Occupations*)

HERESY *(HAIR-uh-see)* is a belief or practice

that is not accepted by the church. It usually involves false teaching about God or his purposes. Those who believe these wrong ideas are called "heretics."

Where to find it: *2 Peter 2:1*

HERETIC (see *Heresy*)

HERITAGE *(HAIR-uh-tej)* is what the older generation gives to the younger. In the Bible it also means those things that are handed down to us from God. Because believers are God's heirs, spiritual blessings are available to them as a heritage. The heritage belongs to the heirs.

Where to find it: *Psalm 16:5-6*

HERMON *(HER-mun)*, **MOUNT,** is the tallest mountain in northern Israel. It is the source of the streams that become the Jordan River. It is snowcapped most of the year and is one of the most beautiful sights in the area.

HEROD *(HAIR-ud)*, called "the Great," was king over Palestine and some surrounding areas about 37 to 4 B.C. At that time, the area was part of the Roman Empire, but Herod was the local Jewish ruler. Jesus was born during Herod's reign. Herod ordered the killing of all baby boys in Bethlehem when he heard a new king had been born.

Herod was also the family name for several rulers after Herod the Great.

One was **Herod Archelaus,** the son of Herod the Great, who became ruler of Judea and Samaria after his father died. God warned Joseph in a dream of the danger from this king. So he took his family and settled in Nazareth when they returned from Egypt. Archelaus's rule was short. He was banished to what is now France in A.D. 6.

Another son of Herod the Great was **Herod Antipas,** who became ruler of Galilee after the death of his father. Jesus called him "that fox." Herod Antipas was the ruler who had John the Baptist killed.

Herod Agrippa I was the grandson of Herod the Great. He ruled most of Palestine from A.D. 40 to 44. He is the ruler who had the apostle James killed and Peter imprisoned. He died suddenly in A.D. 44.

Herod Agrippa II is known in the Bible as

HERODIANS

"King Agrippa." He was the son of Herod Agrippa I. He ruled Galilee and some areas east of the Sea of Galilee from A.D. 53 to 70. He is the ruler who heard Paul defend himself against Jewish charges.

Although all the Herods were under the Roman emperor, they could rule their own country as long as they did not go against the Roman rulers. Many Jews resented them.

Where to find it

Herod the Great orders babies killed *Matthew 2:1-18*
Herod Archelaus rules Judea *Matthew 2:19-23*
Herod Antipas kills John the Baptist *Matthew 14:1-12; Mark 6:14-29; Luke 3:19-20*
Herod Agrippa I kills James and imprisons Peter *Acts 12:2-23*
Herod Agrippa II hears Paul *Acts 25:13–26:32*

HERODIANS *(hair-ROH-dee-uns)* were Jews who supported the rule of the Herod family and therefore the rule of Rome. They did not trust Jesus because they feared he had politi-cal goals. They often sided with the Pharisees to try to trap Jesus with questions.

Where to find it: *Matthew 22:16; Mark 3:6*

HERODIAS *(hair-ROH-dee-us)* was the second wife of Herod Antipas and the granddaughter of Herod the Great. John the Baptist had preached against Herodias's marriage to Herod Antipas because she had first been the wife of Herod Antipas's brother. Herodias didn't like being reminded that she had done wrong.

So she schemed to have John the Baptist killed. Her daughter by her first husband was Salome, who danced for her stepfather. He liked the dance and invited Salome to make a wish. Her mother told her to ask for John's head on a platter. Sadly—she got her wish.

Where to find it: *Matthew 14:1-12; Mark 6:14-29; Luke 3:19-20*

HEZEKIAH *(hez-uh-KY-uh)* was the thirteenth king of Judah. He came to the throne when he

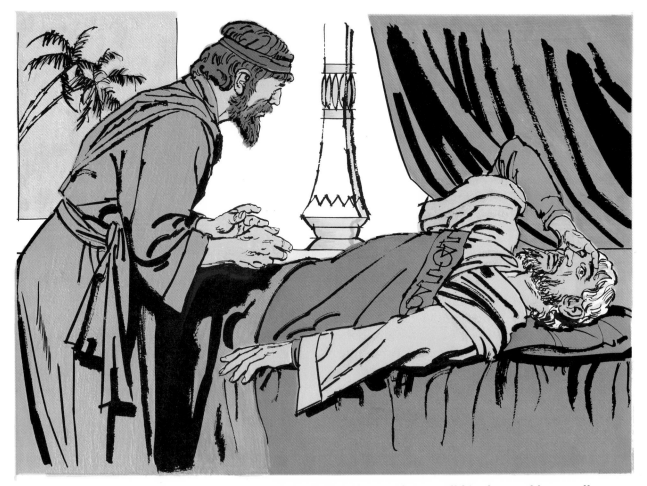

When King Hezekiah was sick, the Lord sent Isaiah the prophet to tell him he would get well.

was 25 and ruled for 29 years, from 724 to 695 B.C. Hezekiah was a good ruler who tried to restore proper worship of God. But later in his life, pride was his downfall.

When Hezekiah came to power, many of the people in Judah had stopped worshiping God. There were also political problems, with both Egypt and Assyria wanting to conquer Judah. Hezekiah started out right as a young king. He reopened the Temple, destroyed pagan altars, and led a Passover celebration.

But he had a hard time. The Assyrians captured many of the cities of Judah and threatened to take Jerusalem. Hezekiah offered to pay them not to attack Jerusalem. He even took gold from the Temple to pay them.

The Assyrians, under King Sennacherib, decided to attack anyway. Sennacherib gathered a huge army outside Jerusalem. But one night, God sent an angel, who killed 185,000 of his soldiers. This saved the city, and Sennacherib and the few men who were left went back home to Nineveh.

Later, Hezekiah became sick. He prayed, and God gave him another 15 years of life. But Hezekiah, as he got older, also became proud. When ambassadors came from Babylon to see him, he showed off his great wealth. Isaiah the prophet scolded him for his foolish pride. He said, ''The days are coming when all that is in your house . . . shall be carried to Babylon.''

And that is exactly what happened—not during Hezekiah's lifetime but to his children and grandchildren.

Where to find it

Hezekiah restores true worship   *2 Kings 18–20; 2 Chronicles 29–32*
God destroys the Assyrians   *2 Kings 18: 13–19: 36*
Hezekiah is given 15 more years   *2 Kings 20: 1-11*
Hezekiah shows his wealth   *2 Kings 20: 12-19*

HIGH PLACES were where ancient people went to worship their gods, because they thought they were closer to them. When the Bible speaks of high places, it means places of worship built on the tops of hills or mountains. Usually these were pagan shrines that the people of Israel were told to avoid or destroy. But sometimes altars to God were also built at these high places.

Where to find it

Israel to destroy pagan high places   *Numbers 33: 52*
Israel worships God on a high place   *2 Chronicles 1: 1-13*

HIGH PRIEST was the most important priest for the Old Testament worshipers. Toward the end of Old Testament times, when Israel had no king, the priest had power like that of a king, because religion and government were

Caiaphas was the high priest who accused Jesus.

tied closely together. The priest was called to be the spiritual leader of the Israelites.

High priests were descendants of Aaron, Moses' brother. After a high priest was consecrated, he held his job for life. The high priest wore elaborate and beautiful clothing. Because he was the go-between for the people and God, his clothes were to reflect the beauty and glory of God.

On the Day of Atonement, the most important day of the year, the high priest put aside his colorful robes. Instead he put on plain linen clothes to enter the Holy of Holies.

Only on this yearly Day of Atonement would the high priest enter the Holy of Holies. He sprinkled the mercy seat with blood to make atonement for his own sins and for the sins of all the people.

Although the high priest was meant to be the spiritual leader of Israel, the high priests Annas and Caiaphas opposed Jesus and worked to bring his death.

HILKIAH

Where to find it

Clothing   *Exodus 28: 1-39*
Day of Atonement duties   *Leviticus 16: 1-28*
Annas and Caiaphas   *John 18: 12-32; John 11: 47-57*

HILKIAH *(hil-KY-uh)* was the name of seven people in the Old Testament. Many of them were priests. Two of the most important were:

1. Hilkiah the high priest in the days of King Josiah. Hilkiah helped Josiah in his reforms by cleansing the Temple. He found the Book of the Law there.

Where to find it: *2 Kings 22–23; 2 Chronicles 34*

2. Hilkiah, the chief of priests, who returned with the exiles from their captivity in Babylon to help rebuild Jerusalem.

Where to find it: *Nehemiah 12: 7*

HIND (see *Animals–Hart*)

HINNOM *(HIN-um)*, **VALLEY OF,** was a low place on the west and southwest side of the city of Jerusalem. It was a place where, in Old Testament times, human sacrifices were offered to pagan gods.

The name comes from *Gehenna,* the word used by Jesus for hell—the place of eternal punishment.

Where to find it: *Jeremiah 19: 1-13*

HIRAM *(HI-rum)* was a friend of David and Solomon. He was king of Tyre, which is now in Lebanon. When David and Solomon were building the city of Jerusalem and the Temple, Hiram supplied materials and builders. He sold some of the cedar and fir trees of Lebanon to Solomon and floated them down to Joppa on rafts.

Where to find it: *2 Samuel 5: 11; 1 Kings 5: 1-10*

HIRELING *(HIRE-ling)* was a laborer who worked for money. Some hirelings were hired for a day, while others worked for longer periods. In the Old Testament, they are pictured as poor, oppressed people.

No doubt some of them worked well, but others took no interest or pride in their work. The hireling in Jesus' parable of the Good Shepherd was a careless worker. In the story, the hireling ran away when he saw the wolf coming, because he didn't really care about the sheep. Jesus is like the shepherd who cares about his sheep, not like a hireling who cares most for his money and his own safety.

Where to find it

Hirelings sometimes oppressed   *Malachi 3: 5*
Story of Good Shepherd   *John 10: 12-13*

HITTITES *(HIT-tites)* were an ancient people who lived in Asia Minor and Syria from about 2000 to 1200 B.C. They were one of the greatest threats to early Israel. They sometimes lived in the same land and often married the people of Israel. In Solomon's day, the Hittites were mostly servants.

Where to find it: *1 Kings 9: 20-21*

HOLINESS *(HOLE-ee-nus)* comes from a Hebrew word that means set apart as sacred, consecrated, or dedicated. It is a word that describes God. God is different from us. He is pure and loving, without sin. Jesus Christ is holy also. He is without sin, dedicated to doing what God wants. His nature is the same as that of God the Father. Even the evil spirits knew Jesus as the holy one of God.

Jesus' death and resurrection give those who believe in him the power to be holy. They can become pure and loving like Christ. A faithful believer separates himself from sin.

All true holiness comes from God. Things, places, times, and persons can become holy as they are used for God's purposes. This holiness always means to become more and more like the nature of God.

Where to find it

God's holiness   *Exodus 15: 11; Psalm 30: 4; Isaiah 6: 3*
Jesus' holiness   *Luke 1: 35*
Evil spirits call Jesus holy   *Mark 1: 24; Luke 4: 34*
Believer's holiness   *Leviticus 20: 7; Romans 12: 1; Hebrews 12: 14*

HOLY GHOST (see *Holy Spirit*)

HOLY OF HOLIES was an inner section in the Tabernacle or Temple. To the Jewish people it was the most sacred place. Only the high priest could enter the Holy of Holies, and he could go in only on the Day of Atonement. He entered to ask forgiveness for his own sin and the people's sins. The ark of the Covenant was kept in the Holy of Holies (see also *Temple, Tabernacle*).

HOLY PLACE was a part of the Jewish people's Temple or Tabernacle. As part of the daily worship service, the priests lit candles and burned incense. In the Holy Place were a table on which fresh bread was placed each week and a seven-branched candlestick to remind God's people of his care during the escape from Egypt.

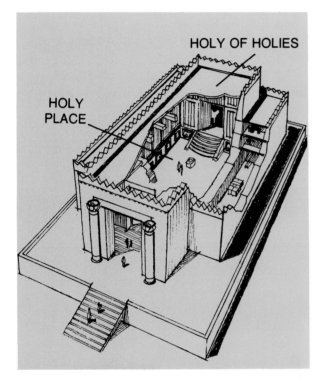

HOLY SPIRIT is God's presence in the world. Jesus Christ was God who became a man in the world. When God is called Father, we speak of his care and love for all of his creation.

Genesis 1:2 tells us that the Holy Spirit helped bring the world into being. In John 16:13, Christ said the Holy Spirit would guide the disciples into all truth. The Holy Spirit explains God's purposes and draws attention to Jesus Christ.

Jesus called the Holy Spirit the helper, comforter, advocate, or counselor. Jesus told his disciples that the Holy Spirit would lead them into truth and would teach them how to share truth with others. The Holy Spirit would convince non-Christians of their sin in not believ-

ing in Christ and would show them the goodness in how Jesus lived. He would show them how Jesus' death defeats Satan.

Many word pictures in the Bible help us understand the Holy Spirit. Wind and breath are the most common. Wind shows the power of the Holy Spirit; breath in the Bible stands for life itself. Other word pictures include a dove, oil, and fire for purification. The dove is a picture of the peace of God; the oil (for a lamp) shows the Holy Spirit as light that shines in darkness. The fire pictures judgment.

In the Bible we read of the Holy Spirit coming upon certain persons to give them power for certain work. This happened to John the Baptist and to his parents.

At the Day of Pentecost, after Jesus had gone back to heaven, the Holy Spirit came in a new way. He gave power to all believers to help them proclaim Christ. He came with a rush of mighty wind and flames like fire to show his power and his desire for holiness.

This power of the Holy Spirit helps us tell other people about Jesus Christ and helps those people believe in Jesus. The Holy Spirit also gives many different gifts to believers so they can serve God and help others. (See also *Spiritual Gifts.*)

Where to find it

Active in creation   *Genesis 1:2*
Holy Spirit with John the Baptist   *Luke 1:15, 41, 67*
Jesus teaches about the Holy Spirit   *John 14:15-17; 15:26-27; 16:7-15*
Holy Spirit comes at Pentecost   *Acts 2*
Symbols:
  breath, wind   *Genesis 1:2; Job 32:8; 33:4; Ezekiel 37:9-10; John 20:22*
  dove   *Matthew 3:16; Mark 1:10; John 1:32*
  oil   *1 John 2:20, 27*
  fire   *Acts 2:3*
Gifts of the Spirit   *Romans 12:6-8; 1 Corinthians 12–14*
Fruit of the Spirit   *Galatians 5:22-23*

HONOR is respect given to another person. God receives honor from all his creation. God also gives honor to specific people. He expects his followers to honor those he honors. Both the Old Testament and the New Testament teach that honor is to be given to fathers and mothers.

Where to find it

Honor to God   *1 Timothy 1:17; Revelation 4:9; 7:12*

HOPE

Honor to Jesus *Hebrews 2:9; Revelation 5:12-13*
Honor to parents *Exodus 20:12; Deuteronomy 5:16; Ephesians 6:2*

HOPE in the Bible means trust and confidence in God's plans. It means being sure about what God will do for us in the future. Our hope in Jesus means we expect and trust that God will let us live with him forever. This hope is based on God's being trustworthy and loving.

Where to find it: *Colossians 1:27; Romans 8:19-25*

HOPHNI and **PHINEHAS** (*HOP-nee, FIN-ee-us*) were sons of Eli, an Old Testament priest and judge. When Hophni and Phinehas became priests, they embarrassed both their father and the Lord by their evil practices. They were immoral and greedy, taking more than their share of the sacrifices given by the people during worship. Their father, Eli, had once been a godly priest, but he did not punish his sons for their wicked ways. As a result, Hophni and Phinehas were killed in battle, their father soon died, and their family was no longer allowed to serve as priests.

Where to find it

Their lives and sins *1 Samuel 1:3–3:13*
Their deaths *1 Samuel 4:4-18*

HOR, MOUNT, is the name of two mountains mentioned in the Old Testament.

1. The mountain where Aaron was buried. This mountain is probably a sandstone mountain in what is now the Sinai Peninsula about 100 miles south of Jerusalem. It has twin peaks.

2. The mountain that marked the northern boundary of Israel's land. It is probably one of the peaks in what we know as the Lebanon mountain range.

Where to find it

Where Aaron was buried *Numbers 20:22-23; 21:4; Deuteronomy 32:50*
Northern boundary *Numbers 34:7-8*

HOREB, MOUNT (see *Sinai, Mount*)

HORSES (see *Animals*)

HOSANNA (*hoe-ZAN-uh*) was a shout used in Hebrew worship to show praise. It means "Save now!" A few days before Jesus was crucified, children and grown-ups shouted "Hosanna" to him as he rode into Jerusalem on a donkey. That day is what we call Palm Sunday.

Where to find it: *Matthew 21:9*

HOSEA (*hoe-ZAY-uh*) was an Old Testament prophet who called his people back to God. Hosea's own life became a picture of God's love for his sinful people.

Many of the people of Hosea's day—about 785 B.C.—were too prosperous. They didn't know how to handle all the good things God had allowed them to have. Other people were too poor, and the rich people ignored the needs of these poor people. False gods were allowed in Israel, and more and more people fell away from worshiping God.

God told Hosea to use marriage as a picture of God's relationship to his people Israel. God was the bridegroom, Israel was the bride. God told Hosea to marry a woman who would be unfaithful to him. Her name was Gomer. They had three children. But Gomer found other men to love, and she left Hosea, just as Israel found other gods to worship.

But Hosea, like God, brought Gomer back to his house and loved her even after what she had done. This pictured God's love and his desire to have his people back with him.

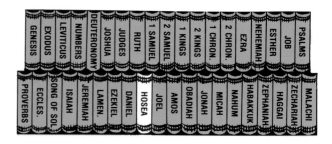

Hosea then begged Israel to repent. "Return, O Israel, to the Lord your God," he said, "for you have stumbled because of your iniquity. Whoever is wise, let him understand these things; whoever is discerning, let him know them: for the ways of the Lord are right."

Where to find it

Hosea's marriage *Hosea 1–3*
He calls the people back to God *Hosea 4–14*

HOSPITALITY *(HAHS-pih-tal-it-ee)* is generous and loving care for guests or strangers. In the Bible, God expected his people to show hospitality. Abraham did this when he entertained three strangers. Though he called them men, they later turned out to be heavenly beings. The Lord with his angels had appeared to Abraham.

Mary, Martha, and Lazarus often showed hospitality to Jesus and his disciples in their home at Bethany.

Many early churches met in homes and so hospitality was important. Christians are told to show hospitality to each other and to strangers as well.

Where to find it

Abraham shows hospitality to God and his angels *Genesis 18*
Mary, Martha, and Lazarus welcome Jesus *Matthew 26: 6-13; Luke 10: 38-42*
Hospitality in the early church *Romans 16: 5; Philemon 1-7; 3 John 1: 5-7*
Christians should be hospitable *Romans 12: 13; Hebrews 13: 1-2; 1 Peter 4: 9*

HOSTS OF HEAVEN usually means God's angels. Hosts of angels sang at Jesus' birth.

But sometimes *hosts of heaven* means the stars and heavenly bodies—all of creation—that are also under God's will and do what he says.

Where to find it

Hosts obey God *Psalm 103: 20-21*
Hosts sing *Luke 2: 13*
All creation *Acts 7: 42*

HOUSE can mean (1) a building where people live; (2) a group of people who live in a certain building; (3) a building where God is worshiped or, (4) a group of people who believe in God.

1. In Bible times, as in our time, the houses where people lived were not all alike. Most of them looked more like boxes than our houses because they usually had flat roofs. There was no need for a slanting roof in a land with so little rain. Walls were usually thick, made from stone or brick. From the street, you first entered a small courtyard that often served as the kitchen. Beyond the courtyard, doors opened into a living room. Small bedrooms were beyond the living room.

The floor of the house would be clay or stone, depending on what the owner could afford. Doors were made of wood, cloth, skins, or woven rushes. The windows were small and high. Since there were no chimneys, smoke from the indoor stoves—used for cooking and heating—escaped through windows or doors.

The flat roofs were important to people of Bible times. They could be used for extra sleeping space, for drying flax, and for other activities. Stone steps often led from the courtyard to the roof.

Houses of richer people sometimes had an upper room built on the roof. Stairs to the upper room were usually outdoors.

Often houses were part of the city wall or

had a wall in common with a neighboring house. The owner and his family often shared the house with farm animals.

2. *House* also meant a group of people who lived together within a certain home. This could include grandparents, aunts, uncles, parents, children, servants, and slaves. The word *household* is also used this way.

3. *House* sometimes meant a building where God was worshiped. The Bible speaks of the Temple as the "house of God."

4. *House of God* also means a group of people who believe in God. It means the same as the "family of God." Hebrews 10:21 says Christ is a "great priest over the house of God." Hebrews 3:6 says that he was also a faithful Son over God's house; Moses was a servant in this same household. Both of these Scripture passages refer to the "house" as the family of believers everywhere. 1 Peter 2:5 says that Christians are to be built into a "spiritual house."

HOUSEHOLD OF GOD

HOUSEHOLD OF GOD refers both to individual churches and to all of God's people in all ages. In New Testament times, when churches met in homes, Christians welcomed other worshipers as brothers and sisters in Christ. Christians see themselves as part of the great family of God, as close to each other as brothers and sisters.

Where to find it: *1 Timothy 3:15*

HULDAH

HULDAH *(HUL-duh)* was a woman prophet in the days of King Josiah. When Josiah first found the Books of the Law while cleaning the Temple, he sent the high priest to ask Huldah what it all meant.

She prophesied God's judgment on the nation. "Thus says the Lord," she said, "I will bring evil upon this place because . . . they have forsaken me." She encouraged Josiah and all the people to follow the Law in the books they had found. Josiah wanted to lead the people back to God. He tore down the altars to the false gods.

But Josiah was too late. The people had been too wicked. God had to send his judgment anyway. But Huldah gave comfort to Josiah. "Because your heart was penitent [sorry], says the Lord, I will gather you to your fathers, and your eyes shall not see all the evil

which I will bring upon this place." Huldah's prophecies of judgment and of Josiah's death came true.

Where to find it

Huldah's prophecy   *2 Kings 22:16-20*
Josiah's reforms   *2 Kings 23:1-25*

HUMILITY *(hew-MILL-i-tee)* means being thoughtful of others, gentle, not proud. Humility comes from realizing what God has done for us through his love.

Sometimes people draw attention to themselves by pretending to be humble. This false humility is really a form of pride and is the opposite of real humility. Jesus told a story about a Pharisee who pretended to be humble when he really was very proud. Humility involves using God's strength to be helpful and kind to other people.

Where to find it

Humility as a virtue   *1 Corinthians 4:21; 2 Corinthians 10:1; Philippians 2:8*
Jesus' story   *Luke 18:10-11*

HUMOR was sometimes used by people in the Bible to tell important messages to others. Their humor was not in side-splitting jokes, but they used situations or wordplays that gave insights into the people or their situation.

Much of that humor is lost to us, because we don't read the Bible in the language in which it was written. Puns or wordplays are very hard to translate into another language. For example, when Jesus said to Peter, "You are Peter, and on this rock I will build my church," he was making a pun with Peter's name. *Peter* in Greek is the word for "stone." The word for *rock* is *petra*. Although what Jesus said was serious, he used a pun to say it. This is lost when it is translated into English.

Jesus seemed to have a sense of humor, for he often painted funny word pictures. Jesus' audience must have chuckled a little when he said it was easier for a camel to go through the eye of a needle than for a rich man to enter heaven. Another time he showed how silly it was for the Pharisees to make a lot of fuss about what amounted to a speck of dust in someone else's eye when they had a whole log in their own!

The Bible is a serious book with a valuable

166

message. But the Bible writers used their wit to help their listeners and readers understand some very important matters.

HUNTER (see *Occupations*)

HUSBANDRY (see *Occupations–Farming*)

HUSBANDMAN means a farmer in the Bible. Sometimes it means the person in charge; a husbandman could be the master of the house.

HUSHAI *(HUSH-eye)* was a spy for King David when David's son Absalom was leading a rebellion against his father. Hushai pretended to have changed from David's side to Absalom's. When Absalom asked him about attacking King David, Hushai gave advice that delayed the attack. Then David had time to escape across the Jordan River.

Where to find it: *2 Samuel 16: 15-19; 17: 5-15*

HYMENAEUS *(hi-meh-NAY-us)* said he was a Christian but had some false beliefs. He tried to turn believers away from their faith by teaching a false doctrine about resurrection.

Where to find it: *1 Timothy 1: 19-20; 2 Timothy 2: 16-18*

HYMNS *(hims)* are Christian songs for praising God. Singing was a part of worship in both the Old Testament and the New Testament. Earliest Christian hymns were psalms from the Old Testament. The hymn Jesus sang with the disciples at the end of the Last Supper was probably Psalms 113—118. Paul and Silas sang hymns when they were in jail. Christians are told to sing hymns to encourage each other as well as to praise God.

Where to find it

Jesus and the disciples singing   *Matthew 26: 30; Mark 14: 26*
Paul and Silas singing   *Acts 16: 25*
Christians encouraged to sing   *Ephesians 5: 19; Colossians 3: 16*

HYPOCRITE *(HIP-uh-krit)* is someone who pretends to be something he is not. He may pretend to be good or to love God when he really only loves himself and his own interests. He is "play-acting" his religion. Jesus called the Pharisees hypocrites because they wanted their religion to be noticed, but they would not listen to God.

Where to find it: *Matthew 23: 13-15; Luke 11: 44*

ICHABOD *(ICK-uh-bod)* was the grandson of Eli the priest. His name means ''Where is the glory?''

Ichabod's father, Phinehas, and his brother let the ark of God be taken into battle with the Philistines as a kind of good-luck charm. The Philistines won the battle, killed Phinehas, and captured the ark.

Phinehas's wife was about to have a baby when news came that her husband had been killed. She died a few moments after her son was born. But she said he was to be named Ichabod, because God's glory had left Israel when the Philistines captured the ark.

Where to find it: *1 Samuel 4*

ICONIUM *(eye-KOH-nee-um)* is a city in what is now Turkey. It still exists but is now known

When Isaac was born,
his parents were overjoyed;
God had kept his promise after all!

168

Perhaps the most famous idol in the Bible was Aaron's golden calf.

as Konya. In New Testament times Paul visited there on his first and second missionary journeys.

On his first visit, he and Barnabas preached to both Jews and Gentiles. Many believed, and a church was formed. However, the two men were forced to leave when some unbelieving Jews threatened to stone them. Some of these unbelievers from Iconium followed Paul to Lystra, where they did stone him and drag him out of the city. But Paul and Barnabas went back to Iconium after a while, preached more, and encouraged the church.

Paul visited Iconium later with Timothy.

Where to find it: *Acts 14: 1-7, 19-23; 16: 1-5*

IDLENESS is condemned in the Bible as a sin. An idle person neglects his own work and lives off others. Proverbs says, "An idle person will suffer hunger." Paul told the Thessalonians to "keep away from any brother who is living in idleness."

Where to find it: *Proverbs 19: 15; 2 Thessalonians 3: 6-13*

IDOL *(EYE-dul)* usually means an image that is worshiped. Such images were usually made of wood, stone, metal, or some other material.

In the Old Testament, the nations around Israel had idols of many kinds. Some were images, others were groves of trees or pillars. The Second Commandment given to Moses was "You shall not make for yourself a graven image or likeness of anything that is in heaven above or that is in the earth beneath, or that is in the water under the earth; you shall not bow down to them or serve them." This was a warning to the Israelites not to worship idols as the nations around them did. However, the Israelites often disobeyed, and God sent many prophets to warn them against this.

In the New Testament, Christians were told not to deliberately eat meat that had been offered to idols, because it might confuse people who did not understand that "an idol has no real existence."

Where to find it

Command not to make idols   *Exodus 20: 4*
Command not to eat food offered to idols
   1 Corinthians 8: 4-11

IDOLATRY *(eye-DOLL-uh-tree)* is the worship of false gods or idols. It includes not only worship of objects made by people, but also the worship of the sun, moon, or stars.

Although the Israelites were told many times not to practice idolatry, they often did. In Judges 17—18 is a story of a Levite who was supposed to be a priest of God but worked as a priest for an idol.

During the time of the prophet Elijah and during other periods as well, many Israelites worshiped the god Baal. Baal worship was common in Israel for hundreds of years.

Sometimes the Israelites worshiped false gods in the ways they were supposed to worship the true God. They offered burnt sacrifices, burned incense, and brought money, grain, and oil as offerings.

In the New Testament, the apostle Paul wrote about idolatry as including putting other things before God. He said that covetousness (a strong desire to have something that belongs to someone else) is one form of idolatry.

Where to find it

Sacrifices *2 Kings 5:17*
Incense *1 Kings 11:8*
Offerings *Hosea 2:8*
Covetousness is idolatry *Ephesians 5:5; Colossians 3:5*

IGNORANCE *(IG-nor-unce)* in the Bible does not mean being stupid. It refers to a lack of knowledge or unwillingness to learn what should be learned.

Where to find it: *Romans 10:3; Ephesians 4:18; 1 Timothy 1:13*

ILLYRICUM *(ill-EAR-eh-kum)* was a province of the Roman Empire that is now a part of Yugoslavia. Paul said that in his missionary journeys he preached the gospel of Christ "as far round as Illyricum."

Where to find it: *Romans 15:19*

IMAGE OF GOD is a phrase that describes men and women as God created them. What it means is not entirely clear in the Bible, but it does suggest that people were created in some ways like God. Some scholars think it includes the authority and responsibility to look after God's creation. It also may refer to the fellowship that God can have with people who love and obey him. Colossians 3:10 suggests that the image of God, which was damaged by sin, can be restored through Christ: "Put on the new nature, which is being renewed in knowledge after the image of its creator."

Since Christ is God, we know that to be like Christ is to be like God. 2 Corinthians 3:18 says that Christians are being "changed into his likeness."

Where to find it: *Genesis 1:27; 5:1*

IMMANUEL *(im-MAN-you-el)* is a name that me ns "God with us." The prophet Isaiah foretold the birth of a child whose name

should be called Immanuel. In the New Testament, this prophecy was applied to the birth of Jesus Christ.

Where to find it: *Isaiah 7:14; Matthew 1:23*

IMMORALITY *(IM-more-AL-it-ee)* in the Bible refers primarily to sexual sins of all kinds—fornication, adultery, homosexuality, incest. Immorality is always condemned in the Bible.

In our modern usage, immorality includes many other kinds of wrongdoing, such as lying, stealing, and murder. These are also condemned in the Bible, but the term *immorality* in the Bible refers to sexual sins.

Where to find it: *1 Corinthians 6:18; 2 Corinthians 12:21; Galatians 5:19*

IMMORTALITY *(IM-more-TAL-it-ee)* refers to life after death. The Old Testament teachings about this are not as clear as those in the New Testament. However, Isaiah wrote, "Thy dead shall live, their bodies shall rise. O dwellers in the dust [the dead], awake and sing for joy!"

Jesus clearly taught there is life after death. He said to the thief on the cross, "Today you will be with me in Paradise." He said to Martha at the death of Lazarus, "He who believes in me, though he die, yet shall he live." The apostle Paul wrote about the new bodies that Christians will have later.

Where to find it

Old Testament: *Isaiah 26:19*
New Testament: *Luke 23:43; John 11:25; 1 Corinthians 15:35-53*

IMPURITY (see *Unclean*)

INCARNATION *(in-car-NAY-shun)* means "becoming human." This term is used of Jesus Christ when he came to earth as a man. Jesus was fully God and also fully human. He was tempted as all people are tempted; he became tired and hungry; he suffered pain and agony on the cross. But Colossians 2:9 also says that "in him [Christ] the whole fulness of deity dwells bodily."

Philippians 2:5-11 says that Jesus, although he was God, willingly became man, accepted the limitations of being human, became a servant, and finally died on the cross even though he did not have to do so. Because of this, God has exalted him, and some day "every tongue [shall] confess that Jesus Christ is Lord."

INCENSE *(IN-sens)* is material made of spices and gum that is burned to make a sweet smell. In the Old Testament Tabernacle and Temple, there was a special altar where incense was burned as a part of worship (see *Incense, Altar of*).

INCENSE *(IN-sens)*, **ALTAR OF,** was a special altar used only for burning incense in the Tabernacle and later in the Temple. It was about 18 inches square and stood about 36 inches high. It had a thin covering of gold. Its upraised sections on each corner were called horns.

Incense burning was an act of worship, but it also improved the smell in the place where many animals were killed and burned as sacrifices.

At first, only the high priest burned incense at the altar each morning. By the time of

Priests burned incense on a special altar each day.

Christ, ordinary priests were chosen to burn incense at a specified time each day. The priest took fire from the altar of burnt offering and brought it into the Holy Place to the altar of incense.

Zechariah was bringing incense to the altar of incense in the Temple when an angel appeared to him. He told Zechariah that he would have a son whose name would be called John.

Where to find it

High priest burns incense   *Exodus 30:1-9*
Zechariah burns incense   *Luke 1:5-23*

INHERITANCE *(in-HAIR-ih-tunce)* refers to property or money that parents give to children or grandchildren.

In Old Testament times, there were strict laws of inheritance, especially regarding land. When the Hebrews went into the land of Palestine, they believed God had given them the land as their inheritance. The land was divided among the 12 tribes. Each tribe and each family within that tribe received certain land. This land was passed on from family to family, one generation after another.

The oldest son always received twice as much of his father's goods as the other sons. Daughters did not receive anything, unless there were no sons. In that case, they inherited the land, but they were required to marry someone within their own tribe so that their land would stay within that tribe. There were many other customs and rules about inheritances.

In the New Testament, some of the same customs were still followed. However, Jesus also talked about the "eternal inheritance" that belongs to those who believe in him. As God's Son, he is the heir (the one who inherits) of God, and believers in him become "fellow-heirs."

Where to find it: *Deuteronomy 21:15-17; Romans 8:17*

INIQUITY (see *Sin*)

INN was not like a modern hotel or motel. There were three main types of inns or lodging places for travelers:

1. A resting place (something like a camp) for individuals or caravans as they traveled. Such inns would be near a well and might have some protection with rocks and trees.

2. A large courtyard with a gate that could be locked. Around the sides were rooms or stalls for animals and travelers. A well would be in the courtyard. Travelers carried their own food for themselves and their animals.

3. Guest rooms in private homes.

We do not know which kind of "inn" Mary and Joseph were turned away from for lack of space at the birth of Jesus.

The main caravan routes had inns with open courtyards and stables for travelers' animals.

Innkeepers of ancient times had bad reputations, especially those who had large inns with a courtyard and a gate. This is one of the reasons Christians were urged to welcome traveling Christians into their homes.

Where to find it

Mary and Joseph turned away   *Luke 2:7*
Christians told to welcome travelers   *Romans 12:13; 1 Peter 4:9*

INNER or **INWARD MAN** is a term used of a person's true self as seen by God. It is sometimes used in the New Testament to mean the opposite of the "outward" person—what we seem to be to others.

Where to find it: *Matthew 23:27; 2 Corinthians 4:16; Ephesians 3:16*

INSCRIPTION *(in-SKRIP-shun)* **ON THE CROSS** were the words written on the sign fastened to Christ's cross. (Such inscriptions usually told the crimes for which the person was being put to death.) For Jesus, the sign said, "This is Jesus of Nazareth, the King of the Jews."

As far as the Romans were concerned, Jesus was charged with plotting to overthrow the government and become king.

Where to find it: *Matthew 27:37; Mark 15:26; Luke 23:38; John 19:19-21*

INSPIRATION *(IN-spur-AY-shun)* is what makes the Bible different from other books. 2 Timothy 3:16 says, "All Scripture is inspired of

God. . . ." The Greek word for "inspired" means "God-breathed" or "energized by God."

To say that God energized the writings in the Bible does not mean that God dictated the words of the Bible to the persons who wrote it. We know this is not true, because the various writers in the Bible have different styles of writing and ways of expressing ideas.

Furthermore, the Bible itself says that the writers worked hard on their material. Luke talked with eyewitnesses of the events of Christ's life. In the Old Testament, the writers often referred to certain histories that are not a part of our Old Testament books.

In the four Gospel accounts of the life of Christ, there are many differences in details, because each writer recorded what he saw or remembered. But in every case he was inspired by God, so that the words he wrote were what God intended us to have.

The Bible does not tell *how* God inspired the writers. It simply states that God did so. And because the Bible is inspired by God, it speaks to us with authority. It reveals God to us in the ways God chose to be revealed.

Most importantly, the Bible tells us about Jesus Christ, through whom God spoke most clearly. "In many and various ways God spoke of old to our fathers by the prophets; but in these last days he has spoken to us by a Son, whom he appointed the heir of all things, through whom also he created the world."

All of the New Testament writers tell us

172

about Jesus Christ, God's most important way of showing us himself. God guided or "inspired" their words so that they teach us truth.

Where to find it

Other histories mentioned in the Old Testament *2 Kings 15: 6; 2 Chronicles 12: 15*
Luke's research *Luke 1: 1-4*
God has spoken through Christ *Hebrews 1: 1-2*

INTEGRITY *(in-TEG-ri-tee)* in the Bible means more than being honest. It means both being devoted to God and being fair and honest with people.

Where to find it: *Psalms 7: 8; 25: 21; Proverbs 2: 6-7; Titus 2: 7*

INTEREST (see *Usury*)

INTERPRETATION *(in-TER-pruh-TAY-shun)* is the process of finding out what something means. In the Old Testament, some men of God had the ability to interpret dreams. Joseph interpreted a dream of the Egyptian Pharaoh that meant there would be seven years of plentiful crops followed by seven years of famine. Daniel was able to interpret the handwriting on the wall of King Belshazzar.

Because the Bible was written by dozens of different authors thousands of years ago, we have to try hard to understand what it really means. Many of the differences in beliefs among Christians are because not all groups accept the same interpretation or meaning of some parts of the Bible.

There are several principles to follow in interpreting or discovering the meaning of the Bible. Three of the most important are:

1. Try to figure out what the part you are studying meant to the first readers or hearers. For example, what kind of problems did they have? What were their habits and customs? What were their religious beliefs? When did they live? Was their country at war, or were they being threatened by war? When we understand the first readers and how this part of the Bible applied to them, we can understand much better what it can mean to us. Reference books such as this encyclopedia can help us understand life in Bible times.

2. Try to understand the total meaning of the book or chapter. If we read one or two verses by themselves without understanding what comes before or after, we can get mixed-up ideas.

3. Think about the parts that *are* clear. Afterwhile, other parts will become clearer.

IOTA is the Greek letter *i*. It stands for the smallest Hebrew letter, which in English is *y*. When Jesus said that "not an iota, not a dot, will pass from the law," he was saying that not even the smallest letter or a little part of a letter would be lost.

The reason it would not be lost was that Jesus had come to fulfill the whole Law in himself. This is a word picture showing that the smallest things in the Old Testament Law would be influenced by Jesus' work and ministry.

Where to find it: *Matthew 5: 18*

IRON in Bible times is much like the iron we have today. It was used to make axes and other tools. When the Israelites first came into Palestine, they had very little iron. This kept them poor, because they did not have good farming tools, or swords and spears for their armies. Later, when they defeated the Philistines and took over the land, they were able to learn how to smelt iron.

ISAAC *(EYE-zek)* was the only son of Abraham and Sarah, born by a miracle of God when Abraham was 100 years old and Sarah was 90. God promised that the nation Israel would descend from Isaac.

When Isaac was a young boy, God told Abraham to sacrifice Isaac to God on a mountain in the land of Moriah. With great sorrow, Abraham went to Moriah and got ready to sacrifice Isaac. When everything was set, God appeared to Abraham and said, "Do not lay your hand on the lad or do anything to him; for now I know that you fear God, seeing you have not withheld your son, your only son, from me."

At age 40, Isaac married Rebekah, a relative from Mesopotamia. He and Rebekah had twin sons, Esau and Jacob.

When Isaac was about 100 years old and his eyesight was poor, he intended to give the

The most frightening day of Isaac's life was when his father offered him as a sacrifice.

usual blessing to his sons. According to custom, the oldest son (Esau) was to receive the birthright, which included a double amount of the inheritance. However, Rebekah wanted Jacob to get that blessing, and she helped Jacob dress up like Esau and pretend to be Esau. Her plan fooled Isaac, and he gave the birthright blessing to Jacob instead of Esau.

Esau became so angry that he threatened to kill Jacob. At Rebekah's suggestion, Isaac sent Jacob to the country his mother had come from.

Isaac died at age 180. Isaac is always mentioned as one of the three ancestors of the Hebrew nation—Abraham, Isaac, and Jacob.

Where to find it

Born when parents are old   *Genesis 17: 17-19;*
  18: 9-15; 21: 1-8
Abraham goes to sacrifice Isaac   *Genesis 22: 1-14*
Isaac marries Rebekah   *Genesis 24*
Gives birthright to Jacob   *Genesis 27*
Dies at age 180   *Genesis 35: 27-29*

ISAIAH *(eye-ZAY-ah)* is an Old Testament prophet who is quoted more in the New Testament than all other prophets combined. More than any other prophet, Isaiah seemed to be looking for the coming of the Messiah.

Most of the Old Testament prophecies that are applied to Jesus Christ come from the writings of Isaiah. Many of the words in Handel's famous oratorio *The Messiah* are found in the Book of Isaiah.

We do not know much about the prophet Isaiah except that he prophesied from 740 to 680 B.C. during the reign of four kings of Judah—Uzziah, Jotham, Ahaz, and Hezekiah.

He was married to a prophetess, whose name we don't know. They had two sons.

Isaiah must have been well known and welcomed in the courts of the kings, for his book mentions talking with them often.

Besides his remarkable prophetic poems, the Book of Isaiah also has sections that tell about the history of Judah and surrounding nations. Chapters 36—37 tell how King Sennacherib of Assyria threatened to overrun Jerusalem. When Hezekiah received Sennacherib's threatening letter, he took it to the Temple, spread it before the Lord, and prayed for deliverance. God answered and destroyed the Assyrian army.

Isaiah was a prophet of great imagination and skill as a writer. He used colorful word pictures to describe the sins of his people: "The ox knows its owner, and the ass its master's crib; but Israel does not know, my people does not understand."

He showed God as the great holy Creator of the universe—one who has great power and knowledge but also loves his people deeply.

Isaiah warned the people that God was more interested in right living than in animal sacrifices. God hates sin and idol worship.

Probably the most well-known chapter is Isaiah 53, where the picture of a suffering Savior seems to describe the life and ministry

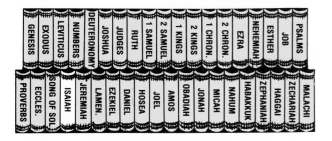

of Christ with stunning accuracy.

The importance of the Book of Isaiah is shown in the fact that Jesus began his public ministry in Nazareth by reading from Isaiah 61. Then he said, "Today this scripture has been fulfilled in your hearing."

Where to find it

Marries a prophetess   *Isaiah 8:3*
Describes death of Christ   *Isaiah 53*
Jesus refers to Isaiah's prophecies   *Luke 4:16-21*

ISHBOSHETH *(ish-BOW-shith)* was the fourth son of Saul. He was king over Israel for two years after Saul and his three older sons died in battle. He was proclaimed king by Abner, the captain of Saul's army.

But the tribe of Judah had made David king. Ishbosheth fought against David for two years, until Abner turned his loyalty to David. Later, Ishbosheth was murdered by his own captains.

Where to find it: *2 Samuel 2:8–4:11*

ISHMAEL *(ISH-may-el)* was the son of Abraham and Hagar. Hagar was an Egyptian maid of Sarah, Abraham's wife.

Ishmael was 14 years old when Abraham and Sarah had a son, Isaac. Sarah did not want Isaac to be brought up in the same house with Ishmael, and when Ishmael was 16, she urged Abraham to send Ishmael and Hagar away. Abraham did not want to do this, for he loved Ishmael. An angel appeared to Abraham, however, and told him it was all right to have Hagar and Ishmael go away, for God would make the children of Ishmael into a great nation.

When Ishmael and his mother went into the wilderness, he almost died of thirst. Then an angel of God appeared to his mother and assured her that God would care for them.

Ishmael and his mother went on living in the wilderness, where he became a skilled hunter with bow and arrow. He married an Egyptian woman and had 12 sons and a daughter.

When his father, Abraham, died, Ishmael went back to Canaan and helped Isaac with the funeral.

Ishmael died when he was 137 years old. He had become the ancestor of the people known as the Ishmaelites. All Arabs claim to be descendants of Ishmael.

Where to find it

Birth of Ishmael   *Genesis 16:1-17*
Ishmael to become a great nation   *Genesis 17:20*
Sent into wilderness   *Genesis 21:9-21*
Helps bury Abraham   *Genesis 25:7-18*

ISHMAELITES *(ISH-may-lites)* were the descendants of Ishmael, the son of Abraham and Hagar. They lived mostly in the desert areas and became known, like Ishmael, for their skill with bows and arrows.

Some Ishmaelites bought Joseph from his brothers and took him to Egypt.

All Arabs claim to be descendants of the Ishmaelites.

Where to find it: *Genesis 37:25-28*

ISRAEL *(IZ-ray-el)* has several meanings.

1. *Israel* is another name for Jacob, the son of Isaac. An angel changed his name to Israel after an all-night wrestling match.

2. *Israel* also refers to the Hebrew people, who were called to a special relationship with God: he would be their God and they would be his people. In the New Testament, Christians are called the new "Israel of God"— people with a special relationship to God (Galatians 6:16).

3. *Israel* was often used as the name of the Northern Kingdom between 930 and 722 B.C. This kingdom, which included 10 of the original 12 tribes, was also called Ephraim—the name of one of the strong tribes.

After the Northern Kingdom was conquered by Assyria in 722, the term *Israel* was used for the Southern Kingdom, made up of the tribes of Judah and Benjamin. The Southern Kingdom was usually called Judah, however. The words *Jew* and *Jewish* come from *Judah*.

4. *Israel* also refers to the land called Palestine or Canaan in the Old Testament. This

✥ MAIN EVENTS IN THE HISTORY OF ISRAEL ✥

APPROXIMATE TIME	EVENT
2000 B.C.	Abraham leaves his home to go toward Canaan.
1876 B.C.	Joseph invites his family to live in Egypt because of the famine in Canaan.
1876—1450 B.C.*	Israelites become slaves in Egypt.
1450—1406 B.C.*	Israelites are led out of Egypt by Moses and wander in the wilderness, waiting for God to give them permission to enter the Promised Land—Canaan.
1406—1400 B.C.*	Israelites fight for control of the land of Canaan under the leadership of Joshua. They conquer enough to divide the land among the various tribes.
1400—1050 B.C.*	Various judges rule the tribes. Frequent war with surrounding enemies and sometimes between tribes. Prominent judges are Deborah, Gideon, Samson, and finally Samuel.
1050—1010 B.C.	Israelites request a king. Samuel anoints Saul. The tribes are drawn together into a unified country.
1010—970 B.C.	David rules all of Israel. He captures the city of Jerusalem, which had never before been a part of Israel. Although there are periods of war, it is considered the "golden age" of Israel.
970—930 B.C.	Solomon rules a prosperous, united Israel. He builds a beautiful Temple. But he also begins to worship other gods.
930 B.C.	Solomon dies, and civil war divides the northern tribes, called Israel, from the southern tribes, called Judah.
722 B.C.	Northern Kingdom (Israel, or Ephraim) is conquered by the Assyrians. Many people are taken away into Assyria. Most of them never return.
586 B.C.	The Southern Kingdom (Judah, or now called Israel) is conquered by Babylon. Many of the people are taken away to Babylon. Jerusalem and the Temple are destroyed.
538 B.C.	Some of the people return to rebuild Jerusalem's Temple and walls.
167 B.C.	Antiochus IV, then ruler of Judea, sacrifices a pig on a pagan altar in the Holy Place of the Temple in Jerusalem. This causes a revolt among the Jews living there that continues until 164 B.C., when the Temple is again consecrated to God. The Jews become largely self-ruling.
67 B.C.	Civil war breaks out in Palestine between followers of two Jewish men who want to rule Judea. The Roman government conquers Jerusalem in 63 B.C.
40 B.C.	Herod the Great becomes ruler of most of Palestine. He rebuilds the Temple in Jerusalem. This is the Temple in which Jesus taught.
5 B.C.	Birth of Jesus Christ.
4 B.C.	Herod the Great dies. He arranges to have his kingdom divided into three parts—one part for each of his sons.
A.D. 30	Crucifixion of Jesus Christ.
A.D. 68—70	Jewish war with Rome. Jerusalem is destroyed. 600,000 Jews are killed.
A.D. 73	Destruction of Masada, the last Jewish fortress in Palestine.
A.D. 70—1920	Jewish people are scattered over the world. During the centuries, many different groups conquer the land—Persians, Muslims, Crusaders, Tartars, Egyptians, Turks.
A.D. 1920	Mandate (rule) of Palestine is assigned to Great Britain.
A.D. 1948	New state of Israel is proclaimed, followed by bitter war with the Palestinian Arabs.

*Scholars do not agree about these dates.

includes most of the country now known as Israel.

The history of the people known as Israel (the Hebrews) started with the time of Abraham, about 2000 B.C.

Abraham, his son Isaac, and Isaac's son Jacob are the ancestors or founders of the Israelites.

The chart on page 176 shows some of the main events in the history of Israel.

ISSACHAR (ISS-uh-car) was the ninth son of Jacob and the forefather of one of the 12 tribes of Israel.

We know very little about him, except that he and his wife and children went to Egypt with his brothers and father. His descendants left the slavery of Egypt with Moses and the other Israelites.

Some of his famous descendants include Deborah (the judge) and two kings of Israel—Baasha and Elah.

ITALIAN COHORT (see *Cohort*)

ITTAI (IT-ah-eye) was one of David's commanders. When David's son Absalom led a rebellion against his father, Ittai stayed loyal to David, even though David urged him to go back to Jerusalem where his friends were.

Where to find it: *2 Samuel 15:18-22*

IVORY (EYE-vuh-ree) is a creamy white material that comes from the tusks of elephants. Since there were no elephants in Palestine, ivory was very expensive. It had to be brought from India by caravans and ships. Kings liked to show off their wealth by using ivory. Solomon's throne was made of it. Ahab had a palace that was called an "ivory house" because he used so much ivory in the decorations and furnishings.

Where to find it

Solomon's throne   *1 Kings 10:18*
Ahab's house   *1 Kings 22:39*

Jesus—Son of God, our Savior—
explained to people such as Nicodemus
who God is and how to be right with him.

JABESH-GILEAD *(JAY-besh GIL-ee-add)* was a city east of the Jordan River where some of the people of the tribe of Manasseh lived.

A king of the Ammonites once threatened the people in the city, but King Saul came to their rescue by gathering an army of Israelites and defeating the Ammonites.

Many years later, Saul and his sons were killed in a battle with the Philistines. Their bodies were left hanging on a wall in the city where they were killed. That was considered a disgrace. Some men from Jabesh-gilead remembered how Saul had saved them. They walked 19 miles during one night to rescue the bodies and bring them back for honorable burial in their city.

Where to find it

Saul saves the city   *1 Samuel 11*
Men rescue Saul's body   *1 Samuel 31: 8-13*

JABIN *(JAY-bin)* was the name of two Canaanite kings of Hazor, a city in northern Palestine.

The first King Jabin led an army from his own city and several surrounding cities to fight Joshua. However, Joshua and his army won, and King Jabin was killed in the battle.

The second King Jabin conquered much of Israel. When Deborah was judge, she brought together soldiers from several tribes of Israel and defeated Jabin's army.

Where to find it

Joshua's battle   *Joshua 11: 1-10*
Deborah's battle   *Judges 4: 1-24; 5: 1-31*

JACKAL (see *Animals*)

JACOB *(JAY-kub)* was the younger of twin sons born to Isaac and Rebekah. His name was later changed to Israel, and from that name came the word *Israelites*. All Hebrew people (Israelites) are descendants of Jacob.

Jacob and his twin brother, Esau, didn't get along when they were young. Because Esau was born first, he was supposed to get the birthright—a special blessing from his father. Jacob wanted that birthright.

One day when Jacob was fixing food for himself, Esau came home tired and hungry. He asked Jacob for some of the food. "Sell me your birthright, and I will give you some food," Jacob answered.

Esau agreed. "After all," he said, "I'm about

to die of hunger. My birthright will do me no good if I'm dead."

Jacob never told his father, Isaac, what he had done. When Isaac was getting old and blind, he decided it was time to give the special birthright blessing to Esau. He asked Esau, who was a good bow-and-arrow hunter, to kill an animal and fix his favorite food.

Rebekah, Jacob's mother, heard Isaac talking to Esau. She wanted Jacob to have the birthright, so she quickly fixed Isaac's favorite food. She told Jacob to put on Esau's clothes. Esau had more hair on his body than Jacob did, so Rebekah fastened some goat skin on Jacob's hands so he would feel hairy.

Then Jacob pretended he was Esau, took the food to his blind father, and received the special blessing.

Esau was so angry when he learned what Jacob had done that he threatened to kill him. Jacob left his home in Beersheba to visit his uncle, Laban.

One night on his way, Jacob dreamed he saw a ladder reaching to heaven, with angels walking up and down. At the top of the ladder was God, who said to him, "The land on which you lie I will give to you and to your descendants. I am with you and will keep you wherever you go."

Jacob called the place where he slept Bethel, meaning, "the house of God."

Jacob's mysterious wrestling match at the brook.

At his uncle's home, Jacob met Rachel and wanted to marry her. Laban said he would have to work seven years to earn Rachel as his wife. At the marriage, his bride wore the customary heavy veil. After the marriage, Jacob found he had married Leah—Rachel's older sister instead! Laban said older daughters had to marry first and Jacob would have to work another seven years to marry Rachel. Jacob did.

After he had stayed with Laban for 20 years, Jacob took his family back to Beersheba. A messenger met him saying that Esau was coming to meet him with 400 men. Jacob was sure he and his family would all be killed. That night he had another meeting with God—he seemed to be wrestling with someone all night. When morning was dawning, God told him that his name would be changed to Israel, which means "he who strives with God."

When Jacob finally met Esau, it was a friendly meeting. Jacob settled in Shechem, in Canaan. He had 12 sons—for whom the 12 tribes of Israel are named. One son, Joseph, was sold into slavery by his jealous brothers, but he later became the ruler of Egypt.

At a time of famine, Jacob and his other sons and families moved to Egypt, where Joseph was in charge of distributing grain. Jacob died in Egypt.

Where to find it

Jacob gains the birthright   *Genesis 25: 27-34*
Deceives his father   *Genesis 27: 1-41*
Sees the ladder   *Genesis 28: 10-22*
Marries   *Genesis 29: 15-30*
Goes back to Canaan   *Genesis 32: 3-19*
Wrestles with God   *Genesis 32: 24-30*

JACOB'S WELL is the place where Jesus talked with a Samaritan woman. The Old Testament does not mention Jacob buying or digging the well, but it does mention his buying land in the area.

The well is still in existence. It is about 75 feet deep and is now owned and guarded by the Greek Catholic church.

Where to find it

Jacob buys land in area   *Genesis 33: 19*
Jesus talks with the woman   *John 4: 6-26*

JAEL *(JAY-el)* was a woman who killed Sisera, the commander of forces fighting against Israel when Deborah was judge.

Where to find it: *Judges 4: 11-21*

JAIRUS *(jay-EYE-rus)* was the ruler of a synagogue whose 12-year-old daughter was raised from death by Christ.

Jairus himself came to Jesus seeking help for his sick daughter. But before Jesus arrived at Jairus's home, messengers came saying the girl had died.

Jairus could do nothing for his sick daughter— except call for Jesus.

Jesus insisted on going anyway, and when he arrived, the people were weeping and mourning. Jesus sent everyone out of the house except Jairus and his wife and Peter, James, and John. Jesus took the girl's hand and commanded her to rise. She was immediately made well.

Where to find it: *Matthew 9: 18-26; Mark 5: 21-43; Luke 8: 40-56*

JAMES was a common Jewish name in the time of Christ. Three important men in the New Testament were named James. Two of the 12 apostles were named James.

1. Perhaps the most famous was James the son of Zebedee; his brother was the apostle John. He was a fisherman in Galilee when he was called to follow Jesus. He was one of the three most well-known disciples—Peter, James, and John. These three were with Jesus at several important moments—such as Jesus' time on the mountain of transfiguration where Jesus' appearance was changed; when Jesus prayed in Gethsemane before his crucifixion; and when Jesus raised the daughter of Jairus from death.

This James was killed by Herod Agrippa I in A.D. **44**.

Where to find it

With Jesus on mountain *Mark 9: 2-9*
Raising Jairus's daughter *Mark 5: 37-43*
In garden of Gethsemane *Matthew 26: 36-46*
Killed by Herod *Acts 12: 1-3*

2. Another apostle named James was the son of Alpheus. He is mentioned only in the lists of the disciples. Nothing further is known about him.

Where to find it: *Matthew 10: 3; Acts 1: 13*

3. Another James was the half brother of Jesus. He probably wrote the Book of James in the New Testament. James and his other brothers were not followers of Christ during his life. But after Jesus rose from the dead, they became believers and were in the Upper Room waiting for the coming of the Holy Spirit.

Jesus appeared to James in a miraculous way after the resurrection. James became a leader in the church in Jerusalem. He was in charge when Paul and Barnabas came to Jerusalem to discuss the serious problems arising when Gentiles became believers in Christ. Should the Gentile believers follow Jewish practices about food and religious ritual?

James said he thought Gentiles should be asked only to stay away from certain practices that offended Jewish believers. James's advice was followed.

When Paul returned to Jerusalem after his third missionary journey, he went to tell James what God was doing in other areas.

James was stoned to death by the Jewish high priest in A.D. 62, according to the Jewish historian Josephus.

Where to find it

Not a believer during Jesus' life *John 7: 5*
Jesus appeared to James after resurrection
  1 Corinthians 15: 7
In charge of Jerusalem council *Acts 15: 1-21*
Paul tells James about journeys *Acts 21: 17-19*

JAMES, LETTER OF, was probably written by James the brother of Jesus (see *James*). It is written in high-quality Greek, and James probably had the help of an excellent secretary. This short book tells believers they must

do more than talk about their faith—they must *do* what is pleasing to God.

James is very plain about the things that do not please God. He says the true believer should be careful about what he says. The Christian should not bless God and curse people. Christians are not to honor people because they are rich. Everyone is to be treated alike.

James urges Christians to pray for each other, to resist temptation, to be humble before God, to seek wisdom from God, and to realize that every good thing we have is a gift from God.

This book shows the difference between true religion and false religion. Beliefs don't mean anything unless they make us act better. "Faith, by itself, if it has no works, is dead" (James 2: 17).

JARS in the Old Testament and New Testament were pottery containers for water, oil, flour, or other foods. They had varying shapes but were often quite large. The jars of water at the wedding in Capernaum each held 20 or 30 gallons.

JASON *(JAY-sun)* was a Christian man at Thessalonica who invited Paul and Silas to stay at his house while they were preaching.

Some of the Jews who were jealous of Paul's success in winning converts gathered a crowd and attacked Jason's house. Paul and Silas were not there at the time, so the mob took Jason and some of his friends to the city judge and accused him of harboring criminals who were teaching there was another king, Jesus. This made it sound as though Paul and Silas were trying to overthrow the government.

The judge "took security" from Jason. This probably meant he made Jason promise that Paul and Silas would leave the city and not come back again.

JASPER

Where to find it: *Acts 17: 1-10*

JASPER (*JASS-per*) is a precious stone. Ancient people used *jasper* as a name for several colors of stone—sometimes dark red like modern jasper, or green, brown, blue, yellow, or white. The "jasper" in Revelation 21:11 may have been a different clear stone, like an opal or a diamond.

JAVELIN (see *Weapons*)

JEALOUSY (*JELL-us-ee*) can be either a good or a bad feeling. Jealousy means "zeal for someone or something." The Bible describes Elijah as being "jealous for God"—meaning that he was very devoted to God. God is said to be a "jealous God," meaning that he badly wants his people to turn away from sin to love and worship him.

Ordinary jealousy or envy is condemned in the Bible as sin. Paul says that jealousy is a "work of the flesh" and that love casts out jealousy.

Where to find it

God is a jealous God   *Exodus 34: 14*
Elijah is jealous for God   *1 Kings 19: 10*
Ordinary jealousy is sin   *1 Corinthians 13: 4; Galatians 5: 20*

JEBUSITES (*JEB-you-zites*) were a Canaanite people who lived where the city of Jerusalem is now. Although Adoni-zedek, the king of the Jebusites, was killed in a battle with Joshua, the people of Israel did not capture Jerusalem, the home of the Jebusites, until the time of David nearly 400 years later.

Where to find it

Adoni-zedek is killed   *Joshua 10: 4, 16-26*
Jebusites not driven out   *Joshua 15: 63*
David defeats Jebusites   *1 Chronicles 11: 4-5*

JEHOAHAZ (*juh-HO-uh-haz*) was the name of two kings—one in Israel and one in Judah.

1. Jehoahaz, the twelfth king of Israel, was a wicked king who worshiped calves as his father had. He ruled from 814 to 798 B.C. Because he did not turn away from idolatry, God allowed the Syrians to defeat him so badly he had almost no army left. Finally he prayed to God for help. God answered his prayer after Jehoahaz's death, and the Israelites were not destroyed by Syria.

2. Jehoahaz, the seventeenth king of Judah, reigned only for three months in 609 B.C. He was a son of a godly king, Josiah, but he did not worship God. After three months as king, he was captured by Neco, the Pharaoh of Egypt, and taken as a prisoner to Egypt, where he died.

Where to find it

Jehoahaz, king of Israel   *2 Kings 13: 1-9*
Jehoahaz, king of Judah   *2 Kings 23: 31-34*

JEHOASH (see *Joash*)

JEHOIACHIN (*juh-HOY-uh-kin*) was next to the last king of Judah. He was 18 years old when his reign began in 598 B.C., and it lasted only three months and ten days. During this time he kept up the wicked practices of his father, the former king. He was taken captive by Nebuchadnezzar to Babylon, where he lived the rest of his life. He was in prison for 37 years. Then he was freed and given an allowance on which to live.

Where to find it

He becomes king   *2 Kings 24: 8-15*
Is released from prison   *2 Kings 25: 27-30*

JEHOIADA (*juh-HOY-uh-duh*) was a high priest and uncle of Joash, a king of Judah. When Joash was a baby, Jehoiada and his wife rescued him from being killed by his grandmother. She became ruler of Judah when Joash's father, King Ahaziah, died. She reigned for seven years.

During these seven years Jehoiada and his wife hid Joash, and no one else knew he was alive. When he was seven years old, Jehoiada told the palace guards that the king's son, rightful heir to the throne, was alive. Jehoiada planned with them to have the boy crowned king when Queen Athaliah was not around. The plan worked.

Jehoiada became an important adviser to Joash. Jehoiada directed the destruction of many of the images and altars to the false god Baal. Jehoiada and Joash also arranged to have the Temple repaired.

Because of his importance and his good work, Jehoiada was buried among the kings when he died at age 130.

Where to find it: *2 Kings 11: 1–12: 16; 2 Chronicles 22: 10–24: 16*

JEHOIAKIM *(juh-HOY-uh-kim)* was the eighteenth king of Judah. He ruled from 609 to 598 B.C. He became king when his brother was taken captive by Pharaoh Neco, the ruler of Egypt. Neco made Jehoiakim king of Judah and told him what to do. Jehoiakim had to tax the people very heavily and give the money to Neco.

His name was originally Eliakim, but it was changed to Jehoiakim by Neco. Jehoiakim was a cruel and godless king during his 11-year reign. He is best remembered for the scornful way he treated the prophet Jeremiah. Jeremiah had prophesied that Babylon would conquer Judah. When the king's princes heard about the prophecy, they told Jeremiah and his scribe, Baruch, to hide. One of the princes took the prophecy and read it to King Jehoiakim.

When the king heard something he didn't like, he cut out those parts with his knife and threw them into the fire. God told Jeremiah to

rewrite the prophecy and to include in it that Jehoiakim would be taken captive and die in disgrace.

While Jehoiakim was king, the Babylonians captured most of Palestine, and Jehoiakim then had to take orders from Nebuchadnez-zar. Later, Jehoiakim tried to rebel against Nebuchadnezzar, but he was taken captive and killed, just as Jeremiah had prophesied.

Where to find it

His reign   *2 Kings 23: 34–24: 6; 2 Chronicles 36: 3-8*
Destroys Jeremiah's prophecies   *Jeremiah 25–26, 36*

JEHORAM *(juh-HOR-um)*, also known as Joram, was the name of one king of Israel and one king of Judah, both of whom lived and reigned about the same time.

1. Jehoram was the tenth king of Israel, reigning from 852 to 841 B.C. He is most re-membered for his many meetings with the prophet Elisha. Elisha disliked him because he was an idol worshiper like his parents, Ahab and Jezebel.

Elisha, however, faithfully prophesied God's word to Jehoram, telling him how God would save him and his army from their enemies. Once the enemy thought that pools of water were blood; another time they heard the sound of armies attacking them, and they ran.

Jehoram later was killed by an arrow shot by Jehu, who became the next king of Israel.

Where to find it

Becomes king   *2 Kings 3: 1-3*
Meets Elisha   *2 Kings 3: 9-24; 6: 24–7: 20*
Killed by Jehu   *2 Kings 9: 14-26*

2. Another Jehoram was the fifth king of Judah, reigning from 848 to 841 B.C. He mar-ried Athaliah, the wicked daughter of Ahab and Jezebel. Although Jehoram's father had been a godly king, Jehoram began worshiping idols when he became king at age 32. He had all of his brothers killed so they could not threaten his rule. The prophet Elijah sent him a letter saying that because of his wickedness he would die of a terrible disease.

Part of the people under his rule, Edom and Libnah, rebelled against him. Later the Philis-tines and Arabs invaded Judah and carried away all of Jehoram's belongings and also his sons and wives. Jehoram did die of a painful disease. At his death, no one honored him as they usually honored kings.

Where to find it: *2 Chronicles 21: 1-20*

JEHOSHAPHAT *(juh-HOSH-uh-fat)* was the

fourth king of Judah. He reigned from 871 to 848 B.C. and was one of the best kings Judah had. He worshiped God and tried to lead his people away from idolatry. He sent priests and princes among the people to teach them the Law of God.

He was also an excellent ruler. He developed a strong army and a system of army posts around the edge of his country for protection.

He improved the system of justice, assigning judges to all important cities in his kingdom.

He also made peace with the Northern Kingdom, Israel. King Ahab of Israel asked Jehoshaphat to help him in a war against Ramoth-gilead. Jehoshaphat would not do so unless he felt it was God's will. Ahab called in his prophets, who said the war would succeed. However, Jehoshaphat was not satisfied that those prophets were seeking the message of God, and he asked Ahab to find another prophet.

Ahab finally agreed to call Micaiah, whom he disliked. Micaiah prophesied failure. However, the war was begun, and Ahab was killed in the battle.

On another occasion, the Ammonites and the Moabites made war on Jehoshaphat. He realized their armies were stronger than his. He called his people to fast and pray. God assured the king that they would defeat the enemy. When the battle began, the enemy forces began to fight among themselves and destroyed each other.

Where to find it

Sends teachers among people *2 Chronicles 17:7-9*
Makes alliance with Ahab *2 Chronicles 18*
Reforms his country *2 Chronicles 19*
Wins against his enemies *2 Chronicles 20:1-34*

JEHOSHAPHAT *(juh-HOSH-uh-fat),* **VALLEY OF,** is a place mentioned in the Book of Joel as the scene where God will judge all nations. Today, the Valley of Kidron near Jerusalem is sometimes called the Valley of Jehoshaphat, but there is no proof that it is the place Joel prophesied about.

Where to find it: *Joel 3:2, 12, 14*

JEHOVAH *(juh-HOVE-uh)* is one of the names

for God. The Jews had a special name for God that was so sacred they would not even say it out loud. When reading the Old Testament, they would substitute another more general name *(Lord)* for their special name for God.

Originally, all Hebrew words were written without vowels. A name such as Peter would be written PTR. The special name for God was written YHWH. Because the Jews never said the name, they eventually forgot how to pronounce it. Hundreds of years later, the vowels for *Adonai,* the Hebrew word for "Lord," were used with the letters YHWH, and from these two Hebrew words (the consonants of one and the vowels of the other) came the word *Jehovah* that is used in some translations of the Bible.

Scholars think that the one Hebrew word that was not pronounced would have sounded something like "Yahweh" if it had been said. Most translations now use the word *LORD* in capital letters for the Jewish special name for God.

JEHOVAH-JIRAH *(juh-HOVE-uh JY-ruh)* means "The Lord provides." It is the name Abraham gave to the place where God provided a ram as a sacrifice instead of his son Isaac.

Where to find it: *Genesis 22:8, 14*

JEHU *(JEE-hoo)* was the name of two important men in the Old Testament.

1. Jehu was the eleventh king of Israel. While he was serving in the army, he was chosen by God to take the place of King Joram, the son of the wicked Ahab. The prophet Elisha told a younger prophet to go to the army post where Jehu was stationed and anoint him king of Israel.

The prophet told Jehu that he must strike down the rulers who were relatives of Ahab. Jehu did as he was told. Joram was killed and so was the wicked Jezebel, wife of Ahab.

Jehu was king for 28 years. He stopped the worship of Baal among the people. However, he still allowed the worship of golden calves, and this displeased God.

We remember Jehu partly because he drove his chariot "furiously."

Where to find it

Jehu is anointed king   *2 Kings 9:1-13*
Destroys the relatives of Ahab   *2 Kings 10:1-27*
Allows worship of golden calves   *2 Kings 10:29*
Drives his chariot furiously   *2 Kings 9:20*

2. Jehu was an Old Testament prophet who denounced Baasha, king of Israel, and Jehoshaphat, king of Judah.

Where to find it: *2 Kings 16:1-4; 2 Chronicles 19:1-3*

JEPHTHAH *(JEF-thah)* was one of the early judges (rulers) of Israel. Because his parents were not married when he was born, his brothers made him leave home, and he was not given his share of his father's inheritance.

But Jephthah was a good leader, and when he went away to a nearby country, he soon had a group of men who formed a small army under his command.

When the Ammonites began making war on Israel, some people from Israel came and begged Jephthah to help defend them. Jephthah didn't want to, but he finally agreed.

Jephthah was a man who tried to please God. He also kept his word. Before he led the battle against the Ammonites, he promised God that he would sacrifice to God the first thing that met him when he came home.

He won a great victory—but the first thing that met him when he came home was his own daughter! Sadly, he explained to her the promise he had made, and she agreed that he must keep it. So he did.

Scholars do not agree on exactly what this meant. Some believe she was killed as a sacrifice. Others think Jephthah knew that God condemned human sacrifices, and so his sacrifice was to have his daughter serve God forever instead of marrying and having a family.

Where to find it: *Judges 11:1–12:7*

JEREMIAH *(JER-uh-MY-uh)* was one of the greatest Old Testament prophets and one of the most unpopular. He spent much of his time in prisons or hiding from angry kings. He was a prophet during the reigns of five kings of Judah—Josiah, Jehoahaz, Jehoiakim, Jehoiachin, and Zedekiah—a period of 40 years.

God called him to be a prophet when he was a young man, but Jeremiah told God he was too young and not a good speaker. God said he would put his words in Jeremiah's mouth, and Jeremiah must speak them.

The messages God gave Jeremiah made people angry. He told people God was judging them for their idolatry and evil acts, and that a great power from the north would soon come and conquer them. When Jehoiakim was king, he became so angry at Jeremiah's prophecies that Jeremiah was arrested and threatened with death. With God's help, he escaped. Later God told him to prophesy that destruction was coming to Judah. He was called a traitor and put in stocks. He was finally released with orders not to speak his terrible prophecies anymore.

But God still spoke to him, so Jeremiah put his words in writing instead, with the help of his friend, Baruch. Baruch gave them to a young man to read aloud at a house near the Temple. The listeners were so shocked that some of them took the writings to King Jehoiakim. He listened as they were read to him and then cut them up and threw them into the fire. He ordered Jeremiah arrested. However, Jeremiah and Baruch went into hiding, and no one could find them.

The next king was 18-year-old Jehoiachin. Soon Nebuchadnezzar, king of Babylon, came with his army, took the young king captive, and left King Zedekiah in charge of Judah.

Meanwhile, God told Jeremiah and Baruch to rewrite all the prophecies that wicked King Jehoiakim had burned in the fire.

Zedekiah thought he could escape from the

rule of Babylon if he made friends with Egypt—an enemy of Babylonia. Jeremiah heard about Zedekiah's plans and warned him not to do it. He told Zedekiah he should save the lives of his people by surrendering to Nebuchadnezzar.

Again Jeremiah was considered a traitor for giving that advice and was placed in a dungeon half-full of mud. Then, Nebuchadnezzar's army surrounded Jerusalem. The people tried to hold out against the army, but they ran out of food and water. Finally the city was defeated, and Nebuchadnezzar's army destroyed everything—including the beautiful Temple of Solomon.

Many people of Judah were killed; others were forced to go to Babylon as exiles. The old and sick were allowed to stay in the battered city. Jeremiah was left in Jerusalem with the others.

The few that were left later decided to go to Egypt and try to make new lives for themselves there. They forced Jeremiah to go with them. In Egypt Jeremiah continued his prophecies, urging the people to turn away from idolatry and worship God again. In Egypt Jeremiah finally died.

Where to find it

Jeremiah called by God   *Jeremiah 1: 4-10*
Threatened with death   *Jeremiah 26: 1-11*
Jeremiah in a dungeon of mud   *Jeremiah 38: 1-13*

JEREMIAH *(JER-uh-MY-uh)*, **BOOK OF,** is the longest prophetic book in the Old Testament. Even though the Book of Isaiah has more chapters, they are shorter than the chapters in the Book of Jeremiah.

It was written by the prophet Jeremiah (see *Jeremiah*) about many events in his life and in the history of Judah (the Southern Kingdom) between 625 and 580 B.C. The book also gives many of the prophecies and sermons that Jeremiah spoke and wrote. However, things are not written in the order in which they occurred.

The book seems to be arranged roughly this way:

1. Jeremiah's prophecies and sermons about Judah (chapters 1—25)

2. Events in the life of Jeremiah (chapters 26—45)

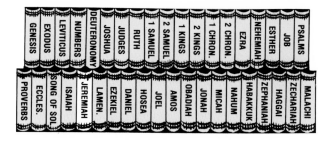

3. Jeremiah's prophecies about other countries (chapters 46—51)

4. The fall of Jerusalem and events that followed (chapter 52)

Much of the Book of Jeremiah is written in Hebrew poetry with colorful words making vivid pictures. Even if we do not always understand what Jeremiah's writings mean, the poetry is so picturesque it is worth reading for its sheer beauty.

But more than that, Jeremiah points out that God judges nations and individuals who do as they please instead of serving him.

Although Jeremiah's prophecies were usually about the bad things that would happen to Judah and other countries, he also wrote about a New Covenant that God would make with his people. God would write his Law in their hearts, and he would forgive their sins. This New Covenant is mentioned in several places in the New Testament.

Where to find it: *Jeremiah 31: 31-34; Hebrews 8: 7-13; 10: 15-18*

JERICHO *(JER-ih-ko)* is the oldest known city in the world—dating 5,000 years before the time of Abraham! About 40,000 people live there today, about one mile southeast of where the city was in Old Testament times.

Jericho is famous because its walls fell down after Joshua and his army marched around it for seven days. At the command of God, Joshua and his men destroyed everything in the city. The city was not rebuilt for more than 500 years. Then it again became an important city. Later it was again destroyed.

The Jericho of the New Testament is near the modern town of Jericho. It was a great city, built by Herod as his winter capital because it has a tropical climate. Jesus often taught and healed there. Zacchaeus, who climbed a tree to see Jesus, lived in Jericho. Jesus' famous story about the Good Samaritan is placed on

Jericho is not only the world's oldest city. It is also the lowest—1,300 feet below sea level.

the lonely winding road between Jerusalem and Jericho—a distance of about 20 miles.

Where to find it

Joshua's battle at Jericho   *Joshua 6*
Jesus heals at Jericho   *Mark 10:46-52*
Jesus sees Zacchaeus   *Luke 19:1-10*
Story of Good Samaritan   *Luke 10:29-37*

JEROBOAM *(jer-uh-BOH-um)* was the first king of the Northern Kingdom (Israel), ruling from about 931 to 910 B.C. He began as a government official under King Solomon. He helped stir up anger against Solomon over the high taxes the people had to pay.

While walking one day, he met the prophet Ahijah. The prophet tore his mantle (robe) into 12 pieces and gave ten pieces to Jeroboam. Ahijah said this meant that soon Israel would split into two separate nations—one with ten tribes, the other with

two—and that Jeroboam would become leader of the larger one. The prophet told him he should obey God's laws.

After King Solomon's death, the prophecy came true, and the people of the ten tribes asked Jeroboam to become king. He did; however, he forgot about obeying God's laws. For example, God had said that once a year all Israelites were to worship at the Temple in Jerusalem. But Jerusalem was in the two-tribe section, and Jeroboam didn't want his people leaving his territory to worship. So he built two places of worship in his country—one at Dan, another at Bethel.

Also, Jeroboam "decorated" his new houses of worship with golden calves and said, "Behold your gods, O Israel, who brought you up out of the land of Egypt." Faithful priests refused to serve at these altars, so Jeroboam got new priests and served as a priest himself.

Once while serving as a priest, a prophet told him that God would judge him for what he was doing. Jeroboam got angry, pointed at the man, and ordered him arrested. The hand that pointed suddenly went dead! Jeroboam pleaded with the prophet to ask God to heal him. The prophet did, and Jeroboam was healed.

But Jeroboam did not return to worshiping God. Instead he led his people to worship false gods.

Where to find it

Becomes government official   *1 Kings 11:28*
Ahijah tells him he will be king   *1 Kings 11:29-39*
Becomes king   *1 Kings 12:20*
Builds two altars   *1 Kings 12:26-31*
Hand is lifeless   *1 Kings 12:32–13:10*

JEROBOAM II *(jer-uh-BOH-um)* was the fourteenth king of Israel, reigning from about 782 to 753 B.C. Like Jeroboam I, who had lived almost 200 years earlier, Jeroboam II kept the pagan worship with golden calves in houses that were supposed to be dedicated to God.

Jeroboam II was a skillful army commander and won several wars for his country. While he was king, some Israelites became quite wealthy, living in large, fancy houses. But there were also many poor people, and the rich did nothing to help the poor.

The prophet Amos warned him that God would destroy the country because of its

Jerusalem's Dome of the Rock (upper right) and the Wailing Wall (lower right), where Jews often go to pray.

many sins, but Jeroboam paid no attention.

Where to find it: *2 Kings 14:23-29; Amos 7:7-17*

JERUSALEM *(juh-ROO-suh-lem)* is the most famous city on earth and in all of history. Its name means "city of peace," and if you visit Jerusalem today, probably at least one person will say to you, "Pray for the peace of Jerusalem."

Jerusalem has not been a city of peace, for it has been involved in many wars and has been destroyed several times. But unlike most ancient cities, Jerusalem has always been rebuilt on exactly the same place.

Jerusalem was the capital of Israel under David and Solomon. In this city, Solomon erected his beautiful Temple to God. After Israel was divided into northern and southern kingdoms in 930 B.C., Jerusalem continued to be the capital of Judah, the Southern Kingdom.

The city was destroyed by King Nebuchadnezzar in 586 B.C. when the Southern Kingdom was defeated and many of its people taken into exile in Babylon.

About 538 B.C. some Jews were able to return to Jerusalem and start to rebuild the Temple. Nehemiah led the rebuilding of the walls of the city, beginning about 445 B.C.

During the next 500 years, Jerusalem was ruled by a number of countries including Greece, Persia, Egypt, Syria, and finally, Rome. It was during the Roman rule that Jesus visited Jerusalem several times and once wept about how it wouldn't listen to his message. He was finally crucified there. After he rose from the dead, he appeared to his disciples in Jerusalem and went back to heaven from a hill near the city.

The first Christian church was formed in Jerusalem after the Holy Spirit came upon the disciples during the feast of Pentecost.

The city was completely destroyed by the Romans in A.D. 70. After it was rebuilt beginning in A.D. 136, it came under the control of many rulers.

Most recently, the entire city came under the control of the modern nation of Israel in 1967. Today it is considered a sacred city by Jews, Christians, and Muslims. The Muslim Dome of the Rock (where Abraham is said to have offered his son as a sacrifice to God) now stands on part of the area where the Temple once stood.

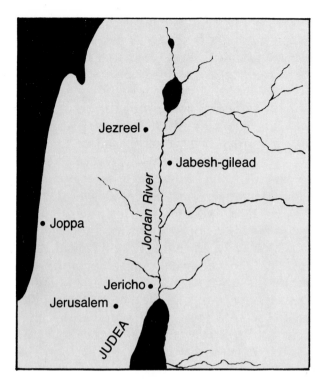

Jerusalem in the Bible has many names that show its special meaning to Jews and Christians. It is often referred to as "the city of God," "the holy mountain," and "Zion." *Jerusalem* is also used as a word picture of heaven, where God lives with his people. Hebrews 12:22 speaks of the "heavenly Jerusalem."

JERUSALEM COUNCIL (see *Council of Jerusalem*)

JESSE (*JESS-ee*) was the father of King David. Jesse was a shepherd, and young David was taking care of some of his father's sheep when the prophet Samuel came and told Jesse that God had told him to anoint one of his sons as the next king of Israel. David was so young that at first Jesse did not even call him in from the fields to meet Samuel.

Where to find it: *1 Samuel 16:1-13*

JESUS (*JEE-zus*) **CHRIST** is the most important person in the Bible. Although he was born in about 5 B.C. and was crucified about A.D. 30, the Bible says he existed before the creation of the world, and he lives forever because he is God.

The name *Jesus* is the same as the Old Testament name *Joshua*, meaning "the Lord is

salvation." Jesus is also called Messiah. In Hebrew this means "the anointed one." The word *Christ* comes from the word *anointed* in Greek. Jesus is called Christ and Messiah because he was anointed or chosen by God for his special work as Savior of the world.

Most of what we know about Jesus' life on earth is found in the four Gospels in the New Testament—Matthew, Mark, Luke, and John. These writings tell us that Jesus was born in Bethlehem, a small village about 4½ miles south of Jerusalem. This was the same village where King David had been born more than a thousand years earlier. Jesus' mother was Mary, a young Jewish girl who was engaged to marry Joseph, a carpenter of Nazareth, a small town about 90 miles north of Jerusalem.

An angel appeared to Mary and told her she would have a son—but that Joseph would not be the father of her son. God by a miracle would cause her to become pregnant. And that is exactly what happened.

At the time of Jesus' birth, a huge star appeared in the sky. Some wise men hundreds of miles away considered the star a sign that a great new king was being born. They made a long journey to follow the star and find the new king.

When King Herod the Great heard about the wise men coming to look for a newborn king, he was afraid this new king would try to take his throne from him. So he ordered all baby boys in and around Bethlehem to be killed. However, God warned Joseph in a dream that he and Mary and the baby should go immediately to Egypt. In this way, Jesus' life was saved. A few years later, King Herod the Great died, and Joseph and Mary and Jesus went home to Nazareth in Galilee.

Although the new rulers appointed by the Roman governor were Jewish, the Jewish people hated them. The Jews wanted to be free to rule themselves and to set up a great kingdom like they had when David and Solomon had been their kings. They believed the Old Testament promised a Messiah (a person anointed by God) who would drive out the hated Romans and restore a new kingdom for them.

When Jesus was about 30 years old, he began to preach and teach. He often taught in synagogues in the small cities. His 12 special

disciples and others (including some women) walked with him from town to town.

Jesus' teachings were different from those of other Jewish teachers and priests. He told interesting stories and used plain words. The people liked to hear him teach. As more and

more people wanted to hear him, Jesus had to teach outdoors on hillsides and beaches.

The people soon learned that Jesus could perform miracles. He healed people who had terrible diseases. He fed thousands of people with just a few loaves of bread and a few fish; he made a terrible storm go away. Because of these powers, many people wanted to make him king of their country. They were sure that he would be able to defeat the hated Romans.

But that was not the kind of king Jesus came to be. His Kingdom was one in which God ruled the hearts of people, who then tried to do God's will. Slowly the religious leaders of his time, the Pharisees, became more and more angry with Jesus. They became angry because he was friendly with people who clearly were sinners. One man who became one of his disciples had been a tax collector for the hated Romans. Also, he and his disciples did not keep the hundreds of religious rules the Pharisees thought were important.

And the leaders didn't like some of the things Jesus taught. He said he could forgive sins; they said, "Only God can do that!" So the Pharisees, scribes, and chief priests began to figure out ways to have Jesus put to death by the Romans.

The disciples were still loyal to him, even though they did not understand many of the things Jesus was saying and doing. He told them that they must be servants of others. (They thought Jesus was going to become king, and they would be officers in his government.) Even though he told them that he was going to suffer and die, they didn't really believe it.

Finally one of his own disciples, Judas, helped the religious leaders have Jesus arrested. He was tried by the Jewish council (see *Sanhedrin*) on charges that he blasphemed God. Because the council could not sentence anyone to death, he was taken to the Roman governor, Pilate, who sentenced him to be crucified.

On the day we now call Good Friday, Jesus was crucified as a criminal along with two thieves. Even on the cross, he thought about others. He asked the apostle John to take care of his mother. He told one of the thieves that he would be in heaven with him. He prayed for the soldiers who had crucified him and for

Today, Jesus' followers are doing the same thing, because Jesus has given them new life and made them part of his great Kingdom of God. We enter his Kingdom when we come under God's control and try to do what he wants. Jesus asked his followers to pray that God's Kingdom would come and his will would be done on earth as it is in heaven.

Where to find it

Angel appears to Mary *Luke 1:26-38*
Jesus is born in Bethlehem *Luke 2:1-7*
Wise men come from the East *Matthew 2:1-12*
Joseph, Mary, Jesus go to Egypt *Matthew 2:13-15*
Jesus performs miracles *Mark 3:1-12*
Crowd wants to make him king *John 6:15*
Judas betrays Jesus *Matthew 26:47-50*
Jesus is crucified *John 19:17-30; Luke 23:32-49*
Jesus rises from the dead *Matthew 28:1-15; Luke 24:1-11; John 20:1-31*
Jesus ascends into heaven *Matthew 28:16-20; Acts 1:1-11*

the people who had wanted all this to happen. After six hours of suffering, he died. The disciples were frightened and disappointed. They thought it was the end of all their dreams.

But on the third day, Jesus rose from the dead and appeared again to women who were his followers, and to the disciples. For 40 days, Jesus appeared occasionally to his followers, talked with them, and taught them. Then he ascended in a cloud to heaven, telling them that he would send "another Comforter"— the Holy Spirit—to be their teacher.

He told them they were to go all over the world, teaching and baptizing people, and that he would be with them.

And the disciples did as Jesus told them. They told the story of forgiveness through Christ to people all over the known world.

JETHRO (*JETH-row*) was Moses' father-in-law. Moses lived with him in Midian or the Sinai Peninsula and shepherded his sheep for 40 years before he went back to Egypt to lead the Israelites out of slavery.

When Moses was leading the Israelites in the wilderness, Jethro came to visit him. He saw how overworked Moses was as he tried to govern and lead the people. He suggested that Moses appoint judges to help him in less important matters. Moses took his advice.

Where to find it: *Exodus 18*

JEW at first referred to anyone who belonged to the tribe of Judah, one of Israel's 12 tribes.

But in the New Testament and even now, it means anyone who traces his ancestry to the Israelites or who is a follower of the Jewish religion.

JEWELRY (*JOOL-ree*) was popular among ancient men and women. They used jewelry not only for beauty but as part of religious festivals. The Old Testament mentions bracelets, necklaces, anklets, rings for fingers, gold nets for hair, pendants, diadems, and jeweled perfume and ointment boxes.

Like modern jewelry, ancient jewelry was made of gold and silver and was set with precious stones such as emeralds, sapphires, diamonds, and amethysts. Jewelry was often

given to a bride by her husband or her husband's family.

When the first Tabernacle was built in the wilderness by the Israelites, the people brought their bracelets, earrings, rings, and jewels to Moses. Many of these had been given by the Egyptians when the Israelites were their slaves. The clothing of the high priest was decorated with many jewels.

In the New Testament, Christians are warned not to give too much attention to "gold or pearls or costly attire."

Where to find it

High priest's clothes *Exodus 39*
Christians not to give too much attention
  1 Timothy 2:9

JEZEBEL *(JEZ-uh-bel)* was the wicked wife of Ahab, king of the Northern Kingdom. She brought the worship of the pagan god Baal into Israel and had 450 prophets of Baal eating in her palace. To please her, King Ahab built a temple and an altar to Baal. She ordered all the prophets of God to be killed.

The prophet Elijah had a famous contest with these prophets of Baal on Mount Carmel. The false prophets were defeated and killed. After that contest, Jezebel ordered Elijah to be killed, but he escaped.

Elijah prophesied that God's judgment would fall on her and King Ahab. Ahab died in battle, and Jezebel died when she was thrown from a window in her palace.

Where to find it

Temple to Baal built *1 Kings 16:32*
450 priests of Baal *1 Kings 18:19*
Jezebel threatens to kill Elijah *1 Kings 19:2*
Ahab and Jezebel die *1 Kings 22:34-40; 2 Kings 9:30-37*

JEZREEL *(JEZ-reel)* was a city about 60 miles north of Jerusalem where King Ahab had a palace. Near the palace, a man named Naboth had a vineyard that King Ahab wanted for his vegetable garden. When Naboth refused to sell it, Jezebel, the wicked wife of Ahab, arranged to have Naboth killed so Ahab could get it.

After Ahab's death in battle, Jezebel continued to live in the palace in Jezreel. She died by being thrown from the window.

Where to find it

Naboth's vineyard *1 Kings 21:1-16*
Jezebel dies there *2 Kings 9:30-37*

JOAB *(JO-ab)* was commander of David's army. He was a skilled fighter, but he was also a cruel man. He killed Abner, the commander of an opposing army, who was trying to make peace with David. When Absalom, David's son, led a rebellion against David, David ordered that Absalom was not to be killed. However, Joab killed him anyway.

David then made Amasa commander of his army instead of Joab. Joab pretended to be Amasa's friend—and then one day suddenly stabbed him to death.

When David was dying, Joab supported Adonijah as the next king instead of Solomon. After Solomon was made king, he ordered Joab to be killed.

Where to find it

Kills Abner *2 Samuel 3:20-30*
Kills Absalom *2 Samuel 18:9-15*
Kills Amasa *2 Samuel 20:4-10*
Solomon orders Joab killed *1 Kings 2:28-34*

JOANNA *(jo-ANN-uh)* was one of the women who traveled with Jesus and his disciples and gave money to support them.

She helped prepare spices and ointment and went to Jesus' tomb to help get his body ready for burial. There she met the angel of God who told her Jesus had risen from the dead.

Where to find it: *Luke 8:2-3; 23:55-56; 24:1-11*

JOASH *(JO-ash)* was the name of three important people in the Old Testament, including one king of Israel and one king of Judah.

1. Joash, the ninth king of Judah, ruled for 40 years, from 835 to 796 B.C. When he was a baby, everyone else in the royal family, including his father, was murdered. He was saved by his aunt and uncle, who hid him for seven years. Then he was brought out and crowned king. At first he took advice from his godly uncle, the high priest, and ruled well. Later he began to worship idols.

When Zechariah, the son of the priest, told him he was doing wrong, he had Zechariah killed. Joash was wounded in a battle with the Syrians, but he was killed in his own bed by his

Joash was only seven years old when he was brought out of hiding and crowned king of Judah.

servants because he had ordered Zechariah killed.

2. Joash, the twelfth king of Israel, was also called Jehoash. He was king for 16 years, from about 799 to 783 B.C. Although he worshiped idols, he seemed to be a successful king. At one time, the king of Judah challenged him to war, and Joash tried to discourage the idea. When the king of Judah insisted on war, Joash led his army in a stunning defeat of Judah. Joash was a friend of the prophet Elisha.

3. Joash, the father of Gideon. When Gideon tore down the altar to Baal in his hometown, the townspeople wanted to kill him. But Joash said, "If Baal is a god, he ought to be able to protect himself!"

Where to find it

The king of Judah *2 Chronicles 24:1-24*
The king of Israel *2 Kings 13:10-19; 2 Chronicles 25:17-24*
Gideon's father *Judges 6:28-32*

JOB *(jobe)* was a man who was wise, rich, and good. Then suddenly terrible things happened to him. His ten children were all killed in a tornado. He lost all his wealth. And he became ill with a painful skin disease.

Three friends came to visit him, and they all tried to explain why these dreadful things had happened. They said it was because Job had some sin in his life and God was punishing him. His wife and friends all thought the same thing.

Job insisted it was not true, but none of them believed him. Job became very discouraged and angry with God for letting such bad things happen, but he still believed in God and trusted him.

In the end, God answered Job in a whirlwind, reminding him that humans can never understand how great God is. After Job heard God speak, he said, "Now my eye sees thee; therefore I . . . repent in dust and ashes." Job realized that his trust in God did not depend on the things that happened to him.

God also told Job that his friends who condemned him didn't know what they were talking about. Finally, God restored Job's health, made him twice as rich as he had been before, and gave him ten more children.

This story is told in the Old Testament Book of Job. It is told in poetry—among the greatest poetry ever written. The poetry is great because its use of words and rhythm is so beautiful, and also because it says important things about suffering. Almost everyone at some point in life asks, "Why did that awful thing happen to that good person?"

Actually the Book of Job never answers the question "Why is there suffering?" But it does show right and wrong ideas and feelings about suffering and the meaning of life.

JOEL

JOEL *(jole)* was an Old Testament prophet who wrote a short book. No one knows exactly who he was or when he wrote.

We do know that he wrote about a terrible plague of locusts that had invaded the land, stripping the crops and ruining orchards. Joel told the people that the locusts had come as a punishment because they had not been faithful to God. The locust plague was said to be the "day of the Lord"—a time of judgment.

The Book of Joel, like much of Old Testament prophecy, is written in poetry. The writer uses some startling word pictures when he compares locusts to an approaching army:

They do not jostle one another,
   each marches in his path;
they burst through the weapons
   and are not halted.
they leap upon the city,
   they run upon the walls;
they climb up into the houses,
   they enter through the windows like a thief.

The most famous part of Joel's prophecy is a section the apostle Peter quoted on the Day of Pentecost:

It shall come to pass afterward
   that I will pour out my spirit on all flesh;
your sons and your daughters shall prophesy,
   your old men shall dream dreams,
   and your young men shall see visions.

Where to find it

Locusts compared to army *Joel 2: 8-9*
Peter's quotation at Pentecost *Joel 2: 28-31*

JOHANAN *(jo-HAY-nun)* was an army captain who was loyal to Gedaliah, governor of Judah, after Nebuchadnezzar had conquered the land. Johanan warned Gedaliah that another man, Ishmael, was trying to kill him, but Gedaliah would not believe it. Ishmael did kill Gedaliah and took captive many of the people in the town. Johanan and a group of men went after him. Although Ishmael escaped to a nearby country, Johanan rescued the captives.

Later Johanan led most of the people left in Judah to Egypt and forced the prophet Jeremiah to go with them. Jeremiah had warned them not to go.

Where to find it

Johanan warns Gedaliah *Jeremiah 40: 13-16*
Gedaliah is murdered *Jeremiah 41: 1-10*
Johanan rescues captives *Jeremiah 41: 11-17*
Jeremiah warns against going to Egypt *Jeremiah 42: 7-22*
Johanan goes to Egypt anyway *Jeremiah 43: 1-7*

JOHN THE APOSTLE was known as "the disciple whom Jesus loved." He was involved in the writing of five New Testament books—the Gospel of John, 1 John, 2 John, 3 John, and Revelation.

John was a fisherman when Jesus called him to become a disciple. Jesus nicknamed him "Son of Thunder." This probably meant that when John was young, he did things on the spur of the moment and had a hot temper. He is the only one of Jesus' disciples known to have lived to old age. When he was older, he was known for his gentleness and loving spirit.

He was one of the three disciples—Peter, James, and John—who were very close to Jesus and saw him do some miracles that no one else saw, such as raising the daughter of Jairus from the dead. Jesus took these three with him into a garden to pray just before his trial and crucifixion. John was the only disciple who the Bible says watched the crucifixion. Jesus saw him and asked him to take care of Jesus' mother.

After Jesus returned to heaven, John stayed in Jerusalem and became one of the leaders of the Christians there. He may have been the same John who was exiled much later on the island of Patmos because of his faith. There God gave John visions. He wrote them in what we know as Revelation—the last book of the Bible. John was probably later released from Patmos and died in the city of Ephesus when he was an old man.

We don't know exactly when he wrote the parts of the New Testament that carry his name.

Where to find it

Called "son of thunder" *Mark 3:17*
Is asked to care for Jesus' mother *John 19:26-27*
On the island of Patmos *Revelation 1:9*

JOHN THE BAPTIST was a prophet who was a cousin of Jesus. His parents, Zacharias and Elizabeth, were quite old when he was born.

When he was a young man, he began to preach in the wilderness near the Jordan River just north of the Dead Sea. There he lived simply, eating locusts and wild honey, and wearing rough garments of camels' hair. He told his listeners that they must repent of their sins, treat people fairly, and share what they had with others. Many thought John was the coming Messiah, but he told them, "No. Another is coming who is mightier than I."

John baptized those who wanted to turn to God and change their ways. One day as John was baptizing, Jesus came and asked to be baptized. At first John refused, but Jesus insisted. Afterwards a voice from heaven said, "This is my beloved Son, with whom I am well pleased."

Some of John's followers became disciples of Jesus after John told them that Jesus was the "Lamb of God who takes away the sin of the world."

Some months later, John the Baptist was imprisoned by Herod Antipas, the ruler of Galilee. John had said that Herod was wrong to have married the wife of his half brother. While in prison, John sent some of his friends to ask Jesus if he really was the promised Messiah. Jesus sent word back, "Go and tell John what you hear and see; the blind receive their sight, and the lame walk, the lepers are cleansed and the deaf hear, and the dead are raised up and the poor have the good news preached to them."

After the messengers went back, Jesus told his disciples that there had been no prophet greater than John the Baptist.

John was killed after Herod's stepdaughter asked for his head as a reward for her dancing at one of Herod's banquets.

Where to find it

John's birth *Luke 1:5-25, 57-80*
John preaches and baptizes *Matthew 3:1-17*
Calls Jesus "Lamb of God" *John 1:29*
Sends friends to Jesus *Matthew 11:2-15*
John is killed *Matthew 14:1-12; Mark 6:14-29*

JOHN, GOSPEL OF, is one of the four New Testament books that tell about the earthly life of Jesus Christ. This Gospel was written by one of Jesus' disciples, the apostle John, probably when he was an old man. It was probably written after the other three stories of the life of Christ—Matthew, Mark, and Luke.

The apostle John tells many things about the life of Christ that the other three do not. Most of John's Gospel is about Jesus' teachings, travels, and miracles in Judea. (The other Gospels tell more about Jesus' ministry in Galilee—the northern part of Palestine.) These are some of the miracles that are described *only* in the Gospel of John:

Turning water into wine at a wedding (John 2:1-11)

Healing a lame man at the pool of Bethesda (John 5:1-18)

Healing the man who had been blind from birth (John 9:1-41)

Raising Lazarus from the dead (John 11:1-44)

John's Gospel also tells many teachings of Jesus that are not in the other Gospels. These include his sermon about the Bread of Life and his teaching that he is the Good Shepherd.

John tells the readers that Jesus is God. In the very first sentence of his book he calls Christ "the Word" and says, "The Word was God."

When Jesus had his last supper with his disciples before his death, he gave them many important lessons. These are recorded in John, chapters 13 to 17, and most of these teachings do not appear in the other Gospels.

The apostle John said in John 20:31 that he

wrote this story of the life of Christ so that the readers would "believe that Jesus is the Christ, the Son of God, and that believing you may have life in his name."

We can be very thankful John wrote his story of Jesus' life, filling in many details that had not been included in the other accounts.

JOHN, FIRST LETTER OF, is a kind of sermon written between A.D. 85 and 100 by a disciple of Jesus, the apostle John. It was probably sent to the churches in Asia (now Turkey) where John lived toward the end of his long life.

In this sermon-letter, John reminded the readers that there were some teachers traveling around who said they were followers of Christ but were actually teaching things that were not true.

These teachers taught at least three false things:

1. that they knew some things other Christians did not know (1 John 2:4).
2. that Jesus had never been truly human—he just seemed to be. They did not believe that Jesus had come "in the flesh" (1 John 4:2).
3. that they never really sinned (1 John 1:10).

John told his readers that all of those teachings were wrong. He also reminded them that anyone who says he is a believer in Christ must live right—he cannot just go on sinning as if it didn't matter. He said that Christians must love God and treat each other lovingly because "God is love."

JOHN, SECOND LETTER OF, is addressed to a Christian woman and her children. The apostle John wrote that he had met some of her children and he was glad they were following Christ. He warned the woman about teachers who said they were Christians but taught wrong things. John said she should not invite them into her home. He encouraged her to love other Christians and to follow the teachings of Christ.

Some scholars think that the "elect lady," to whom this letter is addressed, was really a church and its members. Other scholars believe John was writing to a Christian woman he knew.

JOHN, THIRD LETTER OF, was written by the apostle John to his friend Gaius, who was a leader in one of the churches. John praised Gaius for inviting some of the Christian traveling teachers to stay in his home. He also said Diotrephes, another man in the church, was not pleasing God by the way he was treating John and some other Christians.

JONAH *(JO-nuh)* was an Old Testament prophet who had to be swallowed by a huge fish before he was willing to obey God. His story is told in the Book of Jonah.

When God called him to preach in a Gentile city, Nineveh, in about 745 B.C., Jonah did not want to go. He was afraid the people would repent and God would spare the wicked city. Jonah wanted God to destroy it because it was an enemy of Israel.

Instead of going to Nineveh as God commanded, Jonah took a ship the opposite direction—to Tarshish, probably a city in what is now southwestern Spain. During a violent storm at sea, the sailors prayed to their heathen gods to save them. They felt the storm was due to some wicked person on board. They decided it was Jonah, and Jonah admitted it probably was his fault. He told them to throw him overboard. God sent a huge fish to swallow Jonah whole. Alive inside the fish, Jonah prayed to God, and after three days the fish vomited him up near the shore.

Jonah was now willing to go to Nineveh. Just as he thought, the people listened to his message and repented. That made Jonah so angry that he went outside the city, sat down under a large plant, and complained to God.

The next day the plant withered, and Jonah was so hot he asked God to let him die.

God said Jonah cared more about the plant over his head than he did about all the people in Nineveh.

The Book of Jonah shows that God was concerned for all the people of the world—not just the Israelites, who were his chosen people.

Where to find it

Refuses to obey God   *Jonah 1:1-3*
Is thrown into the sea   *Jonah 1:4–2:10*
Preaches to Nineveh   *Jonah 3*
Argues with God   *Jonah 4*

JONATHAN *(JON-uh-thun)* was the oldest son of King Saul. He was also David's best friend. Jonathan was a skilled and courageous soldier.

When his father, King Saul, saw that David was popular among the people, he hated him so much he plotted to kill him. Jonathan tried to show his father that he had no reason to kill David. But Saul's jealousy was so intense that he refused to listen to Jonathan. Jonathan warned David that Saul planned to kill him, and this helped David escape.

Jonathan knew that David would become

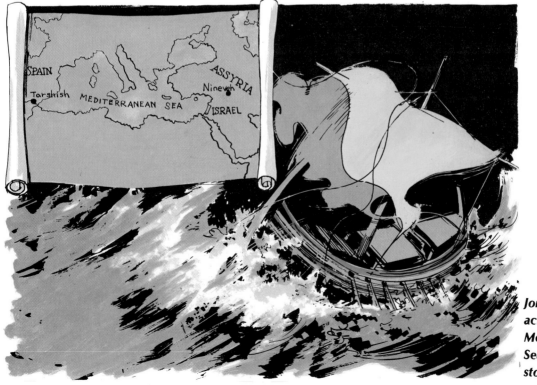

Jonah was headed across the Mediterranean Sea when the storm hit.

197

Jonathan once gave David a secret message while pretending to practice shooting arrows.

the next king of Israel even though, as Saul's oldest son, Jonathan should have been the next king. The love of David and Jonathan for each other was so deep that jealousy over the throne never hurt their friendship.

At the end, Jonathan and King Saul were both killed in the same battle with the Philistines. Later King David wrote a song in Jonathan's honor.

Where to find it

Wins a battle   *1 Samuel 14:1-45*
Jonathan and David promise love to each other   *1 Samuel 18:1-3; 20:17*
Saves David from Saul   *1 Samuel 20:18-42*
Dies in battle   *1 Samuel 31:1-6*
David's song to Jonathan   *2 Samuel 1:19-27*

JONATHAN *(JON-uh-thun)* **THE PRIEST** was a Levite who became a private priest for a man from Ephraim named Micah. Some Israelites from the tribe of Dan came and stayed in Micah's house, stole the images he used in his worship of God, and talked Jonathan into going with them to be their priest.

Jonathan set up these stolen images in Dan, the most northern city of Israel. For hundreds of years, many Israelites worshiped at this shrine. It continued until Israel was defeated by the Assyrians in 722 B.C.

Where to find it: *Judges 17:1—18:31*

JOPPA *(JOP-uh)* was an ancient seaport very near where Israel's largest city—Tel Aviv—

now stands. Joppa is now called Jaffa and is really a suburb of Tel Aviv.

The old Joppa was a walled city that existed before the time of Moses. It was the city where Jonah caught a ship for Tarshish when he was trying to run away from God's command.

Joppa is mentioned in the New Testament as the city where Peter raised Dorcas to life. It was also where Peter saw a vision that made him realize the gospel was for Gentiles as well as Jews.

Where to find it

Jonah sails from Joppa   *Jonah 1:3*
Peter raises Dorcas   *Acts 9:36-43*
Peter sees a vision   *Acts 10*

JORAM (see *Jehoram*)

JORDAN is the name of an Arab nation today and is also the name of an important river.

1. The modern nation of Jordan includes lands that the Bible calls Gilead, Ammon, Bashan, Edom, and Moab. Jordan's people are mostly Muslims.

2. The Jordan River was the most important river in Israel's history. It begins in the mountains north of the Sea of Galilee, runs into the Sea of Galilee, then out and down to the Dead Sea, where it ends. Because it is so winding, it actually travels about 200 miles to cover its 65-mile route. It is not a river that can be used for shipping. It has too many rapids and is only three to ten feet deep.

The nation of Israel had to cross the Jordan

Near this spot in the Jordan, Jesus was baptized.

198

going into Canaan. God miraculously made it possible for them to cross over on dry land.

John the Baptist did his preaching in the wilderness along the Jordan River, and Jesus was baptized there by him.

Where to find it

Israelites cross the Jordan *Joshua 3–4*
John preaches near the Jordan *Matthew 3: 1-5*
John baptizes Jesus *Matthew 3: 13-17*

JOSEPH OF ARIMATHEA *(AIR-im-uh-THEE-uh)* was a rich Jewish man who was a member of the ruling council when Christ was crucified. He secretly believed in Jesus but was afraid to tell others. After Christ died on the cross, Joseph asked Pilate for permission to remove the body. He helped place Jesus' body in a new tomb he owned.

Where to find it: *Matthew 27: 57; Mark 15: 43; Luke 23: 50-53; John 19: 38-41*

JOSEPH, husband of Mary, was a carpenter who lived in Nazareth. When Mary was pregnant before Jesus was born, an angel told Joseph that the Holy Spirit was the father of the child to be born, and Joseph should go ahead and marry her. He was with Mary when Jesus was born in a stable in Bethlehem.

Joseph was warned in a dream that Herod would try to kill the young child, and that they should go immediately to Egypt. The family stayed there until King Herod died. Then they all returned to Nazareth, where Joseph taught Jesus the carpenter trade. Joseph is last mentioned in the Bible in the story of the family going to Jerusalem when Jesus was 12.

Most scholars believe Joseph died before Jesus began his ministry.

Where to find it: *Matthew 1: 18-25; 2: 13-23; Luke 2: 41-52*

JOSEPH, son of Jacob, is one of the most important people in the Old Testament. His story explains how the Israelites became slaves to the Egyptians.

Joseph's father, Jacob, was 90 years old when Joseph was born, and Jacob favored Joseph over all his other sons. The older brothers were jealous and sold Joseph as a slave to a caravan of strangers going to Egypt. They made their father think that Joseph had been killed by a wild animal.

Meanwhile, Joseph was sold to Potiphar, an officer of the Pharaoh. Joseph proved so trustworthy and skillful that he was given much responsibility. Later he was thrown into prison because Potiphar's wife lied about him.

In prison, Joseph became known as a man who could tell what dreams meant. He was finally called to tell the Pharaoh what one of his dreams meant. As a result, he was released from prison. Joseph later became the chief ruler of the land—second to the Pharaoh himself.

Several years later, the brothers of Joseph came to Egypt to buy grain. They met Joseph but did not recognize him. Joseph put them through several tests to see if they were still cruel and thoughtless. Their actions showed that they had changed. Joseph then told them who he was and invited them to bring their father and their families to live in Egypt.

Joseph's brothers never expected to find him ruling Egypt.

Many years after their deaths, new cruel Pharaohs came into power. They made slaves of the descendants of Joseph and his brothers.

Where to find it

Sold by his brothers *Genesis 37: 12-36*
Sent to prison *Genesis 39*
Interprets Pharaoh's dream *Genesis 41: 1-49*
Brothers come to Egypt *Genesis 42: 1–45: 20*

JOSEPHUS *(jo-SEE-fus)* was a Jewish historian who began as an officer in the Jewish army. He was captured by the Romans. He then began writing a long series of books about the history of the Jewish people. He wanted the Romans to understand his people and to stop spreading wrong ideas about the Jews.

His writings begin with the time of Abraham and continue to A.D. 100. His books about the period after 200 B.C. are especially valuable because they tell so much about the life in New Testament times. Many of the rulers Josephus wrote about are mentioned in the New Testament. He was not a Christian, but he did mention Jesus Christ.

Early Christians recognized the value of his work, and Christian scribes copied and preserved his writings for the 15 centuries before the printing press was invented.

The books of this ancient interesting writer are now in many libraries, all put into one book called *The Complete Works of Josephus*. It is 770 pages long!

JOSHUA *(JAH-shoo-uh)* was Moses' assistant and military commander through Israel's 40 years in the wilderness after the escape from Egypt. When Moses died just before Israel was ready to begin its conquest of Canaan, Joshua was appointed the new leader.

He was already at least 70 years old at that time. He led the battle against the city of Jericho and many other campaigns. He also assigned specific areas to the tribes and encouraged each to drive out the remaining Canaanites in their areas. Joshua then dissolved his top command post and retired to an area near Mount Ephraim. He died at age 110.

The Book of Joshua tells about the campaigns of the Israelites in conquering Canaan and explains how the land was divided up among the various tribes. The book begins with Joshua taking over after Moses' death and ends with the death of Joshua.

The first 12 chapters tell about the conquest of Canaan. Chapters 13 to 22 tell how it was settled and how disagreements were worked out. Chapters 23—24 tell how Joshua, when he was nearing death, called all the leaders of

Israel together and reminded them of all that God had done for them. He encouraged them to worship only God and to do all that God commanded. The leaders promised, "The Lord our God we will serve, and his voice we will obey." Joshua took a huge stone and put it in the sanctuary of God at Shechem as a reminder of their promise.

Where to find it

Appointed leader in Moses' place *Numbers 27: 15-23*
Fights battle of Jericho *Joshua 6*
Last words to the Israelites *Joshua 23: 1–24: 28*

JOSIAH *(jo-SY-uh)* was the sixteenth king of Judah and one of the most godly kings in the Old Testament.

He became king when he was eight years old, after his father had been killed by slaves in the palace. The people were worshiping idols and building altars to pagan gods. Worship of the Lord had almost been forgotten. Josiah's father, the previous king, had encouraged idolatry.

When Josiah was only 16, he began to change all that. He ordered his men to break down the images and the altars to foreign gods. When he was 20 years old, he pushed his reform to other areas.

But the most important event occurred when Josiah was 26. At that time some repairs were being made in the Temple of God, and the priest discovered the Book of the Law that had not been seen or read for years. After getting the advice of the prophet Huldah, Josiah gathered all the leaders and many of the people of Judah to stand together in the Temple while the Book of the Law was read to them. Josiah decided to try to do all that the book commanded.

He ordered that the Passover feast should be held again. The Passover had not been observed for hundreds of years. 2 Kings 23: 25 says about Josiah, "Before him there was no king like him, who turned to the Lord with all his heart and with all his soul and with all his might, according to all the law of Moses; nor did any like him arise after him."

Josiah was killed in a battle with Egypt in 609 B.C. when he was 39 years old. After that, many people returned to their old ways and forgot about worshiping God. Twenty-three years

after his death, the kingdom of Judah was conquered by Babylon.

Where to find it: *2 Kings 22: 1–23: 30; 2 Chronicles 34–35*

JOT AND TITTLE (see *Iota*)

JOTHAM *(JO-thum)* was the name of the youngest son of Gideon and also the twelfth king of Judah.

1. Jotham the son of Gideon is best known in the Bible for a parable he told about who would be the ruler of trees. Jotham was the only one of the 70 sons of Gideon to escape death when Abimelech (another son of Gideon) killed the others because he wanted to become ruler. Jotham said his parable showed that Abimelech would fall from power. His words came true three years later.

2. Jotham the king of Judah was one of the few God-fearing kings. He became king when his father, King Uzziah, became ill with leprosy. He was a great builder, erecting better military defenses for his country and building the high gate of the Temple.

Where to find it

Gideon's son *Judges 9: 1-21, 57*
King of Judah *2 Kings 15: 5, 32-38; 2 Chronicles 26: 23–27: 9*

JOY is an intense feeling of good. In the Bible it usually comes with God's triumph over evil, either for an individual or for a nation. It is used this way in Psalm 105: 43-44. "Rejoicing in God" is often a part of public worship, as in Psalm 47: 1. Joy is also mentioned in Galatians 5: 22-23 as one of the results of the Holy Spirit in Christians. A person with joy feels right about his relation to God, to himself, and to others.

JUBILEE *(JOO-bul-ee)* was a year-long observance that came every 50 years. During the year, three things were to happen:

1. All Israelites who were slaves to other Israelites were to be freed.
2. All lands and houses outside walled cities were to be returned to the original owners or their children.
3. No Israelite was to farm. The land was to have "rest," and the people were to live on what had been grown the year before or grew naturally without being planted.

Although the rules about the Year of Jubilee are in Leviticus 25, no one knows for sure whether the Israelites ever really obeyed them.

JUDAH *(JOO-duh)* was one of the 12 sons of Jacob and the head of one of the tribes of Israel. When his other brothers wanted to kill Joseph, it was Judah who persuaded them to sell him as a slave instead. Judah was an ancestor of King David and of Jesus Christ.

Where to find it: *Genesis 37: 12-27; 38: 1-26*

JUDAH *(JOO-duh)*, **TRIBE OF,** descended from Judah, the son of Jacob (see above). When Joshua led the Israelites into Canaan, the tribe of Judah was assigned the land between the Dead Sea and the Mediterranean Sea. It was one of the largest territories, nearly 45 miles wide and 50 miles long. The tribe of Simeon was assigned a large area south of Judah, but a lot of it was almost desert land. Over a period of hundreds of years, the tribe of Simeon became a part of Judah. King David came from the tribe of Judah, and so did Mary and Joseph.

JUDAH *(JOO-duh)*, **KINGDOM OF,** was the Southern Kingdom when the Israelites divided into two separate countries after the death of King Solomon. The kingdom of Judah included most of the land assigned to the tribes of Judah, Simeon, and Benjamin, and also the kingdom of Edom.

This kingdom began in 930 B.C. and lasted until the capital city, Jerusalem, fell to the Babylonians in 586 B.C. The cities of Judah were destroyed at that time, and most of the leaders were forced into exile in Babylonia. They were free to live as they chose, but they could not return to Judah.

About 40 years later, Babylonia was conquered by Persia. The Persian king, Cyrus, allowed the Jews to return to their own land if they wanted to. At least 43,000 went back to live and to rebuild the city of Jerusalem.

The word *Jew* comes from *Judah.*

JUDAISM *(JOO-dee-izm)* is the religion of the Jewish people. Its teachings have been shaped more by the books of Exodus and Deuteronomy than any other part of the Old

It was Judas who led the soldiers to capture Jesus.

Testament. Traditions handed down through many centuries have also been important.

The teachings of Judaism include:
- the worship of only one God (no worship of idols)
- circumcision as a sign of being part of God's special people (the Jews)
- special ceremonies and worship on the Sabbath (Saturday).

JUDAIZING *(JOO-dee-eye-zing)* was the teaching of some people in the early church that Gentiles (non-Jews) who became Christians must also keep the laws of Judaism. The apostle Paul said this was wrong. He said that to be a Christian one must believe in Christ and follow Christ's teachings.

Where to find it: *Galatians 2:14*

JUDAS *(JOO-das)* was a popular name among Jews of Christ's time. Several are mentioned in the New Testament.

1. Judas, the brother of Christ. He is probably the "Jude" who wrote the Letter of Jude—one of the shorter books of the New Testament. He is mentioned in Matthew 13:55.

2. Judas, one of the apostles—*not* the one who betrayed Jesus. In Acts 1:13 this Judas is called "Judas the son of James" (RSV) or "Judas the brother of James" (KJV). Nothing else is known about him.

3. Judas Iscariot *(iss-KARE-ee-ut)* is the disciple who betrayed Jesus. He served as treasurer for the disciples. Although they trusted Judas, Jesus knew all along that Judas would betray him.

When a woman came and put expensive ointment on Jesus' feet, Judas complained that the money it cost could have been used to feed many poor people. However, he did not really care about the poor—he just wanted the money.

We do not know why Judas finally decided to lead the enemies of Jesus to him. The Bible says the chief priests paid him 30 pieces of silver. After Jesus was arrested, Judas felt so guilty for what he had done that he took the money and tried to give it back to the priests, but they refused it. He finally threw it on the floor of the Temple. Then he went and hanged himself.

Where to find it

Treasurer for disciples   *John 13:29*
Complains about costly ointment   *John 12:3-8*
Jesus knows Judas will betray him   *John 6:64*
Leads priests to Jesus   *Matthew 26:47-50*
Gives back the money   Matthew 27:3-5

JUDE is one of the shorter books in the New Testament. This letter was probably written by one of the half brothers of Jesus, who did not believe in Jesus until after the resurrection.

In this short letter, Jude warns the readers to look out for false teachers who say it is all right to do bad things and to live as you please. Jude condemns grumblers, people who are always complaining, boasters, immoral people, and those who flatter others to get them to do what they want.

Jude writes that Christians must stay close to Christ and obey him.

The most familiar part of Jude is the lovely benediction that is often repeated at the close of a church service. It begins: "Now to him who is able to keep you from falling and to present you without blemish before the presence of his glory. . . ."

Where to find it

Warning against false teachers *Jude 3-4, 16*
Teachings about living close to God *Jude 20-21*
Benediction *Jude 24-25*

JUDEA (*JOO-DE-uh*) is the Old Testament name for the part of Palestine to which many Jews returned after they had been exiled in Babylonia. Since most of these people were from the tribe of Judah, the land was called Judea.

In the New Testament, *Judea* refers to the southern part of Palestine. It extended from the southern part of the Dead Sea north about 60 miles. It included Bethlehem, Jerusalem, and Jericho.

JUDGE was a government official who had different duties at different periods of history. In the time of Moses, judges settled arguments among the people.

When the Israelites had settled in Canaan after the death of Joshua, judges were the chief rulers of various tribes or groups of tribes. They not only ruled during peacetimes but they were leaders in wars. Some of the prominent judges were Deborah, Gideon, and Samuel.

After Israel got a king as the chief ruler, judges again became those who settled disputes and took care of official business. Six thousand Levites were appointed to be officers and judges.

Where to find it

Moses appoints judges *Exodus 18: 13-23*
Israel is ruled by judges *Judges 4: 4-5; 1 Samuel 7: 15-16*
Judges during the time of kings *1 Chronicles 23: 2-4*

JUDGES, BOOK OF, tells what happened to the Israelites during the 350 years before Saul became king.

The Israelites began to forget God, who had led them out of Egypt into their Promised Land. They began to worship idols and other false gods like those of the neighboring countries. The Book of Judges also tells how the twelve tribes sometimes fought against each other. Each tribe seemed more concerned about itself than about the nation of Israel as a whole.

There were several small nations or groups of people still in Canaan who often made war against the Israelites. They included the Philistines, the Hittites, the Amorites, and several other groups. Sometimes, when the Israelites had a hard time with their enemies, they called on the Lord for help. God would raise up a judge to lead them and to defeat the enemy. But after the judge died, they would go back to their sinful ways. The Book of Judges tells about 13 such leaders.

The book describes some of the cruelty of the Israelites when they left the worship of God and turned to idols. They became as evil and cruel as the people of the pagan neighboring countries.

Judges 2: 11-19 is a summary of the whole Book of Judges.

JUDGMENT (*JUJ-ment*) is a word that appears often in the Bible.

In the Old Testament it often meant God was punishing a person or a nation for disobeying him. God often "judged" the Israel-

203

ites by letting an enemy country conquer them or oppress them.

In the New Testament, *judgment* is used differently. Sometimes it means to criticize or condemn someone. Jesus said Christians are not to judge each other. However, we are to examine and judge ourselves. God's judgment also means God is examining our actions day by day, recognizing what is good and what is sinful. This is happening now—in the present.

Judgment also refers to the end of the world as we know it, when God will judge (or punish) sin, reward those who have lived for God, and Christ will rule completely.

Where to find it

Christians shouldn't judge each other *Matthew 7:1*

We should judge ourselves *1 Corinthians 11:27-31*

The future judgment *Matthew 12:36*

JUDGMENT SEAT *(JUJ-ment seat)* means the bench or chair where a judge sits to hear arguments in court and to give his decision. Christ was brought to the judgment seat of Pilate, we are told in John 19:13.

Judgment seat is also a word picture to show that every believer is responsible to God. Romans 14:10 says, "We shall all stand before the judgment seat of God." The same idea is expressed in 2 Corinthians 5:10: "We must all appear before the judgment seat of Christ, so that each one may receive good or evil, according to what he has done in the body."

JULIUS *(JOOL-yus)* was a Roman soldier in charge of the ship that took Paul to Rome as a prisoner. When the ship was wrecked in a violent storm, the other soldiers wanted to kill Paul, but Julius kept them from hurting him.

Where to find it: *Acts 27:1-3, 9-44*

JULIUS CAESAR *(JOOL-yus SEE-zur)* was the founder of the Roman Empire. He was born about 100 B.C. and became a government official when he was a young man. As he was being promoted to higher offices, the self-governing Roman republic was growing weaker. Caesar was able to gain more and more power until he became absolute ruler.

In 44 B.C. (when he was about 56 years old) he was stabbed to death. The rulers who followed him took the name *Caesar* as a title to show that they, too, were emperors.

JUPITER *(JOO-pit-er)* was the chief of the Roman gods. The Greeks called this god "Zeus." When Paul healed a crippled man in Lystra, the people gathered around him and Barnabas, his fellow-worker, and called them Hermes and Zeus. Paul and Barnabas insisted they were men, not gods.

Where to find it: *Acts 14:8-18*

JUNIPER TREE (see *Plants–Broom Tree*)

JUSTIFICATION *(JUS-tih-fih-KAY-shun)* is something God does. He declares that those who have faith in Christ are righteous, and he gives them power to live right. He forgives their sins and becomes their friend. The Bible says this is possible because Christ died for sinners.

Where to find it: *Romans 3:21-31; 4:4-8; Galatians 2:15-17; Acts 13:38-39*